INSIDE AUSTRIA

PAUL LENDVAI

Inside Austria

New Challenges, Old Demons

Translated by
Ann Major

Columbia University Press
New York

Columbia University Press
Publishers Since 1893
New York   Chichester, West Sussex
Copyright © 2010 Ecowin Verlag, Salzburg, 2010
Translation by Ann Major, 2010
All rights reserved

The Publishers thank the Austrian Federal Ministry of European
and International Affairs for the generous funding of the translation
from German to English.

Library of Congress Cataloging-in-Publication Data

Lendvai, Paul, 1929–
    [Mein Österreich. English]
    Inside Austria : new challenges, old demons / Paul Lendvai; translated
    by Ann Major.
        p. cm.
    Previously published in German: Salzburg : Ecowin, © 2007.
    Includes bibliographical references and index.
    ISBN 978-0-231-70162-4 (alk. paper)
        1. Austria—Politics and government—1945– 2. Politicians—Austria—
    History—20th century. 3. World War, 1939–1945—Influence.
    4. Austria—Social conditions—20th century. 5. Austria—Social conditions—
    21st century. 6. Social change—Austria—History—20th century.
    7. Social change—Austria—History—21st century. 8. Austria—Economic
    conditions—1945– 9. Lendvai, Paul, 1929– 10. Journalists—Austria—
    Biography. I. Title.

    DB99.1.L4613 2010
    943.605'3—dc22

                                    2010003647

∞

Columbia University Press books are printed on permanent and durable acid-
free paper. This book is printed on paper with recycled content.
Printed in India

c 10 9 8 7 6 5 4 3 2 1

References to Internet Web sites (URLs) were accurate at the time of writing.
Neither the author nor Columbia University Press is responsible for URLs that may
have expired or changed since the manuscript was prepared.

CONTENTS

PREFACE FOR THE ENGLISH EDITION

This is a personal report by a political journalist and author, a work midway between journalism and history about a complex country which since World War II has often been the subject of sweeping generalizations and dangerous oversimplifications. As an Austrian by choice, not by birth I intend to contribute to a more sophisticated and mature approach towards understanding the belated birth of a modern nation with an ambiguous history. As in my previous studies about nationalism in the Balkans, anti–Semitism in Eastern Europe and Hungarian history, I have been determined to remain unswayed by feelings of aversion or of sympathy.

Having survived as a teenager the inferno of the Holocaust in Hungary, I have never been indifferent with regard to the demons of the past, from Hitler's Anschluss to the Waldheim affair and Haider's disturbing ascendancy. Yet at the same time both as Vienna Correspondent of the *Financial Times* (1960–1982) and Editor of a quarterly international journal on contemporary political and economic developments, I could follow closely the fascinating and still little-known story of how after ten years of foreign occupation this land-locked country has become the fourth richest member state of the European Union and at the same time a symbol of social consensus and political independence in the heart of Europe.

I hope that, whatever errors I have committed, I have avoided partisanship for any group or personality at the expense of another. A study of the Austrian odyssey can be properly appreciated only if one, in addition to documents, consults human sources at first hand and checks and counterchecks their statements. Due to my position as a foreign correspondent and political writer, I have known almost all important personalities, in politics, business and the media from personal experience during fifty years.

I have also tried to place the forces operative in Austria in a broader context and historical perspective.

Vienna, January 2010
Paul Lendvai

1

INTRODUCTION

WHY DID I WRITE THIS BOOK?

A very personal preliminary note

On 4 February 1957, on a dreary Monday, I arrived in a second-hand ankle-length blue winter coat, on a Czechoslovak plane from Prague to Vienna. In my pocket I had my Hungarian passport with a valid Austrian visa. I was one of the latecomers; by then the Iron Curtain was almost unnegotiable. My adventurous journey to Vienna via Warsaw and Prague had started on 12 January 1957.

It was my first ever trip abroad; I was twenty-seven. A Polish newspaper had invited me to Warsaw. This trip had been arranged with reform-minded friends as a political mission shortly before the eagerly awaited Polish parliamentary elections. At the time Poland still appeared like a glimmer of hope to our defeated and muzzled Hungary: a country where—so it seemed to us then—the peaceful transformation from Stalinism to reform had succeeded by way of the 'Spring in October'.

Those were unforgettable weeks, marked by the sustained sense of excitement in Warsaw. It soon became clear, however, that the Kádár regime no longer had any intention of a compromise solution and was determined to pursue a merciless campaign of vengeance against the insurgents. When I arrived in Vienna exactly three months after the Russians' full-scale attack against Imre Nagy's revolutionary government, there were already close to 200,000 Hungarian refugees in Austria, and about a tenth of that number in Yugoslavia.

Five, partly difficult, years were behind me: military service, arrest, internment, and three years' ban from my profession. Despite all this I did not at first want to leave my country. As a former young left-wing

1

socialist, persecuted and not 'compromised' during the revolution, at last I could work again as a journalist for a daily paper. Nor had I exchanged any serious words with my beloved parents about defecting to the West before my trip to Warsaw.

The bad tidings from Budapest, the conversations with Western foreign correspondents later to become close friends, and my own impressions in Warsaw changed my view of the situation inexorably. My thoughts turned more and more to an irrevocable decision: I could no longer live a lie!

How could I write on foreign policy issues while my friends, who had helped me out of the internment camp and obtained my rehabilitation, were now themselves behind bars, and admired authors were threatened by long prison terms? Even before my departure for Prague, the next station of my tour, I had firmly made up my mind to start a new life.[1]

Lacking well-to-do relatives or friends abroad, without any qualifications, but with a knowledge of German and English, though by no means good enough for a journalist, and at the age of 27 with no prospect of mastering an accent-free foreign language, I was planning a leap in the dark in the truest sense of the word. I was prepared to jeopardize my newly gained way of life in Hungary, but at the same time I did not have the least idea of my personal future. To the astonishment of my parents and friends, I immediately sought political asylum in Vienna. Without illusions, but also without any apprehension, I prepared myself for the freedom of choice in a free world.

Thanks to helpful foreign colleagues, I belonged to that minority of refugees who could live privately and not in a camp for refugees. I could say together with Michael Blumenthal, the former United States Secretary of the Treasury, who had fled Nazi Germany and settled in the USA via China: 'I had great luck. Life is not only a matter of ambition and work, but also of luck.' I quickly found friends and acceptance in Austria.

For the refugees from Hungary, who emerged from total isolation, and who were received with open arms irrespective of their origins and past, Vienna was not only a showcase of the West, but also—and above all—a beacon of freedom, tolerance and humanity. When decades later Austrian, and particularly foreign, friends reproach me for 'still idealizing the country', I always recall these unforgettable first experiences. At the time the refugees had met with the good Austria, where people did not enquire about who was who or what someone was worth; they simply helped—incidentally, exactly as they would help the Czechs and the Slovaks in 1968, the Poles in 1980–81, the refugees from the collapsed Yugoslavia in 1991–5, and the Kosovo Albanians in 1999.

There is no doubt that the Hungarian Revolution and its bloody suppression by the Soviets was also a political and psychological watershed in Austria's post-war history. That a country after seven years of *Anschluss* and war, after ten years of occupation and so soon after the pull-out of the last foreign soldier but still without its own army, still accommodated the Hungarian refugees so naturally, undauntedly and magnanimously, remains pivotal for an entire generation and has contributed greatly to the self-confidence of the Second Republic. A whole people stood its historical test.

What the Austrians accomplished at the time was unique: from improvised camps and spontaneous fund-raising campaigns to the mobilization of world publicity and the community of states. An obvious sense of guilt by the Western governments that they had so miserably failed the Hungarians in the late autumn of 1956 probably also accounted for the subsequent and never-to-be-repeated willingness of so many countries, from Switzerland to the United States and Canada, to accept refugees. In the relatively short period until the end of 1957, practically all those who wanted to emigrate had left Austria.[2]

According to polls taken over the past fifty years, the refugees' decision whether to 'push along or to stay' was greatly influenced by the Austrians' repeatedly proven empathy for the Hungarians. It tipped the balance for the more than 10,000 Hungarian refugees, among them the author, who remained in Austria. As the political scientist Norbert Leser observed almost forty years later: 'The popular uprising was for Austria and the Austrians a practical test of humanitarianism and a chance to let the living Hungarians benefit from their gratitude that Austria had fared so much better than Hungary.'[3] One can state without exaggeration that, compared to the later waves of refugees, the refugees of 1956 had been privileged precisely because they came from Hungary. As Kurt Vorhofer wrote in the *Kleine Zeitung* on the occasion of the revolution's thirtieth anniversary: 'The Magyars are actually the only neighbouring people who are not targets of wisecracks in our country, let alone scoffed at.'

Numerous former refugees who became Austrians, as I have, regarded it as a kind of obligation on their part to proclaim loud and clear their memory of 'the good Austria' precisely in difficult times (in the Waldheim case in 1986 and in 2000 at the time of the EU sanctions after the formation of the black–blue government).

Already then I regarded the battle against anti-Austrian clichés as part of my journalistic priorities. This brief portrayal of Austro–Hungarian relations in general, and my personal attitude in particular, is merely meant to clarify to the reader from what perspective and based on which experiences I, as the long-standing correspondent of the London *Financial Times* and Swiss newspapers, then as editor-in-chief and later director of ORF, the Austrian Broadcasting Corporation, would like to reveal and analyze from the inside and the outside, as it were, the complexes and anxieties, the formative personalities of the Second Republic.

This book is a profoundly personal trip down memory lane about my recollections of half a century behind the scenes of power in Austria, about my experiences as a foreign correspondent, TV director and editor-in-chief of the quarterly journal *Europäische Rundschau*. It is about my experiences in Austria, especially in the light of meetings with personalities whom I got to know—not least the close relationship with Bruno Kreisky between 1960 and 1990.

I should like to take this timely opportunity to express my gratitude to all those forty-eight personalities who were willing to answer my many questions about their terms in office and their experiences, and at the same time also to impart their opinions about their political friends and foes. They include:

Federal President Heinz Fischer, former Chancellors Alfred Gusenbauer, Wolfgang Schüssel, Fred Sinowatz (†), Franz Vranitzky, Vice-Chancellors Hannes Androsch, Erhard Busek, Susanne Riess-Passer, the Governors of Lower Austria, Erwin Pröll, of Styria, Josef Krainer jun. and of Carinthia, Jörg Haider (†).

I have also used quotes from interviews with the late Cardinal Franz König and Federal President Rudolf Kirchschläger as well as abroad with Uri Avnery (the left-wing Israeli politician), Muhammad Kaddafi (the Libyan leader), Mohammed Hosni Mubarak (the Egyptian President) and Shimon Peres (who became subsequently Israel's President), which were recorded in 2000 for an ORF TV documentary on the occasion of the tenth anniversary of Bruno Kreisky's death.

2

AUSTRIAN CLICHÉS

THE MEDIA CURTAIN

It is difficult, often almost impossible, to ignore the clichés and pre-judices about Austria. The myths of the Second Republic's history explain some things and obscure many more; the clichés range from pride ('Cultural super power') to self-abasement (the 'Austrian *Leb-enslüge*'—the myth that it had been the victim of Hitlerite aggression as asserted in the Moscow Declaration). The years between 1945 and 2005 have been arguably the happiest epoch in Austria's history. How-ever, Austrian involvement in National Socialism and the revulsion felt against the crimes of the Nazi regime distort the outsiders' view of this uniquely positive success story to this day.

It is peculiar that so many declarations of love and of disdain are showered on such a small country from abroad, and that so many Austrian writers maintain a love—hate relationship with their country. The political leadership of the Second Republic basked for a long time, and successfully, in the historical glow of an innocent victim of the Third Reich. The massive and excessive foreign reaction to the Wald-heim case (1986–92) and the Haider—FPÖ's participation in govern-ment (February 2000) almost completely washed away the 'island of the blessed', the Austrians' favoured self-image based on Pope Paul VI's accolade. The downright hysterical reactions at the peak of the two crises have astounded the majority of Austrians, including the fol-lowers of left-wing parties. They confirmed the timeless validity of what Paul Valéry, the great French poet and essayist, wrote in 1942: 'Society lives on illusions. Every society is a kind of collective dream. These illusions become dangerous illusions when they begin no longer to delude. Awaking from this kind of dream is a nightmare.'

The impact of this massive criticism from abroad about Austria's association with National Socialism—beginning already during the Kreisky era and intensified after Kurt Waldheim's election as President—produced far-reaching and contradictory political consequences, which we shall discuss later. At the same time, the delicate tightrope walk between the demonization abroad and the denial at home increasingly infuriated the younger and mainly left-wing historians, writers and journalists.

One of the most perceptive essayists, Karl-Markus Gauß, has since cut to the quick of the matter: 'It was this shrewd opportunism that made it so difficult later for me and many others to shape their own image of Austria in which they would have liked to recognize themselves. However, as we had recognized how much was being covered up in Austria, we instead identified Austria herself with the cover-up. ... Everything about Austria seemed somehow to have turned out badly, and that which did not turn out badly could not have anything to do with Austria. Consequently everything that happened in Austria was Austrian, that is to say provincial and dishonest, or it was not dishonest and provincial, ergo not Austrian.'

For Austria the year 2005, with all its historic links, was a Year of Commemoration, and at the same time a year of reflection in a special way: a commemoration of 1945, that is to say the collapse of the Third Reich and the refounding of the Republic of Austria; a commemoration of 1955, when Austria regained full freedom and sovereignty by concluding the State Treaty; and of 1995, the year when Austria joined the European Union. At the beginning of that year, however, 55 per cent of Austrians and 72 per cent of the under-thirties age group had no idea what was going to be celebrated in 2005.

The findings of a study conducted for the Federal Ministry for Education, Science and Culture in November 2004 fits into this framework: 53 per cent of young Austrians under the age of twenty-four felt they were insufficiently informed. Whether and to what extent the unprecedented flood of commemorative celebrations, exhibitions, conferences, special publications and the many TV documentaries not only reached but truly enlightened young people will probably only be evident from future surveys and research.

As far as the generation of parents and grandparents is concerned, judging by the pertinent letters to editors and voices from rightist-populist circles, one cannot go far wrong by arguing that, because of inherited preconceptions and hostile images as well as ignorance, many Austrians are still not willing to face the whole truth regarding the Nazi era. Still, at the same time it would be unwise to overlook the tendencies abroad towards a blanket contempt of Austria and doommongering. Some outside observers consciously or unconsciously want to trivialize what has happened in the last two decades as far as Austrian critical self-perception is concerned. Recalling for instance the caricatures that appeared three days running in February 2000 on the title page of the Paris daily *Le Monde*, which depicted Austria as Naziland, where a train was arriving at a concentration camp bearing the German inscription *Arbeit macht frei*, or if one thinks of the flood of reports about the punitive campaign by the fourteen EU states against the black–blue government, then one could recall the aphorism of the Polish satirical writer, Stanisław Jerzy Lec: 'Some people lack the gift of seeing the truth, but oh what honesty their lie breathes!'

Of course, the fact that this country is portrayed either as an infinitely rich island of the respectable blessed, or as an Alpine redoubt of incorrigible Nazis, reflects in the first place the complexity of Austria's real history. One has only to evoke Thomas Bernhard's 'Heldenplatz' ('Heroes Square') staged in 1988, or the most frequently shown stills from TV documentaries about this fateful square in the heart of Vienna where, before 250,000 wildly cheering Austrians, Hitler proclaimed the 'homecoming of Austria' into the German Reich. It was this indelible picture that moved me, the young foreign correspondent of the London *Financial Times*, to pose the question some time in the early sixties to the then Foreign Minister Bruno Kreisky in his office on the Ballhausplatz, how fraught with symbolism the oft-quoted elation for Hitler actually was on the Heldenplatz. Kreisky answered, as always in private discussions with journalists, not evasively but candidly: 'Have you ever thought about how many were not there, and how many Austrians, apprehended by the Gestapo, would soon be on their way to Dachau in overcrowded trains?' I had not made any notes during or after that poignant conversation, but I shall never forget the Brecht quotation used by him: 'And you see only the ones in the light / those in darkness drop from sight.'

In an interview in the spring of 1988, that is to say half a century after that mass frenzy, the elder statesman reiterated: 'On the Heldenplatz one saw the ones in the light, and everywhere where they identified with the dictatorship they were in the light, and the others were in the darkness. They were either working in the fields or were praying in the churches, or they were crying at home—at any rate they were not visible. But they were in the majority. There is no doubt about that.' In conversation with us journalists and in his memoirs, Kreisky, an unimpeachable witness, repeatedly pointed out that even at its zenith only one-third of Austrians were for Hitler.[1] The road to the *Anschluss*, the cheering after the entry of the German troops, and the mass frenzy on the Heldenplatz cannot be explained or understood without the profound break in Austria's history associated with the collapse of the Austro–Hungarian monarchy. For me, who had grown up in Budapest with a similar trauma, namely the truncation of historical Hungary enforced by the victors in the Treaty of Trianon, it was always the shock of the Treaty of Saint-Germain-en-Laye of 10 September 1919 that denoted the starting point for the later reflections on the 'special case' of Austria.

'What is history?' asked the eminent British historian E. H. Carr, and replied in a nutshell: 'an unending dialogue between the present and the past'.[2] Bearing in mind that, following the unforgettable words of French President Georges Clemenceau at the peace negotiations, Austria was an 80,000 square kilometre shrunken 'rump' of a more than 670,000 square kilometre empire with just under 7 million inhabitants (instead of over 50 million), one does not need any scientific treatises to understand the deeply rooted doubts about the viability of this small state under the influence of the shock of collapse. In contrast to Trianon-Hungary, in the monarchy's Austrian part it was not 'only' a matter of the loss of millions of German-speaking inhabitants, and of the economic consequences caused by the destruction of this great common market, and by the erection of tariff walls in the succession states.

In this 'state that no one wanted' the dominant issue was 'the Austrian identity problem in the twentieth century', that is to say, that the citizens 'had first to learn to be Austrians',[3] the more so as in the monarchy the German-speaking inhabitants had simply been called Germans. They saw themselves as the actual *Staatsnation* (political nation) not only of the German-speaking part of the empire, but of the entire Habsburg monarchy. This state was reluctantly called the 'German–Austrian Republic', that was 'part of the German Reich'. Referring to this first constitution, Erwin Ringel, the great psychiatrist of the 'Austrian soul', drew this apt conclusion: 'It was a state that with the first sentence it uttered also committed suicide. ... This was the origin of the state that no one wanted and whose repeated death was thereby sealed.'[4]

However, as the victorious Allies denied Austria the right to the *Anchluss*, to the union with the German nation, Austria soon had to change its name from 'German–Austria' to the 'Republic of Austria'. The political elite, with the Social Democrats in the lead, but naturally also the pan-Germans, and to a lesser degree the Christian-Social Conservatives, opposed the rump state. Until Hitler came to power they were all in favour of the *Anschluss* to Germany.

The almost permanent crises led to the radicalization and militarization of domestic conflicts through the formation of paramilitary organizations: the Social Democrat *Schutzbund* (Republican Defence League) against the Christian-Social *Heimwehr* (Home Guard). After the scandalous acquittal of three right-wing war veterans, who had been charged with having shot a disabled ex-serviceman and a child in January 1927 during a clash in Schattendorf, mass demonstrations and political violence erupted in Vienna in July, and the Palace of Justice was burned down. Police intervention with the order to fire claimed eighty-nine lives and hundreds of injured.

The world economic crisis of 1929 hit the rump state particularly hard. The level of gross domestic product in 1913 was reached again only in the mid-twentieth century! A third of the workforce was unemployed, and of these almost every second did not receive any support. Against this backdrop of misery, domestic polarization led to increasingly frequent violent clashes between the hostile political camps.

Eventually the Christian-Social Chancellor, Engelbert Dollfuss, grasped the opportunity offered by the resignation of the parliamentary President and his two deputies, adjourned parliament indefinitely on 4 March 1933, and established a corporative state. His authoritarian course resulted on 12 February 1934 in civil war followed by the outlawing of the defeated Social Democrats and trade unions. Already by July Austrian Nazis encouraged by Hitler's Germany attempted a failed *coup d'état*. There were many fatalities; Chancellor Dollfuss was murdered by the putschists in the Chancellery building. While the Social Democrats and the liberals regard Dollfuss—called the 'Millimetternich' for his short stature—as a Fascist destroyer of democracy and the trailblazer for Hitler, for the Christian Socialists, and today for the ÖVP, the murdered Austrian-minded statesman is a martyr of the anti-Nazi resistance.

The British historian Gordon Brook-Shepherd observed about the First Republic in his book on Austria that: 'Most of its patriots were not democrats, while most of its democrats were not patriots.' The merciless persecution of the Schutzbundists and of the Social Democratic activists, among them the young Bruno Kreisky, has left deep marks. At the peak of the waves of arrest, hundreds of Social Democrats were locked up together with National Socialists and Communists and other people deemed 'subversive' in the notorious internment camp in Wöllersdorf.

Kreisky has often told a story, to me too, about his one-year confinement in 1936, when he was locked up in the same cell with a committed Nazi and a similarly fanatical Communist. The National Socialist consoled himself audibly with the thought: 'It won't last long, and Hitler will come to Austria too, and then I'll be free, and I'm going to do well.' The Communist's reply to this was: 'It's possible that Hitler will come here too, but then Stalin will come and chase Hitler away, and we'll all do well.' 'But I,' Kreisky finished the story, 'did not have a Hitler and a Stalin to look forward to, only the hope of democracy. And it was precisely democracy which prevailed while Hitler and Stalin have long disappeared.'

Dollfuss' successor, Kurt Schuschnigg, continued the authoritarian line and tried by various events and propaganda actions to awaken Austrian national consciousness. His endeavours to stabilize the economic situation were just as unsuccessful as his careful and belated opening up toward the Social Democrats and the trade unions at the end of 1937. When Hitler demanded the *Anschluss* in an ultimatum, Schuschnigg called a plebiscite for 13 March 1938 'in favour of a free and German, independent and social, Christian and united Austria'. Hitler prohibited the referendum, because he knew that it would result in a clear majority of 'No' votes against the *Anschluss*. Before the entry of German troops on 12 March, the frustrated Chancellor concluded his radio broadcast with the words: 'We are yielding to force... God protect Austria.'

No resistance was offered against the German invasion. Time and again Kreisky emphasized that Austrian democracy was not annihilated by Hitler, but by Dollfuss. When Hitler came in 1938, many people did not consider it as an attack on Austrian democracy, because none existed at the time, but against the regime or the system, as they saw it then. 'We have always said it, innumerable times, in all our writings:

the Dollfuss road leads to Hitler', wrote Kreisky in his memoirs. At the time of the great Socialist Trial on 16 March 1936, the then barely twenty-five-year-old Kreisky accused the Austrian variety of Fascism of hypocrisy and short-sightedness. His speech in his own defence was widely quoted with approval in the international press, especially the statement 'that in a serious moment the government has to call on the wide masses to defend the borders of the country. But only a democratic Austria can produce such a popular unity. Only free citizens will fight against subjugation.' According to Kreisky, after the executions of the Schutzbundists and the arrests by the Dollfuss regime, hatred against Dollfuss and the *Ständestaat* was stronger among the Social Democrat activists forced underground 'than fear of anything else'.

Not only while I was working on his biography, but also in the subsequent years, I was astounded again and again by the discrepancy between Kreisky's sharp, uncompromising and emotional hostility against the authoritarian regime, the *Ständestaat* under Dollfuss and Schuschnigg on the one hand, and on the other his downright sympathetic appraisal of former Nazis. The memory of his personal experience of the help received from former Nazi cellmates, from the time of his imprisonment under Schuschnigg, when he was once again arrested—this time by the Gestapo, to his successful departure to Sweden, no doubt influenced his great tolerance shown decades later to some of the former Nazis in political life; an attitude that irritated many of his friends and admirers. His public outbursts of hatred against Simon Wiesenthal, some of which I have personally experienced, can only be understood (but certainly not excused) against this historical and personal background. In 1970 Wiesenthal had uncovered the Nazi past of four members of the first Kreisky government, and in 1975 had disclosed that the leader of the FPÖ, Friedrich Peter, had served in 1941–2 as *Obersturmbannführer* in an SS unit involved in mass murder.

Bruno Kreisky fought Wiesenthal till the end of his days, although both of them, as Wiesenthal once put it, were 'branches of the same tree'. Another reason for the veritable witch hunt of the entire SPÖ leadership against the world-famous 'Eichmann hunter' was the fact that by his exposures the latter had touched on a wound of Austrian social democracy. Karl Renner, the key figure at the rebirth of Austria in 1945, the first State Chancellor of the First Republic in 1918–20, and then from 1945 to 1950 the first Federal President of the Second Republic, belonged first and foremost to the Social Democrats' compromised past. He was the man who, arguably more than any other politician, has trodden the right and the wrong tracks of the unloved First Republic.

In an interview on 3 April 1938, Renner publicly accepted the *Anschluss* with true gratification ('albeit not achieved by the methods to which I subscribe') and confirmed his commitment to the 'Yes' vote in the Nazi-organized plebiscite. His voluntary alignment was undoubtedly a sensational gesture, as was, incidentally, the recommendation by Vienna's Cardinal Theodor Innitzer for a 'Yes' vote. At the same time, prominent Social Democrats in exile, above all Otto Bauer in Brünn—much admired by Kreisky—were still devoted to the *Anschluss*, despite their uncompromising repudiation of Nazism, and dreamed of a 'pan-German revolution'.

The terror actions, prior to the almost 100 per cent approval (99.6%) for the plebiscite of 10 April, were committed against Jews and political opponents. This is how the German dramatist Carl Zuckmayer described those March days in Vienna in his memoirs: 'That evening all hell broke loose ... all the people lost their faces and resembled grotesque masks either of Fear, or of Lies, or of wild, hate-spewing Triumph. ... What was unleashed here was the revolt of envy, resentment, bitterness, blind malevolent vengefulness—and all the other voices were condemned to silence. ... All that was let loose here was the obtuse mob, its blind destructiveness, and its hatred of anything that was ennobled by nature or spirit. It was the rabble's witches' Sabbath and a funeral of every human value.'[5]

After decades of fomented anti-Semitism, the atrocities against the 200,000 Austrian Jews were accepted by the majority of Austrians, and in many cases approved—similarly to what would happen a few years later in the neighbouring Central and East European countries. Innumerable personal stories have confirmed Zuckmayer's observation: 'The netherworld had opened its gates, and let loose its basest, most abominable, its foulest evil spirits.'

It is not to belittle the bestialities of that dark epoch in Austrian history, let alone to pass over them in silence, but rather to evoke the international relevance of murderous anti-Semitism, that I must pose a delicate question. Does not what is being held against the Viennese also apply to Budapest or Warsaw society, to the non-Jewish citizens of Latvia or Lithuania? Were not the demons that erupted in 1944 from the popular psyche in Budapest, and which I experienced as a fifteen-year-old, just as frightening as those six years earlier in Vienna?

Nor does it imply the minimization of Austrian collaboration with the National Socialist regime when I approvingly quote the contemporary historian Oliver Rathkolb, according to whom the frequent allegations of a 'disproportionately high participation of Austrians in the then committed mass exterminations are not empirically verifiable and [are] analytically questionable'. All this does not, of course, excuse the scandalous acquittals by Austrian courts in the 1960s of those who had been involved in atrocities under the National Socialist regime. Nor should one pardon the belated dealing with the grave omissions associated with the Austrian *Opferdoktrin* (victimhood)–omissions affecting the surviving victims and their offspring, as well as education and historiography.[6]

Soon after the *Anschluss* there were also heroic acts of resistance. Up to the end of the war 35,000 Austrians died in prisons and concentration camps: 2,700 were sentenced to death by the so-called People's Courts and executed. More than 70,000 people, functionaries of the *Ständestaat*, but also many Social Democrats and Communists as well as monarchists, were arrested. Already on 1 April, ten days prior to the plebiscite, the Nazis took many of their opponents, among them eminent personalities of the Second Republic's political leadership, such as the later Federal Chancellors Leopold Figl and Alfons Gorbach, Vice-Chancellor Fritz Bock, Vienna mayor Karl Seitz and trade union head Franz Olah, to the Dachau concentration camp. The shameful anti-Semitic excesses were soon followed by the 'proper' Aryanization of some 60,000 apartments as well as of numerous shops and firms. In their satirical one-man play, the legendary *Der Herr Karl*, the authors Carl Merz and Helmut Qualtinger have succeeded in sketching a haunting portrait of a perpetual Viennese opportunist. Some 130,000 Jews were driven away and approximately 65,000 were deported and murdered; 8,000 Roma and Sinti, as well as many mentally and physically challenged people, fell victim to the National Socialists' racist mania.

The prelude to the Second World War unleashed by the Nazi dictatorship was the obliteration of Austria from the map of the world by her degradation to Ostmark, later replaced by the term of Alpen-und Donaugauen (Alpine and Danubian territories). A few figures should suffice to spell out its terrible consequences: of the more than 1.2 million Austrian soldiers, 250,000 fell or died as prisoners of war. The number of wounded was even higher, while 24,320 civilians perished in air raids or other military actions.

The contemporary Austrian historian Günter Bischof, who teaches in New Orleans, holds the view that Chancellor Karl Renner had already constructed all the elements of the post-war victim ideology in the Declaration of Independence of 27 April 1945. This proclaimed that the annexation enforced on the Austrian people in 1938 had rendered them powerless, had led them into a senseless and unwinnable war of conquest that no Austrian had ever wanted. Renner—as said by Günter Bischof—had not devoted a single word to the collaboration of many Austrians with Nazi Germany; no word was mentioned about resistance; not a word about the surprising fact that so many remained tenaciously on the side of the Nazi regime until the very last days of the war; not a word about the participation of Austrians in involuntary euthanasia, the exploitation of forced labourers, in the Holocaust, and the death marches; not a single word about the very well-known participation of many soldiers in the crimes of the Wehrmacht. On the contrary: Renner portrayed all Austrian soldiers as victims.

In one of his historical reflections about the thorny question of Austrians in the Wehrmacht, President Heinz Fischer stated: 'The Austrians were not collectively guilty or collectively innocent between 1938 and 1945; there were millions of different biographies with heroic deeds and misdeeds, with compliance and repudiation, with courage and cowardice. ... There can be no blanket condemnation, but neither can there be a blanket acquittal. We have to take the far more taxing course of differentiation, the course of individual responsibility, the course of saying sorry and of forgiveness, and above all the course of learning for the future.'

Heinz Fischer argued similarly for enlightenment and for historical truth regarding the German Wehrmacht: 'We know today—and it should also be clearly articulated—that not everyone who wore the uniform of the German Wehrmacht has automatically incurred guilt. ... But at the same time we know—and this too should be openly asserted—that the German Wehrmacht was made into the instrument of a criminal war of aggression, and we also know that there is a great deal of evidence of war crimes along the paths of the German Wehrmacht across large parts of Europe, which it is not only legitimate but also necessary to disclose and resolve. And with every war crime there is inevitably a perpetrator and a victim.'[7]

The President's words differed from the political speeches of the preceding decades. Even in view of the time that has elapsed and the awareness of the terrible consequences of the war, the Nazi regime has, until recently, been judged differently by most historians and by a considerable section of the populace. In his analysis, the Salzburg historian Ernst Hanisch used the example of Salzburg to enumerate some major elements of bonding with the Nazi regime: an accelerated surge in modernization with a decline in unemployment, loosening the bonds of the family and the church, pseudo-revolutionary ideological propaganda, the special effect of the Führer myth, socio-political achievements, and the blurring of class barriers through the *Volksgemeinschaft* (national community), the yearning for the *Anschluss* that had been fed for decades, and the victory of German identity. Professor Ernst Hanisch confirmed Kreisky's earlier quoted statement when he characterized the reaction to the *Anschluss*: 'In 1938, not a few workers were filled with secret glee that the hated Schuschnigg regime was getting what it deserved. ... And after 1945 the SPÖ was more willing to forgive a functionary if he had become weak in 1938, rather than if he had sold his principles in 1934.' With the looming catastrophe a growing number of people discovered their hidden Austrian identity. His conclusion: 'However, what caused people to close ranks was fear of the East, that is to say, anti-Communism.'[8]

3

THE VICTIM MYTH AND 'ZERO HOUR' 1945

The discussions of the past twenty years about the pivotal years of the Second Republic dealt in particular with the 'great taboo'–Austria's handling of her past. The shift from the victim myth to the perpetrator myth in the perception of Austria, which often appears astonishing to the younger generation, is linked to the 'Zero Hour' of 1945, i.e. to the end of the war and the National Socialist regime, as well as to the creation of the Second Republic.

The Moscow Declaration of 1 November 1943 was figuratively speaking the international birth certificate of the Second Republic and the actual basis of the victim myth. It recognized that Austria had been the first free country to fall a victim to Hitlerite aggression, and the governments of the United Kingdom, the Soviet Union and the United States agreed that Austria should therefore be restored as a free and independent country. It declared 'the annexation imposed upon Austria by Germany on 15 March 1938 as null and void'. This declaration offered post-war Austria a surprising political chance. In view of many derisive references by foreign critics, it should be clearly stated that the victim thesis in Moscow had come about without any manipulation by Austrian émigré circles.

It was also meant to encourage Austrian resistance through the following: 'Austria is reminded, however, that she has a responsibility which she cannot evade for participation in the war on the side of Hitlerite Germany, and that in the final settlement account will inevitably be taken of her own contribution to her liberation.' Despite forming a 'Provisional Austrian National Committee' and despite the (fruitless) efforts of a few officers (subsequently executed by the SS) to prevent the destruction of Vienna, the Moscow Declaration did not succeed in

17

mobilizing a militarily significant resistance. As an Austrian editor put it: 'It cannot be denied that a broad resistance movement did not have any basis among the population, that the exhortations to hold out and the fanaticism were effective until the very last, witness the horrible example when in February 1944 almost 500 prisoners had escaped from the Mauthausen concentration camp, and the local population took part in the hunt in which almost all of them were murdered.'[1]

Many people—Austrian resistance fighters, escaped forced labourers, deserted soldiers, and first and foremost thousands of Hungarian Jews—did not live to see 'Zero hour'. For the Catholic, Monarchist, Social Democrat, Communist and liberal bourgeois anti-Nazis, and almost certainly for those who had participated in the euphoria of 1938 but who with time had become disillusioned or embittered, liberation by the Allies, coupled with the rebirth of the republic, meant a complete break with the past. The liberation saved the lives of political prisoners, as for example that of the future Chancellor Leopold Figl, and of those approximately 5,800 people who counted as Jews according to the Nürnberg racial laws, but who lived in 'mixed marriages' with non-Jewish partners and were (still) exempt from deportation.

As far as the massive collaboration with the Nazi system is concerned, there is no doubt about the figure of the 536,000 registered former members of the National Socialist party. Still, Professor Gerald Stourzh, the respected Austrian historian, rightly emphasizes that in countries that were deemed to have been victims of Hitler's aggression, as for example in France, thanks to the Vichy regime there was an enormous number of collaborators. In the case of the Third Reich's allies, such as Hungary, Romania, Slovakia and Croatia, tens of thousands of perpetrators, fellow-travellers and informers profited from the 'Aryanization' of Jewish property and the theft of valuables from Jews deported to Auschwitz.

What Jean Améry expressed in his awesome book, *At the Mind's Limits: Contemplations by a Survivor on Auschwitz and its Realities*, applies not only to Germany but equally to Austria and Hungary: 'No one can establish how many Germans were aware, approved of, or themselves perpetrated the crimes, and how many in their powerless dislike let the others get away with them.' In my native country, Hungary, the deportation of 437,000 Jewish citizens within two months in the summer of 1944, and the later death marches to Austria, did not elicit any significant protest.

Contrary to assumptions asserted especially abroad, the Provisional Government of Austria enacted a stringent National-Socialist Prohibition Act and the War Criminals Law. The denazification between 1945 and 1947 meant not only (until 1948) deprivation of civil rights from people charged with having been Nazis. From the liberation of Austria until the end of 1947, a total of 101,714 persons required to register were dismissed from the public service. Atonement measures, such as work and monetary services, bans from professions, and various sanctions were imposed on ranking members of the NSDAP and other highly active supporters of the regime (the so-called *Belasteten* or 'illegals') from the 1933–8 period. More than 23,000 final judgments were imposed, forty-three of them death sentences, of which 30 were executed. The registration of former National Socialists until 1948 was more comprehensive, and the rate of tracing Nazi crimes between 1945 and 1955 significantly higher, than in Germany.[2]

Many studies and touching memoirs have been published about the rebirth of Austria and the enormous difficulties experienced with regard to the 'new beginning'. Excellent TV documentaries on Austrian history were watched by millions of viewers. The important speech made by the then German Federal President Richard von Weizsäcker on 8 May 1985, the 40th anniversary of the capitulation, offers a historical–political background not only for Germans, but also for Austrians, and Europeans in general. Its central message was: '8 May was a day of liberation. It liberated all of us from the dehumanizing system of National Socialist tyranny.'

The collapse of the Nazi dictatorship was, of course, the precondition for the rebuilding of an independent and democratic Austria, even if at the time many people, for a variety of private reasons, would not recognize it yet as liberation. However, in contrast to Austria, for Hungary, as for other future Eastern Bloc countries, the liberation was only a relatively brief transition from one foreign dictatorship to another; from the Nazi occupation to bondage under the red star.

It was the Soviet army that had saved the lives of the Gestapo's prisoners in Vienna, and most of all of the surviving Jews threatened by total eradication in Central and Eastern Europe. Yet one must also remember that it was that same Red Army that had committed shocking outrages against civilians. Note the mass rapes of women from

Budapest to Vienna and Berlin and—even after the consolidation—the numerous abductions of political opponents. These harrowing ordeals, and the memories of the surviving combatants and POWs, became imprinted in the collective memory of generations. Until the controversy over the military past of Federal President Kurt Waldheim, silence predominated about the fate of the 600,000 foreign civilian forced labourers and the 200,000 Austrian Jews.

The denial of the past politics of the Nazis (the oft-cited *Lebenslüge*) already characterized the birth of the Second Republic. The Declaration of Independence of 27 April 1945 by the Provisional State Government, headed by Karl Renner, proclaimed not only the restoration of the republic. It also solemnly established Austria's status of victim without complicity. It took almost sixty-one years before Federal President Heinz Fischer as the first Austrian head of state publicly contradicted the 'unacceptable black—white construction' in the preamble to the Declaration of Independence:

'It is simply not true that the war instigated by Hitler was ever anticipated or wanted by "any Austrians". What is true, rather, is that not a few Austrians were fully aware and frequently warned that "Hitler meant war". But another section of Austrians unfortunately took the risk, and, blinded by his initial successes, followed the *Führer* enthusiastically into the war.

'It is also too simple and incomplete to say that the defenceless state leadership was tricked and forced into the *Anschluss*, without adding that the state leadership was to a large extent defenceless because part of the Austrian population—naturally not all of them—reacted with well-documented enthusiasm to the *Anschluss* and the invasion of German troops at the Heldenplatz and elsewhere.

'And it is painful that in the preamble the many sons of our country who have been "unscrupulously sacrificed" in Hitler's aggressive war are (rightly) mourned, but not a single word is devoted to the murdered Jews, Roma and Sinti, the victims of the concentration camps or those who have been forced to leave their country.'

The Federal President could not offer a 'satisfactory answer' in his speech to the question: 'Why only now?' Still, he frankly stated: 'Better late than never.' At the same time, he referred to the fact that the view expressed in the Declaration of Independence 'had made it more difficult after 1945 to pose the right questions, to find the right answers and to use the right expressions. It had only considered part of the victims and had overlooked part of the perpetrators.'[3]

The Austrians, or rather the then Foreign Minister Leopold Figl, succeeded through sheer doggedness and courage—proverbially at the last minute on 14 May 1955, on the eve of the solemn signing of the State Treaty—in having a phrase contained in the treaty's preamble, even more pointedly referring to Austria's responsibility for the war than the one in the Moscow Declaration of 1943, deleted without substitution. This fact was immediately conveyed by a jubilant Figl to the waiting journalists. The approval by the four signatories to eliminate 'the ominous and for Austria defamatory' reference was celebrated as a stroke of luck and a tribute to the Second Republic.[4]

The joy and gratification of the founding generation was understandable, considering that in Figl's first cabinet, in the first freely elected government after 1945, of the 17 members 12 were former concentration camp prisoners, including Figl himself, and 118 of the 215 representatives in the National and Federal Council were also former political prisoners or resistance fighters. Nonetheless 40 years later the outspoken philosopher Rudolf Burger rightly pointed out that 'since 1955, the ideology about Austria's rebirth based on the concept of the innocent victim, combined with permanent neutrality, which no one had wanted at first, became a key element of national identity'.[5]

If one follows the logic of the Federal President's earlier cited critical argument, it becomes self-evident that the stroke of luck on 14 May 1955, i.e. the elimination of the reference to the partial responsibility for the war, actually completed the repression of the past, further prolonging the overdue facing up to Austrian participation in the National Socialist regime. All the same, the political success of the state was undoubtedly extremely important, and the Austrian attitude tactically and politically very clever. The foremost historian of the State Treaty negotiations, Gerald Stourzh, also argues: 'Had Austria not claimed the status of a liberated country for which the Moscow Declaration offered the chance, but had considered herself as a defeated and conquered part of the Donau- and Alpengaus, as "defeated" Ostmark, then Austria would in fact be … nothing more than one of three—since 1990 of two—German states that has emerged from the bankrupt estate of the Greater German Empire. The consciousness of Austrian independence and identity, which seems so self-evident half a century later, could never have developed.'[6]

And the fact that Austria was spared the fate of Germany's division and, despite a Soviet occupation zone, could assert her democratic

unity was—despite all critical reservations from today's viewpoint—
due in the first place to the political farsightedness and determined
actions of President Karl Renner, one of the most controversial and
enigmatic personalities of Austrian history.

4

FOUNDING FATHER OF MANY FACES

The history of the Second Republic confirms the accuracy of Isaiah Berlin's argument that, contrary to the Marxist-materialist concept of history, crucial political courses are set by individuals: 'I do not believe in historical determinism. At crucial moments, turning points … chance, individuals and their decisions and acts, themselves not necessarily predictable—indeed seldom so—can determine the course of history.' Berlin used the examples of Lenin and Churchill to define the intellectual game of 'what if …'. What if Lenin had died in April 1917 or Churchill had not become Prime Minister in 1940? He added: 'So there *are* turning points in history. At these turning points individuals sometimes swing the issue in one new direction or the other.'[1]

That is exactly what happened when one April morning in 1945 the seventy-five-year-old Karl Renner left his house in Gloggnitz at the foot of the Semmering, without an overcoat but with a walking stick, to protest at the local Russian headquarters against the violent behaviour of the Soviet soldiers and to request a more lenient treatment of the population. It was sheer coincidence that the Soviet political commissar in the office recognized his name and realized that he was talking to the first State Chancellor of the First Republic from 1918. What transpired in the course of the ensuing days, during his conversations with high-ranking Soviet officers, and finally after his personal letter dated 15 April 1945 addressed to 'The Esteemed Comrade; His Excellency, Marshall Stalin', is known to posterity only from Renner's subsequently penned summary. It is puzzling to this day how and why a retired Austrian politician could emerge from oblivion with the help of the Russian occupiers to become a key figure at the Republic's rebirth.

It was Karl Renner's biographer, the prominent Social Democratic journalist Jacques Hannak, who related to me details about this incredible and still somewhat enigmatic story. Hannak, who had returned from his French and American exile to Vienna only in 1946, had written Karl Renner's biography and arranged for the posthumous publication of his works. Hannak was an unusual and outgoing older colleague, who took me, a foreign correspondent 40 years his junior, under his wing. During the late sixties he invited me from time to time to his informal gatherings in a Viennese wine tavern. At these totally informal parties one could meet well-known actors and actresses, journalists and writers, but also interesting young politicians and scholars.

Here, and also at our meetings in various coffee-houses, while I was researching my Kreisky biography, Hannak told me fascinating details about the factional disputes within the Austrian Socialist movement before and after the Second World War, especially about the conflicts between one of the leading thinkers of the left Socialist Austro-Marxist tendency, Otto Bauer, and the spokesman of the pragmatic right, Karl Renner. Despite his close relationship with Renner, Hannak did not hide from me his partiality for the failed great rival, Otto Bauer. Bruno Kreisky also affirmed time after time, in personal conversations as well as in his memoirs, that from the very beginning he had felt committed to him with every fibre of his political thinking, and that 'despite some [of his] misjudgements' Otto Bauer had belonged amongst the greatest intellectuals he had ever met.[2]

The Social Democratic activists, as well as the Viennese workers, had admired and even loved Bauer, the romantic—and respected Renner, the pragmatist. As a historian of the First Republic noted, Renner had been a politician without illusions, while Bauer had lived in the world of illusions.[3] Jacques Hannak never went as far of course—not even in conversation—as the author quoted, who described Renner as 'a political chameleon'. Still, in his biography even Hannak termed it carefully but unmistakably as a 'far-reaching mistake' that Renner had avowed a public and uncoerced commitment to the *Anschluss* and the 'Yes' vote in the plebiscite, expressly 'as a Social Democrat and thereby as a champion of the right to self-determination of all peoples, as the first Chancellor of the German–Austrian Republic, and as former president of the peace delegation to St-Germain'. However, the Nazis could not achieve their goal of compromising Renner in front of the world, as people were (erroneously) convinced that Renner had been forced to make his statements.[4]

Actually at the time all of the leading Social Democrats were in favour of the *Anschluss* to Germany. Otto Bauer wrote even after the German occupation, '... the rallying cry, by which we oppose the foreign rule of the Fascists from the *Reich* over Austria, cannot be the reactionary rallying cry of the re-establishment of Austria's independence, but the revolutionary rallying cry of the Pan-German revolution ...' Still, the effect of Renner's long declaration, published a week prior to the plebiscite ordered by Hitler in one of the Viennese newspapers controlled by the Nazis, far exceeded the importance of theoretical discussions in barely-read émigré papers. In his last article before his death, Bauer criticized Renner for having 'misrepresented the situation in a way which not even the terror under which all Austrians live now can barely excuse'.

In his memoirs, Kreisky, who contrary to most of his comrades had never accepted the *Anschluss*, treated the 'official sanctioning of the *Anschluss*' by Renner with ironic restraint: 'It was unimaginable for him that any facts created by Hitler would still change during his lifetime. History had spoken and one had to bend before it, he believed, I would almost say like a reed in the wind. To what extent personal motives, anxiety for his son-in-law and suchlike, played a part in it, I do not know. There are after all many reasons for a certain political behaviour, subjective as well as objective, and it seemed to me, at any rate, as if Renner would have yielded to any given situation. ... The Nazis let him completely alone ... why should we blame Renner for something that many others have also done, if not in such a prominent position as he.'[5]

Regardless of his chequered past, Karl Renner grasped the opportunity offered personally by Stalin. Through his imaginative and bold reaction he rose like a phoenix from the ashes of the ruins in his homeland to become in April 1945 (again) State Chancellor of the first provisional government, and eventually Federal President in December 1945. His discussions, first with the political officers of the local Soviet high command in Gloggnitz, followed by those with high-ranking political officials, and eventually two days later with Colonel General Aleksej S. Sheltov in the headquarters in Eastern Austria, were drawn out, 'very respectful' from the side of the Soviets, and at the end of the day downright sensational: Sheltov, the actual Soviet political commissar for Austria and deputy to Marshall Tolbukhin, the commander-in-chief of the 3rd Ukrainian Front, invited the seventy-five-year-old retired politician to form and head a new Austrian government.

That the appointment of Renner could only have come about on Stalin's personal instruction, and that Sheltov, as the probable top man of the NKVD's secret service in Austria, had a direct line to the Kremlin, seems in retrospect just as certain as Renner's clearly noticeable and later frankly admitted aspiration, once again as in 1918, to assume the highest office in the interests of his country. His long obsequious letter must almost certainly have confirmed Stalin's belief that the ageing politician would be an easily manipulated figurehead of a satellite government. Why else would he have chosen a right-wing Social Democrat, burdened by his affirmative vote for the *Anschluss*, whom Lenin once reviled as one of 'the most contemptible lackeys of German imperialism' and 'a traitor to socialism', as being now a reliable collaborator for the Soviets in the key position of Eastern Austria?

In his just about forgotten and rarely cited letter to 'Marshall, Excellency, very esteemed Comrade' Stalin, Renner offered, as the last President of the then still free parliament, to speak for the Austrian people, and as the first Chancellor also to establish the official administration. He therefore regarded it as his 'absolute duty' to place his person completely and utterly at the service of this matter. He then affirmed that all of the people were filled with admiration for the enormous achievements of the Soviets and closed the letter with the statement: 'The confidence in the Soviet Republic, especially on the part of the Austrian working class, has become boundless. The Social Democrats will deal with the Communist party in a fraternal manner, and will cooperate on an equal footing during the re-establishment of the Republic. That the future of the country belongs to Socialism is indisputable and requires no emphasis.'

Those familiar with the labour movement and with the Stalinist show trials of the thirties regarded it as particularly odd that at the beginning of his obsequious letter Renner not only prided himself on his personal acquaintance with Lenin, but also on his regular contact during his Viennese years with Trotsky, Stalin's arch-enemy who had been assassinated on his personal orders in Mexico in 1940. According to Jacques Hannak, it cannot be established how much in Renner's letter was genuine and how much cleverly contrived naivety. At any rate, Stalin replied briefly and amicably on 12 May, and even apologized for the belated response.[6]

The fact that the Renner-led provisional government was entirely dependent on the goodwill of the Soviet occupying forces was so obvious that the Western Allies at first totally ignored the Soviet-installed Renner coalition cabinet consisting of Social Democrats (SPÖ), Communists (KPÖ) and representatives of the Austrian People's Party (Österreichische Volkspartei – ÖVP). Apart from Renner himself, very few Austrians or foreign observers believed that Karl Renner would succeed in outmanoeuvring the Soviets and set the crucial course for the future of a democratic and free Austria. With tremendous energy and surprising fighting ability, combined with shrewd tactics and thanks also to the total support of the leading cabinet ministers of the SPÖ and ÖVP, Renner managed to realize his two main demands: the holding of early free national elections and the establishment of an all-Austrian government.

Both sides—Moscow and the West—underestimated Renner. Four years later the British Sunday paper, the *Observer*, acknowledged his historic breakthrough: '... This time the Russians had chosen the wrong man. Renner was mild, friendly and engaging, and also willing to let the Communists have a few cabinet seats, but entirely capable of keeping the reins in his own hands. He gently resigned himself to being described by some of his foreign friends as a Russian puppet; he did not cause any offence to the occupying power, he was flexible, polite, charming. But the subject on which he insisted with steadfast serenity was the necessity of general elections ...'[7]

That Renner could, with a 'masterstroke', gain the Russians' agreement to free elections as early as 25 November 1945 was, of course, due also to the Communists' boundless overestimation of their own strength. Luckily for Austria, the Communists and their supporters in the Soviet occupying force miscalculated the true feelings of the Austrian people: instead of the expected 25 per cent, they received only 5.4 per cent and four seats as against the ÖVP's eighty-five and the SPÖ's seventy-six mandates. The 'Russian Party' never recovered from this debacle. Except for the Communist-inspired great strike in the fall of 1950, which was regarded at the time as a putsch attempt, the KPÖ never again played any significant role. Three years after the Hungarian Revolution of 1956, it completely disappeared from the parliament.

According to Hannak and all other observers, Renner's firmness from the very first in claiming jurisdiction for his government over all of Austria was of vital significance for the country's future. Luckily at the time this demand was in the interests of Soviet politics; after all, it concerned a government appointed by the Soviets. After the Communists' electoral defeat it was not possible to challenge the democratic legitimacy of the Renner government, and the government's recognition by the Western Allies (which took place only on 20 October 1945), put an end to any ideas of dividing the country. The enormous significance of the free elections and recognition of a national government for Austria is shown by the fate of divided Germany up to 1989 and the tragedy of the Central and Eastern European states, turned by the Communists into Soviet satellites. A further important success of Renner's was that he managed to hinder a politically risky discussion about a new constitution planned by the Russians, and instead carried through the restoration of the constitution of 1929. With his 'enormous resourcefulness' (praised also by Kreisky) and negotiating skill, Renner, more than any other politician, contributed to saving Austria from the fate of the neighbouring peoples' democracies. For instance, in the matter of the constitution he gave the Communists the option to resign or to come to terms with the suggested solution. In doing so he was probably aided by a personal trait, which he himself pointed out with unusual candour in a private letter to an official of the Socialist International: 'All my life I could not have cared less—and I consider this a forte of mine—what people thought of me *at the moment* ...' (original emphasis by Renner!)

On that April morning in Gloggnitz, in line with the wishes of Stalin but by virtue of his own initiative, Renner got into the historically unique situation of being as State Chancellor the founder of two republics—those of 1918 and 1945. The man who was discredited as an opportunist and seemed to have been compromised by having declared himself for the *Anschluss* played the role of a widely admired unifying figure as a head of government, and after 20 December 1945 as the Federal President unanimously elected by the Federal Assembly, as in 1918. The above-quoted *Observer* article of 1949 concluded with the sentence: 'If this second Austrian republic remains successful, then it will stand as a monument to Dr Renner.'

It seems a miracle even in hindsight that the seventy-five-year-old Renner, with his inimitable ability to adapt to the ever-changing realities of the times, was available in such challenging times. Kreisky was correct in writing that no one else could have done a better job of it. It was also fortunate that, in contrast to Hungary or to the then Czechoslovakia, Renner had such farsighted and determined personalities behind him as Adolf Schärf (later Federal President) and Oskar Helmer (Minister of the Interior) of the SPÖ, and Leopold Figl and Julius Raab (both subsequently Federal Chancellors) of the ÖVP to ward off the Communists' subversive activities during the four-power occupation of the Second Republic.

The experiences in the neighbouring peoples' democracies provided the best proof of the appalling consequences of the Communist tactic of infiltration. Luckily in Austria there were no Social Democratic collaborators, who in Prague and Budapest served as useful decorations for the various stages of the Communist takeover. Anti-Communism thus became an extremely important basic element of Austrian identity and political stability. This anti-Communism cannot be shrugged off as a remnant of the Cold War. If one knows from one's own experience the destruction of values and of people wrought by the Communist dictatorships, one can only rejoice in the happy chance that not only the western provinces but also the Soviet-occupied part of Austria were spared this fate.

5

THE ROLE OF A FOREIGN CORRESPONDENT

The relationship between journalists and politicians belongs amongst the most controversial aspects of the professional—social sphere. I subscribe to the view of the eminent German journalist Klaus Harpprecht, 'that journalism is the most wonderful, the most terrible of professions ... with the blessing of unquenchable curiosity. Journalism is the chance to live many lives'.[1]

During the course of half a century I too seized this chance in Austria. As a foreign correspondent I have gained an insight into the small and relatively transparent world of Austrian politics and economics.

After my arrival in Vienna—for as long as my mother did not receive her exit visa from Hungary—I wrote articles about the Eastern Bloc for English- and German-language newspapers under three different pseudonyms. Then, in the summer of 1960, I started to work as the Vienna correspondent of the British *Financial Times*. My first report appeared at the beginning of May 1960, the last almost twenty-two years later. Since then I have also been writing for Swiss and Austrian newspapers as their commentator on East European affairs. This was an incredibly lucky break for a Hungarian refugee. Through contacts I had made while still in Warsaw, many a door was opened for me in Vienna.

Because of the different and, for the readers, confusing pseudonyms (which the Hungarian secret service managed, of course, very soon to decipher), my early contacts with Austrian politics and economics were haphazard. I began to forge closer contacts with leading personalities of Austrian politics and business only when I started to work as a foreign correspondent for the *FT* (the *Financial Times*). The opinions of the prestigious foreign newspapers have been, as they still are, of particular importance for the small Austrian economy.

At the *FT* the correspondents learned the clear division between facts and comments, the priority of informing the reader fairly and without missionary zeal, concisely and in a balanced way. Our task was to disseminate information, irrespective of one's own political conviction or sympathy, and not professions of faith. In view of the fact that economic journalists are particularly exposed to inducements, not to say overt or covert bribery, the complete separation between the business of advertising and the editorial staff was in this respect a first-rate safety mechanism at the *FT*.

During the twenty-two years as its Viennese correspondent, the head office of the *FT* never interfered with my work. The same applied to the copy-editing. Giving the finishing touch to a report, or cutting the text, never meant changing its content. Only once did I have to make a protest in London. That came about because a foreign editor, who frequently cooperated with me in writing the Austrian supplements, had softened a critical reference in my report about the conflict between Chancellor Kreisky and his controversial Finance Minister Hannes Androsch. Apart from that, in my time the *FT* was—and remains most likely to this day—a citadel of journalistic independence.

During these years I was close enough to the events and the protagonists to get to know them from personal experience, and not to have to work out everything from history books and biographies. On the other hand, I was not influenced by any institution or personality, let alone dependent on them—not even on Bruno Kreisky, whose biography I published in 1972—in a way that would have induced me to reflect their viewpoints in my articles. As an Austrian by choice, not by birth, I still write about the distant or recent past of this complex and so successful country in accordance with my own convictions, but always determined to remain unswayed by feelings of aversion or of sympathy.

I discovered relatively early in the game that covert corruption is the chief danger that threatens political and economic journalists in Austria. At a meeting with the then president of the Austrian Industrialists' Association, the general manager of a large textile mill in Vöslau, I complained about the seeming lack of interest from Austrian enterprises in the foreign press. As an example I cited the tyre factory Semperit. I had rung them to make an appointment for an interview for a lengthier article I was planning to write, but after a considerable time I received the laconic answer that they were not currently interested in a contact with the *Financial Times*!

As a greenhorn I was flabbergasted by this information. After I had told the story to the jovial president of the industrialists, he placed his hand on my shoulder and asked me: And what is the cost of such an article, my dear friend? Taken aback, I replied: In my case, nothing at all, Mr President! I am only interested in information about the economy and not in advertisements for my paper ... When the *FT* advertising department sent someone to Vienna to obtain advertisements for an Austrian supplement, I had absolutely nothing to do with it, nor did any other correspondent in a similar situation. The fact that, through my relatively frequent reports, the *FT* became known in Austria might have helped the advertising revenue, but I was paid a monthly retainer only for my work as a correspondent.

Invitations for domestic or even foreign jaunts, as well as Christmas presents for economic journalists, were ubiquitous then too. Some colleagues received expensive watches and even shares from successful enterprises. During my twenty-two years as a correspondent I never personally experienced any attempt at bribery.

In the meantime the media situation had changed for the worse. It was not a matter of curtailing editorial freedom, but of subtle pressures, such as the cancelling of advertisements or the refusal of information or interviews. The demise of independent newspapers and the consolidation of interests in the media sector combined to worsen the working conditions of journalists even before the triumphant advance of the internet.[2]

One must never forget, of course, the antagonism between politics and journalism; they are hostile brothers, who are nevertheless dependent on each other. Since the year dot, Austrian political and economic circles have always asked in a crisis situation: What do they say about us abroad? The reports of correspondents of important foreign papers are particularly often quoted before national elections.

If the article is relatively positive, it is promptly claimed in various press releases by the respective government as proof of its correct policies. On the other hand, criticism from abroad is immediately heralded by the opposition. That is what happened to the *FT*, for instance, at the beginning of 1970, when the ÖVP government placed my article about the healthy economic situation in the form of a large advertisement in the leading papers, with the comment: Compliments which we gladly pass on. At the beginning of 1975, the Kreisky government proclaimed in large advertisements that, according to the *FT*, Austria could win a World Cup for its economic performance. There was a great flurry in the Austrian press, and malicious comments opined that a paid article was at the bottom of it all. In fact, it was only a single sentence by a London editor in a routine introductory article, which was partly also critical, to an Austrian supplement. Incidentally, we were right on both occasions: the general economic situation in Austria compared to the rest of Europe was really good in 1970 and 1974.

Apart from the international news agencies, only a few foreign newspapers had permanent correspondents with their own offices in Vienna during the 1960s and '70s. The foreign correspondent had to be accredited by the Press Service of the Federal Chancellery and subsequently obtain a press card with a photo from the Association of Foreign Correspondents. Yet more important than these identity cards and the attendance at the press conferences organized by the Concordia Press Club were the direct contacts with decision-makers and their immediate entourage. In contrast to the foreign colleagues on flying visits to international conferences or on the coat-tails of a government delegation, we, the permanent Vienna correspondents, knew that the dies are often cast not in the Council of Ministers on the Ballhausplatz, but in the inconspicuous offices of the presidents of the Federation of Trade Unions and the Chamber of Commerce.

6

COMPROMISE

THE BASIC PRINCIPLE OF SOCIAL PARTNERSHIP

Compromise, wrote the prominent German sociologist Georg Simmel, is one of the 'greatest inventions of humanity' because it constitutes the basic principle of democracy. The notion that no one can completely assert his interests, and that everyone has to lower his sights in favour of the other, provides in fact for the non-violent settlement of interests and with it for a relatively fair and peaceful coexistence.[1]

The willingness to compromise was the connecting link between the founding fathers of the Second Republic. The shared memories of the terrible years in the Nazi concentration camps (Dachau) and the Nazi prisons always proved to be stronger than the supposed advantages to be gained from the prevailing infighting. The fact that the ÖVP and SPÖ have worked together as coalition partners for twenty years after the Second World War, i.e. even after the conclusion of the State Treaty, was eloquent proof of the strength of this tradition.

Hermann Withalm, the long-standing General Secretary of the ÖVP, feared by his opponents because of his toughness and acclaimed by his followers, wrote in his memoirs: 'I am fascinated again and again by the fact that the two great camps in this country, which had fought each other on 12 February 1934 in a bloody civil war, realized eleven years later that only democracy, cooperation and tolerance could constitute the foundation of a concerted effort for the reconstruction of Austria. ... Although I was doubtless a tough and very unpleasant opponent, especially for the Socialists, I should like to declare with great personal satisfaction and pleasure that it is precisely with those political opponents with whom I had the fiercest conflicts that I now have the most unclouded human relationships.'[2]

As head of the ÖVP club in parliament, Withalm, called by a journalist the 'Iron Hermann', had waged the most heated battles of words with his opposite number, the head of the SPÖ group, Bruno Pittermann. When the latter fell seriously ill, Withalm visited him in hospital every week. It was a profoundly human gesture, which became known only much later. 'What we all need the most is tolerance, the attempt to understand the other, the exchange of ideas', wrote this open-hearted politician in his last book.

The willingness to carry on a dialogue at every level, combined with the joint defence against the Communists' united front tactic and the Soviet attempts at intimidation, formed the basis of that Social Partnership which, in my opinion, was the precondition of the Austrian economic miracle. After five successive agreements on prices and wages involving the major economic interest groups between 1947 and 1951, the Parity Commission of Wages and Prices was established in 1957 with the appropriate subcommittees, and finally the Advisory Council for Social and Economic Affairs was set up in 1963. The system of Social Partnership was a profoundly Austrian specialty and it was never easy to explain it to foreign readers. Bruno Kreisky called the conflict of interests between trade unions and trade associations a 'sublimated class war' fought at the negotiating table.

The Chambers of Economy, Workers and Peasants, firmly established in the constitution, as well as the voluntary interest organizations such as the trade unions and the Industrialists' Association, make up the pillars of this corporate system. Though the former leader of the ÖVP and at present successful businessman Josef Taus held that the Social Partnership was not a 'secondary government', it was at any rate 'a unique construct, which represented a sort of amalgam of government and stakeholders. The social partners took part in governing. The conflicts were acted out at the negotiating table. Not everything was good, not everything was right, but it functioned rather well.'[3]

The system of the Social Partnership, partly admired and partly almost disdained by foreign political scientists and observers, has survived all the shifts and changes of Austrian politics. One of the conservative observers pointed out already thirty years ago that by maintaining social peace, the social partners had contributed greatly to that general social stability which far transcends monetary stability. Thanks to the Social Partnership, domestic consensus and labour peace were the basic prerequisites of economic growth and of rising prosperity.[4]

A Social Democratic thinker also described the Social Partnership as the unquestionably most important institutional innovation in post-war Austria.[5] This neo-corporative system (*Kammerstaat*) was unique for other reasons as well. There were, and are, also many cases of 'personal union', that is, of one person holding two or even three posts at the same time in different parts of the network: in the government, as member of parliament and as an active official of the trade unions or other professional organizations. This meant in fact that the same politicians appeared in different roles in the political decision-making in ministries, in parliament and also in the various committees and boards. The multiple functions of these key figures were from a democratic perspective of course also questionable, because the main focus of economic policy has shifted from the government itself to the complex web of overlapping organizations on both sides. The 'personal union' simplified the seemingly complicated procedures of decision-making.

There were two key figures during my time as *FT* correspondent. One was Rudolf Sallinger, a master stonemason, who led the Chamber of Commerce for twenty-six years, and at the same time was a member of parliament and chairman of the ÖVP's Economic Union (*Wirtschaftsbund*) which provided the bulk of financial support for the party. The other was the electrical fitter Anton Benya, who during the same period was president of the Austrian Federation of Trade Unions (1963–87), SPÖ member of parliament (1956–86) and even president of the parliament (1971–86). During the Sallinger—Benya era the following rule applied almost unreservedly: 'There were no economic laws in the broadest sense against the will of the corporative state, nor any labour laws, nor for that matter anything at all of importance.'[6]

I have known both men well. My first 'official' meeting as *FT* correspondent with Sallinger took place at a lunch in the exclusive Jockey Club at the Palais Pallavicini. We sat in a spacious private room, at opposite ends of a long table, while the waiters served us in white gloves. Between the two of us, almost as a go-between, sat the press officer of the Economic Chamber. He made sure that even in difficult situations the viewpoint of the economy should attract interest in the domestic and foreign media.

The power of these two basically simple people can only be properly understood if one also considers their positions within their respective parties. In an article written in the mid-sixties for the *FT*, 'The double life of Rudolf Sallinger', I described the working day of this busy-bee functionary, who appeared regularly at 6.00 a.m. in his small fifty–men stonemasonry firm inherited from his Italian father-in-law in Vienna's fifth district. There he checked the workflow and the orders, before receiving the first visitors two and a half hours later in his spacious office on the Ring. The fact that at the time his wife and three sisters ran the business left him with ample time and energy to concentrate on politics and the power games within the ÖVP.

Once, in a conversation, Sallinger suddenly, out of the blue, mentioned the name of a fellow Conservative MP and asked my opinion whether this man should become the new Minister for Trade. Taken aback, I gave a noncommittal answer. The ambitious Mitterer MP, the owner of a wholesale watch business and at the same time elected functionary of the Chamber of Commerce, became several years later Minister of Trade for a short while, and spent twenty-three years in parliament without having made any impact at all. Already at that time the question itself was more interesting than the person. It showed how politics were in fact subcontracted behind the scenes to the lobbies of businessmen and bureaucrats, and how the political barons running the People's Party-dominated Federal Economic Chamber and the party's Economic Union apply their power and pull the strings outside parliament.

The Sallinger family's home stood next to the workshop. The rustically furnished cellar was the setting for important decisions made by a small circle about questions such as the nomination or replacement of an ÖVP chairman or an ÖVP minister. As head of the financially strong Business League, at the time one of the ÖVP's 'iron triangle' of lobbies,[7] Sallinger was one of Austria's most powerful politicians for a quarter of a century.

The worldwide network of eighty-three offices of trade delegates subordinated to the Chamber was a unique institution. A total of 4,000 small and medium firms could avail themselves of the professional help of experts proficient in foreign languages. The trade delegates were, and are, as a rule better informed and more approachable than diplomats. They constituted one of the most important factors behind the impressive export successes of the Austrian economy. Over the years the Federal Economic Chamber had also invited numerous Austrian journalists to excellently organized European and overseas tours.

President Sallinger himself was a tireless world traveller. Although he spoke no foreign language, by virtue of his position he managed to gain access to even the loftiest personalities. Thus for instance he personally presented to President Reagan a magnificent Lipizzaner stallion as a gift from the Austrian economy. The presentation took place on the South Lawn of the White House in the glare of the press photographers' flashbulbs and TV cameras. He was received also by the Emperor of Japan and various kings. Ambassadors and trade delegates shook in their shoes prior to a visit by the 'fireball' in case something were to go awry.

I can still recall the atmosphere of crisis at the Austrian embassy in Belgrade, when in the early 1980s they were unable to arrange a meeting for Sallinger with the then Yugoslav Prime Minister in time before the Winter Olympics. On the other hand, a lightning visit to New Delhi served as a launching pad for the career of the trade delegate as his Hungarian-born wife surprised the boss with an excellent veal goulash...

In the Economic Union, in the actual political lobby group,[8] Sallinger had set the course for the advancement of two great political talents of the People's Party: Erhard Busek, the future Vice-Chancellor and ÖVP Chairman, served as his Secretary-General between 1968 and 1975; he was succeeded by Wolfgang Schüssel from 1975 until his appointment as Minister for Economic Affairs in 1989. To this day both politicians unreservedly value Sallinger's role as a pillar of the Social Partnership. Sallinger had an almost 'father and son relationship' with both Busek and Schüssel. 'He was a man of instincts. When his gut feeling warned him that something was wrong, he applied the brakes,' said Busek, and added: 'He showed this method in a quite delightful way—I grew a beard once, and he said there were two options: you can be Secretary-General or you can wear a beard! There was no further argument.'

Yet the boss of the Economic Union also had a certain admiration for people who were a bit more colourful. Thus he had been willing to accept Schüssel—despite some objections against his somewhat unconventional appearance at the time—as Busek's successor at the latter's recommendation. 'I did not like [Schüssel's] looks at all, with his checked shirts and trendy suits; on top of it he was also too much of a leftist for my liking ...', said Sallinger twenty years later in an interview. According to Busek, another of his objections was: 'If Schüssel wants to get somewhere, he must eat a bit more; he looks so scrawny ...'[9]

How does Schüssel regard his long-time boss, who, although giving him a long leash, laid down the law when necessary? According to Schüssel, Sallinger was one 'who liked to know about everything; one of his legendary bits of advice was always: to be in the know is power. It was not so much the visible exercise of power, but rather pulling the strings behind the scenes and always knowing what goes on that really signified power to him. He was very circumspect, cautious, one who applied the power that he possessed—and he certainly was a very powerful man—very carefully but sometimes also very resolutely.'

The golden era of the Social Partnership coincided with the single-party government of Kreisky (1970–83), and at the time Sallinger played a particularly important role, also as a counterbalance to the powerful president of the Austrian Federation of Trade Unions, Anton Benya. Only the insiders of the political and media elite knew that the personal relationship between Sallinger and Kreisky was more intimate than that between Kreisky and Benya, although the two most powerful representatives of the SPÖ conferred each Monday morning for a full hour or even longer. Yet for the Chancellor, Rudolf Sallinger was the trusted partner. In his memoirs Kreisky repeatedly paid tribute to him, for example in connection with their successful cooperation in preventing a looming metalworkers' strike in November 1974.

Already on the occasion of a visit to the USA in 1965, when Kreisky was Foreign Minister, a 'personal rapprochement' developed between the two of them during the return flight from Washington. The Sallinger couple could be seen at the parties hosted by Kreisky in the wine tavern near his home. Both Busek and Schüssel confirm in almost identical terms that President Sallinger had profoundly respected Kreisky, for his personal style as well as for his intellectual superiority.

For the Federal Chancellor, in turn, the 'honest and amicable relationship' with Sallinger was important, in order to keep the sensitive three-way arrangement between government, trade unions and private sector in balance. Despite the outwardly smooth cooperation with Benya, he had always nurtured a deep mistrust of the union leader. At the decisive SPÖ party convention on 1 February 1967, Benya made a vituperative speech against Kreisky's candidacy for the party leadership. Benya also played an important role in the conflict between Kreisky and his erstwhile crown prince, Hannes Androsch. During our conversations when I interviewed him on economic issues, Benya never uttered a critical word about the Federal Chancellor. At the same time, however, he always praised Androsch to the skies.

Kreisky was convinced that Benya, together with the then Minister of Justice Christian Broda, supported the intra-party intrigues against him, perhaps even initiated them. Moreover he was of the opinion until the very last that latent anti-Semitic resentment was a contributing factor in shaping the attitude of the trade union boss and later Speaker of the Parliament. To the best of my knowledge there is no concrete evidence for Kreisky's suspicion, which he mentioned to me on several occasions. It is nevertheless interesting that, during a conversation with the former ÖVP Vice-Chancellor Erhard Busek, he described Kreisky's suspicion to me as 'undoubtedly accurate'; he could recall Benya's tone.

Be that as it may, the relationship between these two symbols of the Social Partnership, namely Benya and Sallinger, was totally devoid of friction. They met once a week at 7.30 in the morning, alternately in the Chamber or in the ÖGB head office. Despite their partnership they never addressed each other informally. Schüssel describes their relationship today as 'a very intimate and at the same time respectful association. Benya and Sallinger took very great care never to upset each other, never to say anything negative about each other in public, and they also knew perfectly well that if they agreed to something then they had to keep to it even if all hell broke loose at home.'

It has to be emphasized, irrespective of the protagonists, that already in April 1945 the Social Democrat, Christian Democrat and Communist trade unionists reduced the number of forty-two organizations that had competed against each other in the First Republic to sixteen specialized organizations, and at the same time merged all the various factions into a non-party Trade Union Federation. Although the Social Democrat group always played the dominant role in this umbrella organization, this never meant a monopoly. This close bond of the unions with the SPÖ—which Victor Adler, the first leader of Austrian Social Democracy, dubbed the 'Siamese twins'—ensured the preconditions for economic advancement as well as for the political integration of workers and employees in the Second Republic.

The fact that on the occasion of the ÖGB president's birthday his opposite number on the employers' side, namely President of the Chamber Sallinger, was interviewed in the Austrian Television's newscast, and that on the following day Sallinger gave a dinner in honour of Benya, is the best proof that the previously unimaginable social peace had become the most stable basis for the normalcy admired by the West and envied by the Communist East. French, British and Italian colleagues were downright fascinated by the system, and above all by the successful shift of the class struggle from the street to the nego-tiating table. I was repeatedly asked to explain this phenomenon and its roots in the special supplements of the *Financial Times*.

There were, of course, also visiting foreign correspondents, for example from France, who, accustomed to fierce social conflicts at home, twaddled about the 'merry province of Austria'. In a longish conversation with me on the occasion of the 25th anniversary of the State Treaty, Bruno Kreisky replied indirectly to such flippant remarks: '... The type of conflicts we used to have, not only in the First Republic but also in the monarchy, those hate-filled fights at the universities between young people of various languages and religions, all that has been overcome, that does not exist any more, no one wants that any more. And after all, that shows a certain greatness, a sort of quiet greatness, if I may say so, that the Austrians have learnt from history, hopefully for some time to come. Else they would not repudiate all that. It is possible that this appears boring and uninteresting to some. But those who have witnessed the 'interesting times' of the thirties are happy that politics have become so boring now.'[10]

This 'quiet greatness' of the much-tested Austrians marked also the decisive period of the reconstruction until the State Treaty.

7

THE ECONOMIC MIRACLE

In contrast to the much-publicized German *Wirtschaftswunder* (economic miracle), Austria's rapid economic ascendancy was almost a secret. At any rate, for years it did not really register in the international media. At the time the following oft-cited anecdote was making the rounds at the Foreign Press Association of Vienna: What is the difference between the German and Austrian economic miracle? The Austrian was the real economic miracle—the Germans did work ...

In my reporting for the *Financial Times* I tracked the economic development from 1960 onwards. My first important interview with the then Foreign Minister Bruno Kreisky appeared in the *FT* at the beginning of my career as a foreign correspondent, on 21 June 1960. The topic was the role of the neutral member states of the European Free Trade Association (EFTA) in building bridges between the European Economic Community (EEC-predecessor of today's EU) and EFTA. This subject had for decades dominated Austrian foreign and foreign-trade policies, and proved from time to time to be an explosive issue within the various coalition governments and even within the two big parties.

I covered in those years the following major themes in several variations: the relationship with the Soviet Union—the most difficult signatory to the Austrian State Treaty of 1955—and particularly the efforts for the reduction of reparations (above all of the crude oil deliveries); the long-standing conflicts concerning the construction and control of the Trieste–Vienna pipeline; the political battles over the reform of the oversized nationalized industry; the political controversies in the government's eyes regarding the capital market; and the consolidation of the budget, as well as the liberalization of the monetary and foreign-trade policies.

As the *Financial Times* published several special supplements annually, for example about Austria's economic and political situation, but also about special topics such as the city of Vienna, the banks and the financial world, the export economy and investments, I was able in the course of time to meet all the Federal Chancellors, Finance Ministers, National Bank presidents, trade union and chamber bosses, as well as the general managers of the largest banks and nationalized businesses. Since the conclusion of the State Treaty and after the Hungarian Revolution of October–November 1956, the foreign press's interest in Vienna abated, and the London papers' freelancers (the so-called 'stringers') had to limit themselves to reporting short news items about ski and traffic accidents involving British tourists. I was lucky in as much as my work for the *FT* coincided with the paper's growing interest in European affairs. Numerous short reports and gradually longer and longer articles appeared in it 'from our Viennese correspondent'. Reports by correspondents carried only as of 1 June 1970 a byline in the *FT*; before that time it followed the practice of its 'sister' weekly *The Economist*, where to this day articles almost never carry a byline.

As a result of growing British commitment in Europe and the political initiatives launched by Federal Chancellors Josef Klaus and Bruno Kreisky in Eastern and Southern Europe, I managed to gain space for reports on Austria well beyond the country's actual importance. Although I regularly wrote reports also for Swiss newspapers, and have been engaged in editing the international quarterly *Europäische Rundschau* since 1973, the *FT* became the most important factor in my journalistic life.

During a discussion about Austrian provincialism, the theatre critic and author Hans Weigel (1908–91), who had returned from Swiss exile in 1945, castigated the 'disposition to negative generalization, Austrian self-distrust, the Austrians' negative patriotism. ... The real meaning of Austrian achievements is that in spite of this they do take place; more often than not with the exclusion of domestic public opinion. The by-products are provincial, the achievements are not.'[1] Weigel wrote this exactly thirty years ago. The inclination to 'self-criticism, self-accusation and self-flagellation', criticized by him, has undoubtedly become even more *en vogue* during the last years. The only sensible criterion for the assessment of the Second Republic's economic accomplishments is the comparison with its own past and with the neighbouring countries. As far as Hungary is concerned, we Hungarian refugees regarded Austria as a virtual consumer paradise already in 1956–7. This view was naturally moulded by our own dismal past and present, and we did not even know that in 1945 Austria had begun building a flourishing state out of a hopeless political and economic situation. Sitting in his third-floor apartment in the old town in Vienna with a wonderful view of the Stephansplatz on a New Year's Eve sometime in the 1970s, my best friend Kurt Vorhofer read out the touching 1945 Christmas message of Leopold Figl, the first Federal Chancellor of free Austria. For all those who had a radio and electricity at the time, but also for the generations who have since read it and learned about it, the oft-quoted text was an unforgettable speech:

'I cannot give you anything for Christmas. I cannot give you any candles for your Christmas tree if you have one at all. I cannot give you any gifts for Christmas. Not a piece of bread, no coal for heating, no glass for your windows. ... We do not have anything. I can only ask you: believe in this Austria! ...'[2]

The books, newspaper supplements and articles that appeared on the occasion of the jubilee year 2005 contained revealing facts and figures about the living conditions and the macroeconomic background 60 years ago. Two weeks before Christmas 1945, a reporter in the town of Wiener Neustadt, about an hour's drive from the capital, recorded the daily menu of an eight-year-old boy. Breakfast: a cup of black coffee and a roll; lunch: half a litre of soup as a school meal; evening: again a cup of black coffee. The average daily calorie intake in Wiener Neustadt at the end of 1945 had sunk to 760 calories; 1,600 calories were considered as subsistence level. There is hardly a better proof for the international acknowledgment of this sad situation than the 2 May 1946 statement of the Director-General of the United Nations Relief and Rehabilitation Administration, Fiorello LaGuardia, that 'the Austrian people belong to those peoples of the world that are closest to starvation stage'. At the time the GDP was only 60 per cent of the 1937 level that had already been depressed by mass unemployment.

After the end of the 'starvation period', the currency reform, and the stabilization as a result of the five wage and price-fixing agreements, things were looking up. In his book *Austria's Economy and Economic Policy after the Second World War*, the economist Hans Seidel notes: 'In the first decade after the Second World War, an economic entity evolved, which was far more effective than the one during the pre-war era. This phase was followed by the 'golden age', a long period of historically unique economic growth and full employment.'³ The most important agenda set for the future, and at the same time also the fundamental decision in the economic sphere, was the population's massive rebuff of the Communists at the first free elections, and with it also a vote cast for a Western-style free market economy.

In contrast to the neighbouring countries such as Hungary and Czechoslovakia, subverted and dominated by the Communists in the Soviet sphere of interest, Austria between 1945 and 1955 could use massive foreign aid to the value of 1.92 milliard US dollars (in 1955 dollar terms) for essential imports and the financing of a comprehensive investment programme. Some 80 per cent came from the USA; the Marshall Plan alone, initiated in 1947, yielded about 1 milliard dollars. On a per capita basis, each Austrian received more than any other of the participating West European countries (with the exception of Holland and Norway). The economy was stimulated through the concentrated input of substantial funds in the key sectors. Between 1948 and 1953, Austria also received close to 1 milliard dollars in the form of gifts.

At the same time, however, until the State Treaty, Austria had to pay occupation costs and reparations—primarily to the Soviet Union (by dismantling factories and by way of ongoing production)—as well as transfer fees and compensation payments in connection with the State Treaty, to the value of a total of 1.83 milliard dollars. For the return of the so-called former 'German assets' (involving 59,000 blue- and white-collar workers in the Soviet zone), from 1955 Austria had to deliver to the Soviet Union goods to the value of 150 million dollars annually for six years, and for a further ten years (later reduced to six years) 1 million tons of crude oil.

My first press trips in the early sixties to Lower Austria and Burgenland frequently showed me the indirect traces of Soviet occupation, especially in regard to the great headstart of the western provinces as far as investments and pro capita income were concerned. Of course, what caused the greatest amazement in the London head office was the fact that at the time Austria had the highest degree of nationalization in the free world. Time after time I had to explain in lengthier articles the historical background.

In Austria the ÖVP, the great Conservative party, also agreed to the two Nationalization Acts of 1946 and 1947 in parliament. It was the only means by which the industries that came under the heading of

'German assets' could be maintained in Austrian ownership. To protect them from Soviet appropriation as German war reparations—and not for any ideological reasons—Seventy enterprises were nationalized by unanimously passed acts of parliament, including the major steel concern (VOEST), the oil refinery sector (ÖMV), the three large banks, as well as the aluminium and electric power company. The idea of nationalization was suggested by the Americans, and the two other Western Allies endorsed this sole chance for protecting the vital sectors from seizure by the Soviets.

The question of what should happen to the relationship between state and economy in a country with a market economy, and especially with a large 'nationalized industry', has grown over the following decades into the major economic and domestic political bone of contention in Austrian politics. Moreover, the tug of war over the fate of the 'nationalized industry' has split—even if frequently in a covert form—the decision-makers, and their adherents also, within each of the two great coalition parties. After all, in the seventies it was an issue affecting 20 per cent of the domestic industry with some 125,000 employees, who produced 25 per cent of the export revenue. Added to this came the so-called industrial holdings of the preponderantly nationalized banks, which also controlled an additional 15 per cent of the country's industrial capacity.

It was therefore understandable that in a country where the great pre-war Austrian writer Robert Musil had already noted the precedence of the personal factor over the factual, the traditional *Weltanschauung*, and convictions, judgments and prejudices of the economic politicians, managers and unionists, carried more weight than long-winded party programmes and theoretical treatises. For all their differences about politics and the economic course, the relationship during the post-war years between Federal Chancellor Julius Raab (before and after chief of the Federal Economic Chamber) and the then union boss (and second President of the Nationalrat) Johann Böhm was just as amicable as between their respective successors. Böhm's famous statement after a joint vote in parliament was: 'He is the builder, I am the foreman.' Raab said once, he 'would rather have the Reds at the negotiating table than in the streets'. In an historic lecture to the Industrialists' Federation (as early as 1947!) Böhm summed up the partnership as follows: 'Despite all the differences we might have ... we still sit on the same branch, from which—if one of us saws through it—we both have to fall.'

To illustrate the change between the First and the Second Republics, the eloquent long-standing general secretary of the Austrian Industrialists' Federation, Herbert Krejci, told of a profoundly symbolical personal experience: 'When in the spring of 1959 Johann Böhm was carried to his grave, the first part of the state funeral ended at the Schwarzenbergplatz. The Guard Battalion of the Republic, carrying the traditional flag of the Empire, was lined up below the windows of the House of Industry to pay its last respects to this great architect of the Second Republic. This "second" army, commanded by the Republic, would never again be deployed against "interior enemies" from the camp of the labour movement. Does one need anything more to highlight the difference between then and now?'[4] Krejci's words reflected the—now almost incredible—memory of 1934 when the Austrian army was the principal instrument for suppressing the unions and Social Democrats. That was why the attendance was of such profound symbolic significance.

Without the famous 'Raab–Kamitz course' (named after the Federal Chancellor and his Finance Minister) in the second half of the 1950s, and without its continuation under the Kreisky–Androsch government; without the reorganization measures taken in the eighties and nineties under Chancellor Franz Vranitzky and subsequently under Wolfgang Schüssel, Austria's virtually breathtaking catching-up and overtaking process would not have been possible.

Some time in 1973, when I dictated a report over the telephone to London about the fact that, after lagging behind in 1960 by 20 per cent on a per capita basis, the Austrian economy had overtaken Great Britain in 1972 by 8 per cent, the stenographer in the editorial office was so shocked that I had to repeat this fact three times. Outstripping Britain in economic performance did not imply of course that the average Austrian had immediately become richer in assets than his British counterpart.

At the time I could draw on the study of the statistical expert Anton Kausel, which appeared in 1973 in the first issue of the *Europäische Rundschau*. In his impressive balance sheet of the catching-up process, the author evaluated the achievements on the basis of five standards: GDP growth rate, balance of payments, full employment, price stability and incomes policy. In conclusion Professor Kausel wrote that Austria had an excellent chance through new growth successes to forge ahead in a relatively short time and get into the top bracket of Europe's affluent nations. And so it happened.

More than two decades later, Kausel, as the 'champion of well-founded optimism', affirmed that 'no other country in the world but Austria could so perfectly and purposefully combine solid growth, general prosperity for all, social harmony and fairness, a healthy environment, enviable internal and external security, and the highest quality of life'. Between 1950 and 1994, with an annual growth rate of 3.6 per cent, Austria showed one of the highest rates of economic growth in global terms after Japan. After the endorsement by two-thirds of the electorate, Austria, as one of the world's richest countries, joined the European Union on 1 January 1995.

Incidentally, in spite of the deeply pessimistic predictions, the catching-up and overtaking process continued even after the so-called 'black–blue' government took office in 2000. The latest data show that in 2005 Austria overtook West Germany in gross domestic product (GDP) per capita (adjusted for purchasing power) by 3 per cent (in 1960 it had still lagged behind West Germany by 20 per cent). With regard to unified Germany, the margin is even bigger: 12 per cent. For the past ten years Austria's growth rate has been between a half and 1 per cent higher than that of Germany. Compared to the EU-15, Austria's per capita GDP is 10 per cent higher; and compared to the EU-25 it is 20 per cent higher. In conclusion, a word about Switzerland: at the beginning of 2007, the Swiss newspapers made the unbelievable announcement in three-column headlines: according to the International Monetary Fund 'Austria is richer than Switzerland!' Thirty years earlier Switzerland still had a lead of 21 per cent over Austria.[5]

What are the causes of this sensational catching-up? The head of the Austrian Institute of Economic Research, Professor Karl Aiginger, sees the main reasons in three areas:

- Opting for openness, joining the EU, wage restraint, and the hard currency policy, reduction of budget deficits and the export offensive. The highest export increases are recorded since 1980. The export quota has risen from 16 per cent in the 1960s to 38 per cent in 2005.
- The Social Partnership, security for the entrepreneur and for employment, the climate of certainty, of confidence and cooperation, all these promote pragmatic solutions.
- The high investment quota and technology import. The deficit of trade, direct investment and of quality balance is eliminated; for a

long time now Austria has been a major investor in Central, Eastern and South-East Europe.[6]

One need not accept a vulgar Marxist materialistic worldview in order to link Austria's national identity, and in particular its relationship to Germany, with the economic success story. The rump of Austria which was left over on the ruins of the Dual Monarchy in 1918 was (as Karl Renner said) like a piece of driftwood cast up on the shore after a great storm. As mentioned earlier, interwar history was dominated by the uncertainty of whether or not Austrians were Germans, and if they were, what being German meant. Since the *annus mirabilis* of 1955 and the signing of the State Treaty as an identity-establishing event, the 'state that no one wanted' gradually became 'one that everyone wants' (Rudolf Burger). Reliable polls reflect the inexorable process of the Austrians' complete identification with state and nation. Thus the proportion of respondents who believed that the Austrians were a nation increased from 47 per cent in 1964, to two-thirds by 1970, and to three-quarters since 1987. At the last survey in 2004, only 16 per cent believed that the Austrians were only beginning now to feel like a nation, while 76 per cent held that they were already a nation.

For many years now there can be no question therefore of a pan-German or a monarchist nostalgia. The Austrians' pronounced national pride in their country is particularly evident at sporting events. As a matter of fact, international opinion surveys indicate that the Austrians' national consciousness is even stronger than that of the French or Swiss.

8

THE CRISIS YEARS OF THE COALITION

A glance at the political history of 'consensus democracy' and the out-standing architects of the Second Republic confirms that programmes and institutions are no substitute for the drive, courage and sense of responsibility of true leaders. The first outstanding and controversial public figure whom I met in my capacity of economic journalist was Josef Klaus, the long-standing Governor of the province of Salzburg, who was appointed Federal Minister of Finance on 11 April 1961. In order to understand his position in the government at the time and his later comet-like ascendancy to the pinnacle of the Austrian People's Party, one has briefly to look at the times of the preceding Chancellor, Alfons Gorbach.

Born in Tyrol and raised in Styria, Gorbach (1898–1972) was an extraordinarily likable, open-hearted and friendly person (even toward journalists). After the retirement of Chancellor Julius Raab, the archi-tect of the 1955 State Treaty, Alfons Gorbach was appointed Party Chairman in 1960. One year later, the disabled ex-service-man Gor-bach had lost a leg in the twelfth Battle of Isonzo in 1917, and since then walked with the help of a prosthesis and a stick—became Federal Chancellor. He was regarded as a reformer and a representative of a harder line toward the Socialists. Although the SPÖ won the most votes in 1953 and in 1959, thanks to the electoral mathematics the ÖVP was able to maintain a relative majority of seats.

With the help of clever slogans ('It stands at 79:78—one more red seat and the Socialist regime begins') the ÖVP won the elections out-right on 18 November 1962. It now had five more seats than the SPÖ. The longest negotiations for forming a government in Austria's post-war history ended only on 23 March 1963 with the political defeat of the victorious People's Party.

Federal Chancellor Gorbach soon turned out to be rather a 'soft' and conciliatory negotiator, who disappointed the expectations of the reformers from Styria, Carinthia and Salzburg. The Chancellor's attitude, shaped by give-and-take and not by rigidity, was closely linked with his own personal and political past. He had spent more than five years in the Dachau concentration camp. That he could endure these 'times without mercy' was proof of his stamina. He was also a man who urged a forgive-and-forget attitude toward ex-Nazis not guilty of specific crimes. Precisely because of his concentration camp experiences, Gorbach was not willing to jeopardize the coalition with the Socialists. In the end the ÖVP gained only insignificant concessions, among them two additional state secretaryships.

Gorbach's hobby was collecting and telling jokes, even while he was in the concentration camp. When he met us foreign correspondents he used occasionally to read out from his 'joke booklet' or relate anecdotes. No wonder that Gorbach's state visits abroad also proceeded smoothly in an atmosphere of joviality and abundant alcoholic consumption. His press secretary later described the atmosphere during a visit to Moscow in the summer of 1962, when Khrushchev warned the Austrians against a treaty association with the EEC: 'Subsequently, in a conversation during a reception at the Embassy of Austria between Gorbach, Khrushchev and Mikoyan (the First Deputy Premier), there was no end of speculation among the diplomats and foreign correspondents standing at a respectful distance, because they could hear repeated hearty laughter coming from them. Obviously the differences over the EEC question were after all not that serious. For me, who had leant forward, the few snatches of Gorbach's talk that I overheard sufficed: as was his wont, he was telling jokes, accompanied by copious refills of Austrian wine.'[1]

Journalist colleagues told me how, during a side trip to Siberia, the jovial Chancellor brought to an end a night of drinking vodka and wine at three in the morning only out of consideration 'for the biological condition of his younger attendants'; or on a state visit to London, where after a dinner at the Embassy of Austria he kept on cheerfully drinking for hours with his entourage, although the ambassador and his wife had long ago excused themselves and retired.

Gorbach was very popular, and he visibly enjoyed the pleasant aspects of his three years as Chancellor, not only abroad. As he usually went to sleep late, the meetings of the small top circle, which Gorbach not quite aptly dubbed 'morning prayers', were scheduled for 11 a.m. at the ÖVP's federal headquarters. During his entire Chancellorship, he was essentially a figurehead without a power base. The undisputed strong man in the province of Styria was Josef Krainer snr, the Governor 1948–71. He was also one of the principal driving forces of the ÖVP's reform efforts.

The actual head of the reform group was Hermann Withalm, the notary from Lower Austria who was elected in February 1960 (concurrently with Gorbach as Party Chairman) as General Secretary. In retrospect he appears to have been the most gifted party organizer of the Second Republic. Between 1960 and 1963 he built up a party apparatus that functioned with Swiss clockwork precision. His reform of the ÖVP made the Palais Todesco, i.e. the party headquarters—and not the Ballhausplatz ensnared in endless coalition conflicts—the actual power centre of political life. The daily one-hour briefings in the morning with his closest colleagues and the monthly two-day conferences in the regions with the local party secretaries prepared the ground for the successful election campaign in the late autumn of 1962.

The fact that Withalm had not signed the March 1963 coalition agreement, and that Josef Klaus, the Finance Minister, who had gradually emerged as the key figure of the People's Party, was no longer part of the second Gorbach cabinet, were unmistakable signs of ferment within the ÖVP. Already during the arduous coalition negotiations two delegates of the young reform group—the then twenty-five-year-old Prince Karl Schwarzenberg and a politician from Tyrol—convinced Josef Klaus that he should no longer participate in the old 'Grand Coalition'. At the time Klaus was isolated among his own party colleagues in the government, due to his tough belt-tightening policy. During the night-time secret meeting in the Finance Ministry, the former winter palace of Prince Eugene of Savoy, the two young reformers managed to persuade Klaus to hold himself in readiness as 'Reserve Chancellor' after the inevitable fall of the weak Chancellor Gorbach.

More than forty years later, Schwarzenberg's biographer tells us: 'When Karl Schwarzenberg talks about this meeting, about his first personal involvement with the machinery of politics, his eyes still light up. ... It was Karl's crucial experience that, if you will, 'got him hooked' on politics—it had a lasting effect on him and whetted his appetite for more; for a life with and in politics.' Who would have thought at the time that the young prince (he was always a Czech and a Swiss citizen) would play an important role (albeit now officially called Karel instead of Karl!) in Czech and international politics, first for three years (1990–93) as Secretary-General of Czech President Václav Havel, and then in 2004 as senator, and eventually between January 2007 and May 2009 as Minister of Foreign Affairs of the Czech Republic?![2]

The heated conflict that broke out in 1963 regarding the entry permit for Otto Habsburg seems in hindsight incomprehensible and bizarre. Here is its background in brief. After the founding of the Austrian Republic, the national assembly passed the 'Habsburg Law' of 3 April 1919, banning all Habsburgs from entering Austria unless they renounced all dynastic claims and swore allegiance to the republic. This anti-Habsburg law was preserved in the 1955 State Treaty.

Following the death of ex-Emperor Charles I, who had embarked on two unsuccessful restoration attempts in Hungary in 1921, Otto Habsburg became head of the House of Habsburg-Lothringen. From Paris he called on Austrians to resist after the German occupation, and helped refugees, including many Jews, to obtain visas to the United States, Cuba and the Dominican Republic. He spent the war years in the USA.

The mistrust felt by the Socialists and republican Conservatives was based on Otto's activities against the Renner government and his subsequently declared political intentions. Thus in a letter to US President Harry Truman dated 2 July 1945 he demanded the non-recognition of the Provisional Government as it was a Trojan horse of the Communists. Eventually the Habsburg family settled in the Bavarian town of Pöcking. From there Otto Habsburg pursued his efforts for a return to Austria. Some suggestions of his possible role as 'state notary' or *Justizkanzler* (ombudsman) handed spurious arguments, as it were, on a silver platter for the so-called 'Habsburg cannibalism'.

The fuse of the Habsburg crisis was set alight in June 1961, when for the first time in the history of the Second Republic no agreement was reached in the council of ministers on a question of principle: Federal Chancellor Gorbach moved that the Declaration of Loyalty handed to him by Otto Habsburg be recognized. The Socialists rejected it. Two years later, in May 1963, the Supreme Administrative Court, to which Habsburg had appealed because of the declared lack of jurisdiction of the Constitutional Court, resolved that the declaration was sufficient and adequate. The Socialist campaign against the judges turned out to be an explosive charge for the coalition. The Socialist

Justice Minister, Christian Broda, spoke of a 'judicial coup in robes'. The Socialists tried to depict a possible return by Otto Habsburg as a grave danger for the Republic. On 4 July 1963 there were serious disturbances in the National Assembly. At the same time, that day was a moment of glory for Hermann Withalm as a parliamentarian. In an exceptionally brilliant and calm speech—in spite of 156 interjections ('Fascist', 'gravedigger of the Republic', etc.)—the convinced republican Withalm demonstrated with exact quotations from the Socialist and Liberal side that the issue in the case of Otto Habsburg was the respect of fundamental rights and freedoms.

It was on this day that the SPÖ and the opposition FPÖ (Freedom Party of Austria) voted together for the first time since 1945 in a key question against the ÖVP, in order to obstruct Otto Habsburg's return despite a ruling by the Supreme Court. It had never happened before that one of the two partners in the Great Coalition was overruled by the other one in a motion for a resolution with the help of the FPÖ.

In view of the real danger of a Small Coalition between the SPÖ and the FPÖ under the pretext of the 'Habsburg spectre', Withalm simply got into a car and drove to Pöcking in March 1964 to defuse the tense situation. He managed to persuade Otto temporarily to forgo (for one legislative period) his rightful entitlement to return to Austria. As a result the SPÖ lost the passionately fought battle: when two years later the ÖVP achieved an absolute majority in the national elections, Otto Habsburg received an Austrian passport on 1 June 1966 on the basis of his loyalty declaration. On 31 October of that year he set foot again on Austrian soil for the first time; there were no mass demonstrations. On 4 May 1972, on the occasion of a reception at the Federal Chancellery of the Republic of Austria during the 50th jubilee congress of the Pan-European movement headed by Habsburg, there came a symbolic face-to-face encounter with Chancellor Kreisky and their 'historical handshake'.[3]

During the Habsburg crisis of 1961–4, several one-sided and sometimes absurd reports appeared in the neighbouring Eastern Bloc countries' state-controlled media. Thus, for instance, the Hungarian Communist paper *Népszabadság* alleged in dead earnest that the fact so many dry-cleaning establishments in Austria carry the name 'Habsburg' is a clear indication of the monarchist restoration movement's strength! The appeal of the Dual Monarchy nowadays perceptible in Austria and Hungary—naturally only as far as the tourist industry and in part cultural kinship is concerned—has become an important bond between Budapest and Vienna since the collapse of Communism. This, however, is in no way a sign of nostalgia for the monarchy in a political sense. A serious royalist movement is not an issue in either country. Incidentally, Otto Habsburg was a member of the European Parliament for the Christian Social Union of Bavaria (CSU) for twenty years (1979–99). He was brought up by his mother Zita in preparation for the future role as King of Hungary, and accordingly was instructed in the languages of the countries of the Habsburg Empire, and had to complete the curricula of Austrian and Hungarian schools at the same time. Directly after the change of regime, Otto Habsburg paid a visit to Hungary. He took that occasion to give his very first public address to the Jewish congregation in Budapest; a highly symbolic act. When I heard him in 1995 in Budapest at a conference for Hungarians abroad, I was surprised—as were so many other participants—at his perfect command of the language. He pleaded extremely passionately for national unity, 'as only then can we Hungarians act for our interests in the world'.

Today, almost ninety years after the end of the Austro-Hungarian monarchy, the famous photograph of the Kreisky–Habsburg handshake in the history books remains the only reminder of the great ado caused by the 'Habsburg question'.

Nothing could more convincingly illustrate the reconciliation reached with the Habsburgs than the fact that, a few months after his election as head of state in July 2004, President Heinz Fischer, a livelong Social Democrat invited Otto Habsburg to the Hofburg. They 'had a long and amicable conversation' in the President's study, which 'somehow had a symbolic character ...' Fischer then added that Austrian social democracy was often referred to in Emperor Franz Joseph's time as 'k. u. k. social democracy' (*kaiserlich* und *königlich*), because to begin with it had an absolutely pragmatic relationship with the monarchy.[4]

9

THE REFORMER JOSEF KLAUS

In the atmosphere of open animosity within the coalition, the Conservative ÖVP functionaries and adherents pinned their hopes increasingly on the fairly new Finance Minister, Josef Klaus. After a short spell as a practising lawyer, he held the office of Governor of Salzburg for twelve years. He was the only local governor in Austria's post-war history who was willing to take up a ministerial post in a federal government in Vienna. During his barely two years as minister, the profoundly religious politician with deep-seated Christian-social views proved to be a man of absolute integrity and total independence. Klaus never considered tactical questions, he did not belong to any leagues within the ÖVP, and was not beholden to anyone for anything. From the very beginning he behaved like a merciless Scrooge even vis-à-vis the ÖVP ministers from his own party.

As foreign correspondent I had met him already in the spring of 1961, shortly after he took over the finance portfolio. As so many of his later interlocutors, I too was surprised when in my presence the minister promptly noted down my questions or critical remarks about government policy in a yellow exercise book. As a matter of fact he kept on doing that, even as Chancellor, albeit by then he used a handier black filofax. I was fascinated by his great willingness to learn. The minister and later head of government, who would assiduously make notes during conferences and conversations, naturally made himself the target of derisive remarks on the proverbially slippery Viennese political stage.

Once when I asked him in his office whether it was true that he had actually threatened to resign a few months earlier, because the Ministers of Education and Agriculture, what is more, from the ÖVP side, had rejected his appeal for strict measures of economy, Klaus did not refute the accuracy of the information. However, he added: 'I am a representative of absolute budget discipline, meaning that I have to deal with the people's money exactly as if it were my own.' He did not have a close, let alone a particularly cordial relationship with high-ranking civil servants, nor with the Industrialists' Association. As from time to time I also used to visit his predecessor, then the president of the National Bank (1960–67), the legendary Finance Minister Reinhard Kamitz ('Raab-Kamitz course'), I sometimes queried him about the coalition government's budgetary policy. Kamitz was not only a brilliant national economist, but also a conversationalist of inimitable charm. Once when I asked him about the critical attitude of well-known industrialists toward Klaus, Kamitz replied, with a smile, that in the eyes of the Finance Minister profit was somehow suspect. I confronted Klaus at our next meeting with this statement, without mentioning Kamitz's name. Klaus answered in a friendly manner that this opinion was not incorrect.

His speech-writer and close adviser, Josef Taus, was of the same view: 'Klaus was much closer to the little people, the small tradesmen and to commerce, than to industry.'[1] Tempers rose in the first Gorbach government between Klaus and his fellow ÖVP ministers and the regional party chiefs. Klaus did not eschew even direct conflict with Chancellor Gorbach and torpedoed his agreement with the union of public employees, dominated by the ÖVP. Klaus himself wrote in his memoirs: 'Gorbach was credited with generosity and conciliatoriness, while I was regarded as excessively sensitive and full of Alpine obstinacy.' Josef Klaus was intensely influenced in his inner independence and character by the Catholic youth movement of the interwar period, with its revivalism and rejection of real and putative manifestations of corruption and decadence.

Klaus could be relaxed and friendly during informal, tête-à-tête exchanges, especially if he had thought he could trust his partner. On the other hand, during discussions about subsidies and budget allocations he used a 'certain didactic missionary approach', observed a former high-ranking official from the ÖVP headquarters. 'Gorbach reacted almost allergically when Klaus rang him, and always held the receiver as if saying: Now I am again being lectured on what I should not do and what line I should take with the Socialists. Both of them grew apart from one another psychologically as well as literally.' In his memoirs Klaus himself admitted that he 'soon became the most hated man' in the government.

Ever since the clinching of the State Treaty, the drawbacks of the coalition system became increasingly evident. The price of the consensus was the principle of unanimity in the bipartisan coalition committee. This led frequently to shady deals between the two parties. Above all the discredited *Proporz*, the so-called proportional system, the practice whereby the ruling parties hand out to their supporters positions and jobs in public service and in the nationalized economy in accordance with the proportion of their political strength, aroused the indignation of the reform-minded Conservative ÖVP politicians. The political deals went so far that even government or official delegations going abroad had to be made up on a 1:1 basis. Mutual mud-slinging and veto threats led more and more frequently to a reciprocal blockade.

The independent newspapers sharply criticized the spin-offs of the sclerotic system. The coalition agreements reached after national elections spelled out the precise allocation of seats, not only of the supervisory and executive boards of nationalized industries and banks, but also the appointments of the editors-in-chief and their deputies at the Austrian Broadcasting Corporation to their party-colours.

The attempts of the two coalition parties to subject the state radio and television to total party control, by way of a secret pact, caused an outcry among the journalists and led to the first petition for a referendum in the Second Republic. Well-known editors demanded a new law for the creation of an independent broadcasting corporation. Supported by fifty-two independent newspapers and periodicals, 832,353 Austrians signed the petition.

Already a year earlier, the ÖVP candidate at the federal presidential elections in April 1963, ex-Chancellor Julius Raab, visibly afflicted with health problems, had been soundly defeated by the incumbent Socialist Federal President Adolf Schärf. Many ÖVP functionaries were increasingly dissatisfied with Chancellor Gorbach's weak leadership and the party's lack of clout. Their resentment erupted in an unprecedented manner at the September 1963 ÖVP party congress in Klagenfurt. The delegates enforced for the first time an open ballot on the leadership positions.

General Secretary Hermann Withalm—who acted as the motor of renewal—and the Governors of the provinces of Styria and Salzburg took the initiative for nominating Josef Klaus as Party Chairman. The young reformers, who were present as guest delegates, received Klaus with demonstrative acclaim. Withalm appealed in a passionate speech for the regeneration of the party and for a self-confident stance vis-à-vis the SPÖ, even at the price of breaking up the 'Great Coalition'.

The ballot took place after Klaus's keynote speech, but still before the request to speak by the rival candidate: Klaus received 251 votes, his opponent 144. Withalm, the actual driving force of reform, was confirmed in his post as General Secretary with an even greater majority, namely 278 to his opponent's 116. Gorbach was deposed as Party Chief. Most of the commentators in the domestic and foreign press expected also his early replacement as Federal Chancellor. After a lengthy intra-party tug-of-war, and after regularly leaked newspaper reports about Gorbach's 'impending resignation', this came to pass, as expected, in February 1964. Klaus was sworn in as Chancellor at the beginning of April 1964.

The new strategy and the new course aimed at a free interplay of forces with alternating majorities in parliament, marked a turning point in the history of the Second Republic: Klaus and Withalm had in fact already set the course in Klagenfurt for the later electoral victory of 6 March 1966 and the formation of the ÖVP's one-party government. The international press gave more attention to the appointment of Klaus as Federal Chancellor than to the only too well-known infighting in the coalition government.

A few extracts from an article I wrote in February 1964 may indicate the prevailing atmosphere: 'As Finance Minister in 1961, Klaus, who had never studied economics, got down to work with fantastic determination to straighten out the national budget. When his subordinates arrived in the ministry in the morning, the minister was already sipping his morning tea, because he started work daily at 6 o'clock. During his two years in the ministry, comprehensive concepts were worked out for the creation of a capital market, for the elimination of double-taxation of shares, and for boosting the small and medium enterprises. However, he could not assert himself, because the jovial and relaxed head of government, Chancellor Gorbach, with all his amiability, never had an overview of the complicated processes in a modern industrial society, and was always willing to accept without energetic objection first the thinning out and then the quiet burial of the Klaus concepts by the socialists. ... In a country where ministers retire from office on their own accord only in exceptional cases, Klaus gained prestige, authority and the people's sympathy by his civil courage ...'

'Since his election to Party Chairman, the modest son of a Carinthian master baker and a peasant woman had prepared himself with an iron will and his legendary diligence for taking over the Chancellorship. Unlike Raab, Figl and Gorbach, Klaus represented the new leadership generation not only agewise but also by his views. He is neither a neo-Dollfuss nor a pocket edition of de Gaulle, as one of the SPÖ ministers spitefully described him, but an Austrian model student, who became over the years in a sense an apolitical politician. Since many Austrian politicians, with a few honourable exceptions, tend rather to chattering than to methodical work and hardly read any books, let alone textbooks, Klaus has already been portrayed by fellow party members as well as by opponents as a power-hungry fanatic, an ascetic, even a missionary. Although he is not a jovial type like for example Dr Gorbach, he is a music-lover, a connoisseur of architecture and an enthusiastic skier. He is a lawyer who does not know any tricks, a politician who is willing to fight for his principles, an "un-Austrian Austrian", who is just as repugnant to the Socialists as to some industrialists. At the same time the Socialist party paper *Arbeiter-Zeitung* attacked him as an 'enemy of the coalition allied with West German capitalists and monarchists'.

My portrait of Josef Klaus concluded with the following sentences: 'It seems that in this paradoxical country the fourth post-war Chancellor also has to cope with contradictory tasks. In the forty-one-member federal party leadership there are at present only thirteen members who count as genuine adherents of Klaus; the others are in part wavering, in part overt or covert enemies of the new "strong man". ... It remains to be seen whether, in addition to the so far often sorely missed principled toughness, Dr Klaus wants to and can acquire the flexibility and give-and-take that is just as essential in coalition politics.'[2]

These totally opposite appraisals of his political and human profile even today reflect the opinions of his erstwhile companions, colleagues and historians. Quite apart from the assessment of the individual measures and the personal attitudes of comrades-in-arms and rivals, one has to contradict the thesis whereby the Klaus government has not left any traces. Also, the assertions that Klaus was a 'right extremist', an extremely Conservative 'Alpine king', even a 'mini—Mussolini' (according to SPÖ's parliamentary secretary of the time, Heinz

Fischer), were out of place. The Socialists' main concern was to wipe out the mistake of November 1962, to divert attention from the looming infighting within the party and to force the new Chancellor onto the defensive from the very beginning.

The Socialist leader at the time, Bruno Pittermann (1905–83), was as Party Chairman a failure, but as Vice-Chancellor in the coalition government he could make his ÖVP opponents from Raab to Klaus livid by his tactical manoeuvres and his sarcasm. Klaus had several times recalled in writing, and also in conversations with me, that shortly after his assumption of office as Chancellor, Pittermann had threatened him: 'We shall cause the Klaus government to die in the agony of the coalition.' Klaus and Withalm had indeed made no bones about the fact that, although they envisioned the free play of forces in parliament with alternating majorities instead of the rigid coalition, they imagined all this only in the framework of a loose cooperation between the two great parties. One must not forget that, despite the coalition's twenty years, the country still lived in the shadow of the trauma of the 1934 civil war. This was the reason why the SPÖ leadership had built up the whole Habsburg question as a bogeyman to paint the devil of another civil war or putsch on the wall in order to distract attention from its own crisis.

In addition to the looming electoral contest, a new presidential election took place on May 1965 after the death of Federal President Schärf. The campaign was exceptionally interesting politically and humanly touching for us correspondents, as we had learned to admire the toppled Gorbach as a noble politician. The ÖVP had now nominated him—the recently deposed Federal Party Chairman and Federal Chancellor—as a candidate. Contrary to our expectations Gorbach lost, even if only by a slight margin with a shortfall of a mere 63,000 votes, to the colourless SPÖ candidate, the Viennese mayor Franz Jonas. In a private conversation, Foreign Minister Kreisky praised Jonas as a 'kindly man', but he did not contradict me when I stressed the advantages of the more suitable Alfons Gorbach. In his memoirs Bruno Kreisky highlighted Gorbach's merits for the office of Federal President, and made derisive remarks about 'the stupidity and narrow-mindedness of many an ÖVP politician'.

Despite, or perhaps even because of, Gorbach's defeat,[3] the ÖVP was initially well placed on the eve of the parliamentary elections that had been brought forward from the autumn to the beginning of

March 1966. The aim of the Klaus—Withalm course was 'renewal' and not the end of the coalition. A 'clear majority' for the ÖVP would see to that.

On 14 January 1966, in the press club Concordia, Josef Klaus, a pioneer in many fields, presented his famous 'Aktion 20', the organized and future-oriented alliance between science and politics. One of the most unusual press conferences took place in that small Baroque palace, which also houses the Foreign Press Association.

Seated next to him were some outstanding scientists. The walls were covered with large statistical charts and diagrams: displays of the situation and prospects from educational to health care policy, from economic and social policy to foreign policy. It was all about an institutionalized dialogue between politics and science and the setting up of working parties for the creation of future-oriented projects. There was a sign in giant lettering behind the table, where the ministers and professors were sitting, which read: AKTION 20. The mysterious name 'Aktion 20' was supposed to signify several things: today's twenty-year-olds and the next twenty years, in which 'they did not want to be steamrollered by the future'.

It was the presentation of a new political style by a politician without populism. During the following months and years there followed gatherings of scientists with lectures and discussions, which produced interesting concepts in the working parties. It was obvious to us journalists that it was not a matter of a carefully orchestrated media event but a commitment to a 'politics of relevance'.

In view of the general mood on polling day, 6 March 1966, most observers expected electoral gains for the ÖVP. Yet the end result late that evening was a sensation: with eighty-five seats out of the 165, the ÖVP had scored an absolute majority against the SPÖ's seventy-four. There had already been an absolute majority once, on 25 November 1945. Admittedly unusual conditions prevailed at the time (almost half a million former National Socialists and hundreds of thousands of POWs respectively could not appear at the urns); moreover during the time of occupation there simply was no alternative to a coalition government. A cheering crowd received Klaus as he arrived at around 10 p.m. from the central electoral office in the Interior Ministry to the Palais Todesco and addressed his enthusiastic followers from the Kärntnerstrasse balcony while the Deutschmeister band struck up.

There followed hectic days of deliberations to prepare the delicate coalition negotiations. Most observers believed that the SPÖ would, despite everything, not go into opposition, but cling to the coalition for the sake of power politics. Klaus, the victor, closed his eyes to the fact, not only then but also later, that the unexpected success of the People's Party was first and foremost due to the grave mistakes committed by a deeply split Socialist leadership. One of these factors was the power struggle that had erupted around the person of Interior Minister Olah and his expulsion from the party on a flimsy pretext. Olah's newly formed group, the Democratic Progressive Party (DFP), notched up 150,000 votes, in Vienna even 8 per cent. In addition, there were the turbulent incidents in Fussach at Lake Constance. The SPÖ Minister of Transport, Otto Probst, insisted that a new ship be named *Karl Renner*, although the Vorarlberg state government had unanimously asked for the name *Vorarlberg*. 'Fussach' became a political slogan when 30,000 Vorarlbergers demonstrated against Minister Probst in the Fussach shipyard and succeeded in renaming the ship *Vorarlberg*, so the SPÖ was once again severely routed.

The fact that, in contrast to the ÖVP, the Socialists openly opposed the petition for a law about an independent broadcasting service, and during the parliamentary discussion declared that they 'had no intention … of letting themselves be degraded to bootlickers of certain presumptuous hacks', certainly contributed to the alienation of many independent journalists. The failed attempt of the Socialist trade unionists to occupy the editorial office of the mass circulation popular daily (*Kronen Zeitung*)–supported and allegedly co-financed by the rebel Olah—by way of an interim injunction, and to install an official administrator, stirred up protests all over the country.

In addition to all this, the SPÖ leader and Vice-Chancellor Bruno Pittermann also committed a fatal mistake in the final phase of the campaign, which had far-reaching consequences. The minuscule Communist party of Austria, which had not been in parliament since 1959, stood for election only in one suburban traditional Vienna stronghold, and advised its followers to vote for the SPÖ in all other constituencies. The SPÖ leadership did not reject this offer; the Social Democrats tacitly took notice of it. The Communist votes might have been useful in theory, but, according to media experts, they were 'in practice far outweighed by the voters' instinctive anti-Communist reaction. The ÖVP slogan "The red popular front threatens!" proved to be by far the most successful one of the election campaign.'

The shock of electoral defeat sealed the demise of the twenty-one-year coalition for the SPÖ: with thirty votes against ten, the party leadership in April declined the last ÖVP offer to negotiate. Josef Klaus was the great winner. Yet he soon had occasion to quote from first-hand experience the saying of a Conservative minister: 'What is economically right is politically wrong!' The formation of the single-party government of the ÖVP was unquestionably a watershed in Austria's post-war history. On the one hand, the wise restraint of the winners and the low-key reaction of the losers proved the maturity of Austrian democracy. On the other, the victory carried the seed of future defeats.

10

THE SPLENDOUR AND MISERY
OF THE ÖVP GOVERNMENT

The evening hours of 6 March 1966 signalled the end of Austria's post-war coalition era. The press centre of the Interior Ministry was bursting at its seams. I stood, crowded together with colleagues and officials, in front of the neon signs on the façade of the hall, which displayed the progress in counting the votes. The inexorable trend had become apparent from the start, when the first results reached party headquarters by telephone and were mostly added up by hand. Despite the victors' manifest willingness to enter into new coalition negotiations with the losers, the final result of ÖVP eighty-four, SPÖ seventy-four, FPÖ twenty-one seats was a political landslide, which meant the inevitable end of twenty-one years of coalition.

Josef Klaus, the fifty-six-year-old lawyer and by now professional politician for twenty-one years, had arrived at the peak of his career and was overwhelmed by the jubilation of his followers. As the election winner, he was in the centre of the media spotlight. After the breakdown of the coalition negotiations with the SPÖ, he had to decide quickly about filling the six portfolios that had so far been held by the Socialists. Klaus was the first Federal Chancellor to promote a woman into the government: Grete Rehor, the former textile worker, war widow and trade union secretary, was appointed Minister of Social Affairs: a symbolic move, as was the appointment of the thirty-three-year-old Josef Taus as State Secretary of Transport, also in charge of the reorganization of the nationalized industries. These measures were welcomed by the media.

Few people knew that Chancellor Klaus had to cope in those very days of triumph with the consequences of a family tragedy. His twenty-one-year-old daughter Hildegard, who had been suffering from a congenital heart defect, died as a result of a bacterial infection barely a week after the electoral triumph. This blow afflicted above all his wife Erna, who—because of the hectic pace in Vienna—felt abandoned during these difficult days. Her husband's incessant political activities from morning till late into the night had put the relationship of the deeply religious couple several times in jeopardy, the more so as Erna Klaus with their four other children continued to live in Salzburg and did not move completely to Vienna. This hidden tension probably contributed to the fact that Klaus could not always control his choleric temperament.[1]

Quite another problem emerged on account of the real estate deals undertaken by his wife. Klaus was called the 'embodiment of personal morality' and a 'downright moralist'. Erna Klaus came from a family of merchants and had been engaged in the real estate business all her adult life. A Viennese tabloid paper accused the 'Klaus family' of shady business transactions, which deeply wounded and embittered the Chancellor. I recall that in those days at the end of one conversation Klaus suddenly asked me: 'What should I do? My wife is simply good at business. I have nothing to do with her transactions, but after all one cannot forbid her that. She was always opposed to it that I should come to Vienna and leave the family on its own …' The allegations against Erna Klaus of dishonest property deals turned out to be untenable, and the journalist involved was later convicted.

From the beginning to the very end of his political career Josef Klaus was a man with a sense of mission, or as he himself put it, a 'reformer stuck between objectivity and messianism'. In his memoirs he openly admitted how gravely his family life had suffered from his 'chronic workaholism and restlessness'. Already as Finance Minister, he could not offer his wife more for their silver wedding anniversary in 1961 than a low mass in the recently renovated chapel of the Finance Ministry followed by a small breakfast. This subsequent abrupt goodbye hurt Erna Klaus's feelings very badly. Her husband admitted many years later: 'She never forgave me that.' Precisely because the 'Klausian obstinacy and Alpine messianism' (his self-definition) was not suited to the Viennese political stage, when he moved into the Viennese apartment on the Stephansplatz opposite the archbishop's palace, Erna Klaus hung a portrait drawing of Mahatma Gandhi above the desk in his study: 'In order that he should not forget humility.'

One of the new Chancellor's significant and future-oriented decisions was the introduction of a modern management style in the People's

Party and the government. Gifted, dedicated and loyal young associates moved into the Chancellor's office. Political decision-making was 'outsourced' to a smaller circle, instead of the statutorily designated and far too large federal party bodies. The general staff work and the entire coordination between the government and party leadership were prepared and implemented at discussions on topical matters held several times a week—at the time regarded as a novelty, today taken for granted—with four presentations and briefings as well as once a month at a 'small cabinet meeting' with his closest colleagues. No other Austrian head of government had ever discovered and encouraged so many political talents as Josef Klaus. We foreign correspondents heard for the first time the names of many a prospective top politician, federal minister and general manager 'from the Klaus nursery'.

The government policy statement proclaimed as a motto: 'politics for all Austrians'. Yet apart from the non-party Justice Minister, it was a purely ÖVP government, in which most of the ministers and secretaries of state were additionally members of the so-called *Cartellverband* or CV (Union of Catholic student organizations). The student association, rich in tradition, was particularly powerful between 1934 and 1938. During the Nazi period its members were persecuted. Only Catholic students could join the CV; no Protestant, Orthodox or Jewish students are admitted to this day. Admittedly, this was not implemented on a racial basis, i.e. converted or baptized Jews could become members. After 1945, the CV played an important role in the newly established ÖVP. 'Many of its members were sitting in government, which some people saw as a kind of Catholic freemason lodge', wrote Klaus in his memoirs. Not only he, but also all post-war ÖVP chancellors except Wolfgang Schüssel were CV members. At the time of the Klaus government, 2,142 'actives' and 5,800 'old boys' belonged to the thirty-five CV fraternities in Vienna and the other university towns. To this day all affiliates of the CV, irrespective of age and position, address each other with the familiar *Du*.

This Catholic network with an *esprit de corps* has always sharply detached itself from the 'fencing', pan-German fraternities, which still have many points of contact with right-radical groups. At any rate, during the fifties and sixties the CV influence was particularly strong in the public administration, especially in the Federal Chancellery, but also in the trade and agricultural chambers, in some of the state and district administrations, as well as in the free professions and in some of the universities. At one stage, ÖVP General Secretary Withalm was the highest-ranking functionary of the CV.

At the time of the Klaus government 23 per cent of the People's Party parliamentarians belonged to the CV. Of the six section heads in the Federal Chancellery, four were CV members. By the way, it was at this time that the ÖVP decreed in its statutes that 'the incumbent Federal Chancellor' had to be a member of the party executive. Obviously in 1945 they could not imagine that there could ever be a Socialist Federal Chancellor. Bruno Kreisky is said to have jokingly declared sometime during his Chancellorship in the seventies that he would now be going to a meeting 'in the Kärntnerstrasse' (i.e. the then headquarters of the ÖVP). This outdated reference had to be erased of course from the statutes.

At present the CV no longer plays such a significant role in the selection of elites and in the political networks. However, without familiarity with the CV and also about the occasional not so cordial relations between the CV on the one hand and the members of the Catholic High School Students' Association and the *Katholische Studierenden Jugend* (KSJ or Catholic Studying Youth) on the other, one can hardly understand the background to some important decisions in the Conservative camp. In those years important politicians such as the ex-Vice-Chancellors Josef Riegler and Erhard Busek, the long-standing Governor of Styria Josef Krainer jr., and the former Federal Chancellor Wolfgang Schüssel were all active in the KSJ and not in the CV. Moreover, the membership of a CV-fraternity was by no means a pledge of true friendship. For example, at the time of Federal President Thomas Klestil's personal tragedy, some of his 'CV brothers' were the actual wire-pullers who intrigued against him behind the scenes.

The youngest member of the Klaus government, State Secretary Josef Taus in the Federal Ministry of Transport and Nationalized Industry, was responsible for one of the most significant reforms, the restructuring of nationalized industry. He created a new holding structure, and then left the government in March 1967 to carry out the reform as chairman of the supervisory board. At the same time he was appointed CEO of the Girozentrale, the central institute of the savings bank sector. He successfully carried out the first large-scale privatization, that of the Siemens Works. I have come to know and esteem Josef Taus in both his functions—as top banker and as reformer of nationalized industry. It is thanks partly to him that over the decades I managed to gain unique insights into Austria's politics and economy and the mentality of the Austrians. Klaus had already admired his capacity as Finance Minister the economic competence of his brilliant assistant. His ability and integrity impressed Klaus so much that, after his resignation as Finance Minister in 1963, he suggested to Chancellor Gorbach the not yet thirty-year-old as one of his possible successors—to no avail. During the following years Taus played a prominent role in Austrian politics as Party Chairman of the ÖVP (1975–9), subsequently until 1991 as economic spokesman of his party as well as a successful entrepreneur. He would undoubtedly have made an excellent finance or economic minister in a one-party or even in a coalition government.

Yet against an exceptional personality like Bruno Kreisky, Taus—elected ÖVP Chairman overnight after the fatal traffic accident of the former leader—had no chance in the forthcoming elections. The striving for power of some regional governors, the short-sighted intrigues of the divergent interest groups in the party, and the deficient loyalty of some of his fellow party members made matters worse. Taus has remained a man of modest tastes and absolute personal integrity. He has lived in the same house with the same furniture for the past thirty years.

In contrast to Taus, Lujo Tončić-Sorinj, who as Kreisky's successor had been appointed Foreign Minister in the ÖVP one-party government, was something of a problem case for Chancellor Klaus. It was mainly the lifestyle and the penchant for social functions of the multilingual and elegant politician with a Croatian noble background that irritated the introvert Chancellor.

Returning from a trip on a summer's day, Tončić appeared, for instance, in a white suit in parliament. Klaus was shocked and regarded that as totally inappropriate. 'If you come into parliament you must be dressed completely inconspicuously', he told Tončić, to which the latter curtly replied: 'What should I do? After all I can't dress badly just because I'm going to parliament.' The wish of the Foreign Minister, who had only a small two-room apartment in Vienna, to have an official residence befitting his status where he could give receptions, or his fondness for French wines, seemed 'hair-raising' to Klaus.[2]

As a foreign correspondent I had two indirect experiences with Tončić. The Foreign Press Association had invited the new Foreign Minister to a lunch at the Hotel Imperial as a sort of celebration of his new post. Each of us had to contribute a rather large sum. The illustrious guest was so late that we eventually started the lunch without him. At the time there were no mobile phones; only after an hour and a half when we had reached the dessert and the anxious president of our association had made enquiries did Tončić send a brusque message through his secretariat that he was in parliament and could no longer get away. His behaviour irritated all of us, and some of my colleagues paid him back later with derisive comments about his difficulties with regard to European integration.

Sometime in 1967 the Klauses gave a large reception in Schönbrunn on the occasion of an international conference. Klaus and his wife stood in front, and next to them Tončić with his wife. Both of them were very tall, very good-looking and very elegant. The two Tončićes outshone the staid Klaus couple in every respect. A bold comparison occurred to me: in the Soviet Politburo no one could be taller than Stalin. After his replacement by Kurt Waldheim during the government reshuffle in January 1968, Tončić was elected Secretary-General of the Council of Europe (1969–74). Later he became the centre of an unfortunate controversy: 'because of his family connections to Dalmatia' he decided to take Croatian citizenship, but as a result was deprived of his Austrian citizenship and lost his politician's pension. Only after a lot of ado and the submission of documents to prove that the Croatian citizenship had 'not been lawfully acquired' did Tončić-Sorinj become an Austrian citizen again.

It has already been forgotten, or hardly ever mentioned even in Austria, that in a remarkable speech before the Council of Europe in Strasbourg in the mid-sixties Josef Klaus had already initiated an opening to East Europe (*Ostpolitik*). The Federal Chancellor introduced himself with the words: '*civis europaeus sum*' ('I am a European citizen') and exhorted the international audience that while building the 'European House' one must not forget about the 'East Wing'. He was the first Austrian Chancellor to travel to Yugoslavia, Hungary, Romania and Bulgaria. One can confirm in retrospect what Klaus rightly emphasized in his memoirs, that 'by their moderation the Austrian contacts with the East, just as free of illusions as of hysterical mistrust, served as pioneers for the countries of free Europe'.[3]

What distinguished Klaus's trips from other similar diplomatic excursions by other Austrian heads of government were the human touches and the endeavours to make direct contact with people in foreign countries with at least a basic knowledge of the relevant language.

I witnessed and described this for my British- and German-speaking readers in March 1965 at the time of a memorable state visit by Klaus and Foreign Minister Kreisky to Belgrade. In order to emphasize the regional politics, the Chancellor was accompanied by the Governors of the neighbouring provinces Styria and Carinthia. The Belgrade daily *Politika* described this first visit by an Austrian Chancellor after half a century as 'not the event of a day, but of a generation'. Klaus was not only optimally prepared for the negotiations; he went so far as to 'rehearse' in a vacant compartment of the train the Serbo-Croat text of the scheduled TV address, and with the help of the commercial attaché put 'the finishing touches' to the pronunciation.

I still remember clearly the impression that the Chancellor's speech in Serbo-Croat made, not only on the official contacts, but also on the 'man in the street'. At a lecture in the Belgrade Institute for International Politics and Economics, Klaus spoke the introductory personal words in Serbo-Croat. His discussions with Marshall Tito were conducted partly in German. During his later visit to Moscow, Klaus delivered his TV and radio addresses in Russian. The fact that, apart from his linguistic efforts, he sought contact everywhere with the people, and not least with representatives of the Church, was also a special feature of his visits to the East. That he was willing to do so despite the then still intact monitoring systems by secret police of the Communist dictatorships made Josef Klaus a highly unusual visitor in this respect as well.

His extremely positive relationship with the Slovene minority in Carinthia also needs to be emphasized here. As a student, Klaus had chosen Slovenian as an elective subject at his grammar school in Klagenfurt. In the closing paragraph of an extremely warm-hearted and constructive speech on the occasion of a festive session of the Council of Carinthian Slovenes in May 1965, he promised in Slovene that he would do everything to guarantee their rights. The most important objective, he emphasized, was mutual trust, and the second, perhaps even more important, one was the fact that it was a matter of the preservation, the future and the existence of the ethnic group: 'In the final analysis all the small things, all the single measures have only one purpose: to ensure the continuance and future of the ethnic group. We want to solve all the problems in the future too with the collaboration of the minority, because we know that this is the best for the Slovenes, for Carinthia and for Austria.'[4]

Therefore, when taking stock of the short Klaus era one should—instead of the nowadays fashionably negative assessment of his personality—emphasize the politician's amazing achievements and reform initiatives. Some of these were indisputably the active neighbourhood politics and the conclusion of the South Tyrol agreements with Italy, the Capital Market Acts and the start-up of the reform of nationalized industries mentioned earlier, the gradual introduction of the forty–hour week, the definitive abolishment of the death penalty and the reduction of the voting age.

Nietzsche's aphorism is valid for the Klaus government and its place in Austria's contemporary history: 'Not when it is dangerous to tell the truth does truth lack advocates, but when it is boring to do so.'[5] Perhaps the greatest accomplishment of one-party government was what a close observer so aptly called 'the introduction of the normality of democratic changeover'.[6] The evaluation of the historian Ernst Hanisch is true for the future: 'Although Klaus and Kreisky represented two totally different political types, from a historical viewpoint the Klaus Kreisky era formed an entity, especially from the mid-sixties to the mid-seventies—a reform period rare in Austrian history.'

It should not be forgotten that, after more than twenty years of coalition governments, many leading functionaries of both parties were apprehensive about the path-breaking experiment of a single-party government, and these misgivings were shared by quite a few journalists as well. Added to this was the deliberate scaremongering by the losing SPÖ. The spectres of a general strike, even a civil war, were raised initially. For me, 'coming in from the cold' of a dictatorship, the maturing process of Austrian democracy was an unforgettable experience. Although Gerd Bacher, who became Director-General of the new ORF (Austrian Broadcasting Corporation), was the beneficiary of the Broadcasting Act that the Klaus government had adopted as promised, there is no doubt that he is correct in his praise for Klaus as a media politician: 'To this day the Broadcasting Act is the only major achievement of any federal government with regard to the media.'

Bacher often tells the story of how the first telephone call he received on the evening of 9 March 1967, straight after his election as head of ORF, came from Klaus. Having congratulated him, he said: 'You know that originally you were not my candidate. I promise that I shall never interfere, and should I do so, remind me of this promise.'[7] Even later Klaus and Withalm have never meddled in ORF matters. For example, the editor-in-chief of the socialist *Arbeiter-Zeitung* was appointed as the new TV editor-in-chief in the ORF, although in a recent television discussion forum he had described Chancellor Klaus as a 'nonentity'.

The ORF reform turned out to be a boomerang for the ÖVP, mainly for two reasons. Firstly, as Klaus himself admitted, he 'was paralysed with stage fright by interviewers, in front of the microphone and the TV camera'. Secondly, Bruno Kreisky, who was elected Chairman of the SPÖ and candidate for the Chancellorship on 1 February 1967, was 'a world champion in the media ring and did not win only on points'.[8] While by his dynamic leadership Kreisky seized the initiative in the ensuing years, barely a year and a half after the unexpected victory the 'catastrophically discordant' (as Klaus put it) ÖVP team was already in turmoil.

The ÖVP's defeat in the Upper Austrian state elections in October 1967 (minus 3.4 per cent) created a near-panic reaction. As early as January 1968, Klaus decided on a radical government reshuffle. The Foreign, Interior, Trade and Finance Ministers were replaced. The parliamentary faction leader and ÖVP General Secretary Withalm, nicknamed 'Iron Hermann', added the Vice-Chancellorship to his responsibilities. The new Finance Minister, Professor Stephan Koren, tried to reduce the budget deficit and to stimulate investments in one fell swoop. He rescinded parts of his predecessor's tax reforms and introduced a 10 per cent temporary special tax on wine and on new cars, with a simultaneous reduction in customs duties. They came into force in the autumn of 1968. In addition, as of January 1969, payroll, income and corporate taxes were increased by 10 per cent, and there was an increase from 0.5 to 0.75 per cent in the wealth tax. These measures hit the core of the ÖVP's followers, namely the middle class and the farmers, particularly hard.

The enraged peasants drove up with hundreds of tractors in front of the Federal Chancellery. However, Klaus refused to negotiate under pressure in the street, let alone to revoke the necessary belt-tightening measures. All the important Conservative politicians are convinced even in retrospect that the effect of the tax package on the public was catastrophic. In that hour the Klaus government relinquished all its trump cards.[9]

Meanwhile the tireless Klaus tackled a new project. He was one of the first politicians in Central Europe to size up the fundamental shift brought about by the triumphant advance of the computer. For almost half a year he took private lessons several times a week in the early hours of the morning in the IBM laboratory in Vienna, in order to become familiar with cybernetics and computer science.

Soon after the government reshuffle, Klaus committed a grave tactical error. Faced with growing criticism, he wanted to stress at a meeting of the ÖVP parliamentary group that he was not clinging to this position and announced that Vice-Chancellor Withalm would 'in the foreseeable future' succeed him as head of the government and the party. Thus unexpectedly Klaus had opened a Pandora's Box. Instead of strengthening his authority, it was irrevocably damaged by his impetuous remark. Henceforth the question of the succession was raised at every single press conference.

Contrary to the rumours and assumptions, Klaus was never a power politician. 'I did not have a personal relationship to power', he wrote in his memoirs, and cited the adage of the poetess Marie Ebner-Eschenbach: 'He who appears in the limelight cannot expect or demand lenience.' It did not come to a power struggle within the ÖVP leadership, because, despite his considerable power base (vice-chancellor, party chip whip, and general secretary) and his growing doubts about the government's course, Withalm remained absolutely loyal to Klaus to the end. He observed in his memoirs that he had several times warned the Chancellor and the ministers about the consequences of 'flooding' parliament with 600 draft bills between 20 April 1966 and 31 October 1969! After the series of setbacks at various regional elections, Klaus committed a further error by putting all his eggs in one basket and announcing that he would not want to lead another coalition government.

Events in foreign and domestic politics contributed to the negative image of the Klaus government. Despite the traditionally first-class intelligence service of the Austrian army, the Warsaw Pact intervention in Czechoslovakia on the night of 21 August 1968 was just as much a total surprise for the Austrian government as for the whole world. There was absolutely no coordination, no 'contingency plan'. The Chancellor was in his weekend house in Wolfpassing without a telephone, Vice-Chancellor Withalm was hunting at Gösing, Federal President Jonas was in his official residence in Mürzsteg, the State Secretary for Information was in Tunisia and the opposition leader, Kreisky, on holiday in Dalmatia. While most of the other governments were already mobilizing their emergency task force, the secretary to the

Chancellor, Thomas Klestil (the future Federal President), had to drive to Wolfpassing at 4.00 a.m. to pick up his boss.

During these days the government appeared overtaxed and out of its depth. Together with the correspondents of the *Frankfurter Allgemeine* and *Der Spiegel*, I was invited to a confidential briefing with the Chancellor, Foreign Minister Waldheim and the Defence Minister, as well as some high-ranking officers. Klaus had already been criticized before our meeting, because in his first statement he had not immediately condemned the invasion and had also phrased his subsequent statements too cautiously. Moreover, there were uncertainties regarding the mobilization of reservists and the competence and division of labour between the Federal President (according to the constitution, the supreme commander of the military), the Defence Minister and the government.

During our press briefing at the Ballhausplatz, the three politicians did not come across as very impressive in the way they answered our questions. After a while they admitted a delay of some eight hours before the Austrian border had been protected, i.e. the time lag between the readiness to march and the turn-out command. In addition there were ambiguous reports about alleged preparations in case of an emergency to move the Klaus government with high-ranking officers to Zell am See in Western Austria. At the time we did not know anything yet about the Foreign Ministry's instruction to the Austrian ambassador in Prague, Rudolf Kirchschläger (later Foreign Minister and Federal President), to stop issuing Austrian entry visas to Czechoslovak citizens. Kirchschläger ignored the instructions and asked the ministry to reconsider the order. Kirchschläger has never criticized his predecessor Waldheim by name for the inhumane instructions, but has alluded to him in a cable: 'If we abandon the humanitarian approach, we lose the moral justification for neutrality.'[10] At any rate, many years later as Federal President, Kirchschläger confirmed to me that this directive had been personally issued by Waldheim as a sign of opportunistic 'giving in', but was subsequently reversed.

As the leader of the Socialist opposition, Bruno Kreisky used the Warsaw Pact invasion of the ČSSR for a large-scale political campaign, which also comprised humanitarian measures. In a brilliant speech before 3,000 SPÖ functionaries in the Vienna Guildhall, he pointed to three lessons of the tragedy: hopes that a Communist dictatorship can be 'democratized' are illusory; military intervention is part of every dictatorship's inventory; and finally, compliance and pussyfooting do not impress dictatorships, only closing ranks and a determined approach. The significant 'Eisenstadt Declaration' against dictatorship and any collaboration with the Communist party followed a year later. With it he corrected the grave tactical error of the year 1966, when the Communists' endorsement of the SPÖ had not been explicitly repudiated.

Why did the Klaus government lose not only the absolute but even the relative majority on 1 March 1970, despite a positive economic and socio-political record? Karl Gruber, the former Foreign Minister and State Secretary under Klaus, concludes: 'Klaus's was a decidedly good government for the Austrian people, but—absurd as it might sound—it was a catastrophic government for the Austrian People's Party. ... Josef Klaus was simply too much of an idealist to cope with the motley crew, from which a part always steps out of line when there is a lack of strong authority.' Klaus was a reform politician without a power base, who 'never really felt at home' in the ÖVP parliamentary group.[11] This is how one of the talented 'Klaus boys', Heinrich Neisser, sees him today: 'He was a man who attempted but did not quite achieve a turnaround, a man who regarded professionalism as the core of politics but who, in the event, did not have the strength to enforce it. It was a transition to a new era. However, this transition was accomplished through Kreisky.'[12]

Josef Klaus surprised us journalists on the night of the election in the large hall of the central electoral office in the Interior Ministry, and outraged (in secret) many attending party dignitaries, when in front of the TV cameras he tersely turned down a 'coalition of the losers' as an option with the FPÖ. The statement struck his Vice-Chancellor and General Secretary Withalm 'like a bolt from the blue'. An ÖVP–FPÖ coalition would have given the coalition eighty-four seats against the eighty-one of the SPÖ, yet—as Klaus said many years later in an ORF interview—he would never have done that; that would have been 'indecent'.

Klaus retired from politics at the age of 60 without resentment or regrets. He might have been a transient phenomenon compared to Bruno Kreisky, yet his attitude to power, his voluntary, fast and painless withdrawal from politics, as well as his unusually frank and self-critical memoirs written within the year, remain proof of that human greatness which we media people witnessed both then and later.

11

KREISKY'S SECRET POWER BASE

A quarter of a century after Bruno Kreisky's resignation as Federal Chancellor and almost two decades after his death, the Austrian Public is still fascinated by the Kreisky era. What more proof than the flood of sundry books, articles and opinion pieces about him with attacks and vindications, memories and reflections. Who was Kreisky? Son of an upper-middle-class Jewish family, who witnessed the funeral of Emperor Franz Joseph; as a Socialist he was imprisoned for two years and then forced into Swedish exile for twelve; he lost twenty-one family members during Nazi times; then became the longest serving Socialist Federal Chancellor in a Conservative country, as well as the long-term leader of a social democracy that was also prone to anti-Semitism.

Bruno Kreisky was first and foremost a victor. He led his Socialist party to a series of five electoral victories (1970–83) unmatched in modern European history, which reached their zenith in the attainment three times (1971, 1975 and 1979) of an absolute majority of seats and—for the first time in Austrian history—also a majority of votes. During two decades as Foreign Minister and Chancellor he raised Austria's status in the world to unprecedented heights.

The phenomenon of Bruno Kreisky has fascinated such varied people as Norbert Leser, the critical historian of Austrian social democracy; Kurt Vorhofer, a foremost Catholic journalist; and Armin Thurnher, the left-liberal editor-in-chief of the Viennese paper *Falter*; but also some of his explicit political opponents. Despite all his personal disappointments, Leser saw him (1988) as 'an epoch-making presence' in Austrian history and international socialism: 'I am firmly convinced that without the special charisma of Kreisky, without his commitment and his Protean complexity, the historic chance which the

79

Socialist party had in the seventies of becoming a leading political force would not have been exploited, or at least not with such an intensity and for such a length of time.'

Kurt Vorhofer has coined the epithets 'Journalist Chancellor' and 'Sun King' for Kreisky. Shortly before his death in May 1995, Vorhofer (an ÖVP member!) said at a discussion meeting that Kreisky was for him 'the last glitter of the fairytale city', that is to say, of *fin de siècle* Vienna. He was 'like an unusual natural phenomenon ... incredibly gifted—half a dozen capable politicians could have comfortably lived from his endowment of talent'.

And lastly the diagnosis by Armin Thurnher (b. 1949): 'In 1970 Bruno Kreisky won the elections—not the new SPÖ, but Bruno Kreisky, the upper-middle-class Jew. He would never have imagined—he once said—that a Jew could become Federal Chancellor in Austria, when his rival, the middle-class Josef Klaus, had advertised himself as a "real Austrian". It did not help him. Instead the voters must have had an inkling of another real Austria, the notion of an Austria beyond German nationalist narrowness and state-authoritarian bureaucracy. The "Sun King", as Kreisky was called respectfully by his scoffers, is in the judgement of both his critics and followers the most significant politician produced by the Austria of both republics.'[1] These assessments are particularly significant because they stem from extremely critical and independent political observers long after Kreisky's retirement. Though I am aiming at objectivity in dealing with Kreisky's personality and his era, I should not conceal my close rapport with Bruno Kreisky. Thirty years of my life were linked to his, sometimes closely, at other times loosely, occasionally visibly, now and then behind the scenes, often in harmony, sometimes also in conflict, but never at an indifferent distance.[2]

Very soon after my appointment as correspondent of the *Financial Times* I visited Bruno Kreisky, then Foreign Minister, and made my first longer interview with him on 21 June 1960. While leafing through the forty-four volumes of my newspaper clippings, I found dozens of interviews with, and articles about, Kreisky. His brilliant intellect, his political erudition, his tactical gift and his sensibility by which he grasped the currents of the times, coupled with his proficiency in foreign languages, caused him to be more appreciated at first outside Austria than in his own country and especially in his own party, dominated at the time by narrow-minded functionaries of the old school.

It is difficult, almost grotesque, to imagine today that, after the cata-strophic defeat of the SPÖ at the general elections in 1966, barely 63 per cent of the party executive's members and subsequently 70 per cent of the delegates voted for Kreisky as Party Chairman at the decisive party congress on 1 February 1967. The party establishment's initial rival candidate was a long forgotten political mediocrity called Hans Czettel, at the time Deputy Governor of Lower Austria. He declined the candidacy at the last moment before the voting.

The minutes of the party convention make weird reading today. After the diatribes by the union leader Anton Benya (who reproached Kreisky for malicious gossiping and informing the foreign press), the failed Party Chairman Bruno Pittermann and other powerful men from Vienna, Kreisky was eventually made leader by the representatives of the provinces and 'dissidents' from Vienna. In an improvised and therefore particularly impressive speech after the ranting and raving of the deadly enemies masquerading as 'comrades', the new Party Chief quoted the words of Abraham Lincoln as his motto for the following years: 'With malice toward none, with charity for all.' After his elec-tion Kreisky dictated a furious tempo for the implementation of the reform programme, and gained already 97.5 per cent of the votes at his re-election at the next party congress in October 1968.

This unique personality at the head of the SPÖ–and there is no doubt about that—was primarily responsible for the series of successes in democratic elections unprecedented in the history of Austria as well as internationally. No other Social Democratic party in Europe had gained approval so often and to such a degree. At the 1972 party con-vention in Villach, Kreisky pronounced the following famous words about the many people 'who want to go a large part of the way with us, without necessarily committing themselves completely to our aims and objectives'. He regarded himself as the belated executor of liberal reforms, as the destroyer of the taboos within and outside his party and the relics of the authoritarian state. During a lengthy conversation about his objectives, Kreisky once told me that he considered it a very great piece of luck that 'perhaps also through my contribution, Aus-trian social democracy is gaining a larger portion of the liberal legacy, which had partially become abandoned property'.

After the decisive second electoral victory on 10 October 1971, two publishing houses decided apparently independently from each oth-er—or was it rather a hint from Kreisky?—to bring out a biography of the victorious Chancellor. The Viennese publishing house Paul Zsolnay and the German Econ Verlag, whose owner had been Kreisky's high school classmate, planned a joint coffee-table book with two biographical essays. One of these was to be written by the distinguished Conservative editor-in-chief of the *Salzburger Nachrichten*, Karl Heinz Ritschel, and the other one (both on Kreisky's suggestion) by me. At the time I had no idea that another Austrian publisher was entertaining similar book plans.

Before these two biographies, a brochure about Kreisky commissioned by the SPÖ appeared under the pen-name 'Spectator'. Well written, full of details about Kreisky's career, this nevertheless completely uncritical book had been distributed in large numbers before the decisive polling day in the autumn of 1971, and served as campaign munition for the SPÖ. All this was a useful warning for me. Before signing the contract, I formally notified the publisher that I was only willing to accept stylistic amendments, but no substantial changes without my prior agreement.

I and the two other authors were given piles of documents, which gave evidence that Kreisky's ancestors, the Kreisky and Felix families (on the maternal side), had rendered valuable service as physicians, teachers, soldiers and industrialists for more than 200 years, one of them even as a cavalry captain of the Moravian dragoon regiment and later as a magistrate in Vienna, and a great-uncle as liberal MP in the Austrian Imperial Assembly. Luckily, as a result of my private understanding with the co-author, I could deal mostly with foreign policy and ideological questions, even though the two essays overlapped here and there. The only person who would have read all three manuscripts on completion as well as during the final editing process was probably Kreisky himself.

In the introduction I thanked those twenty-nine 'critical friends' and 'friendly opponents' of Bruno Kreisky who were willing to grant interviews to me. Some of the most influential partners, such as Finance Minister Hannes Androsch, Justice Minister Christian Broda, Trade Union Federation President Anton Benya etc., formed an intra-party faction against Kreisky a few years later for various reasons. But when the two biographies appeared in the autumn of 1972, these conflicts were still under wraps. At the conclusion of my essay I wrote: 'Kreisky has reconciled his party with the intellectuals and with youth, with the Catholics—and with the former Nazis. Therein lie the strength and the weakness of his unique position; a charismatic leader who can preserve the contradictions of his position only as long as he is able to stand the test of time by miracles and successes.'

The superb strategist and tactician Kreisky could never fall back on networks, clans or an organized clientele in his party. Despite his phenomenal successes at the polls he was never an all-powerful party leader, and especially toward the end of the seventies time and again he was the target of coded attacks within the party. I have known him in all phases, from his election triumphs to his embittered retirement, ailing and abandoned by his closest comrades. The terse saying attributed to the party's founder, Victor Adler, could also apply to him: 'I am the loneliest man in the party.'

That he could hold his ground so masterfully for such a relatively long time can only be ascribed to the fact that he 'was indeed the greatest communicator produced in Austria's history'.[3] What a prominent German political commentator wrote about the legendary Foreign Minister Hans-Dietrich Genscher is true also of Bruno Kreisky: 'He realized that public relations belonged to the substance of politics itself and that it must not be tacked on to it afterwards like an advertisement for a car or a brand of cigarettes. ... He was the unmatched master of the art of influencing and forming public opinion.'[4]

Kreisky's power base was the spoken and written word: his inimitable way of casting a spell over world-famous publicists, but also over the young reporters of tabloids or the TV. The fact that in his younger years while in Swedish exile he had worked as a journalist, among other papers for the Tribune in London and for the TAT in Zurich and under a pseudonym for Swedish papers, helped him to appreciate the work of the foreign correspondents in Vienna. Already as State Secretary after 1953 and more than ever as Foreign Minister, leader of the opposition and Federal Chancellor, he was not only the architect, but also in a sense even the salesman of his political ideas: responsible both for 'production' and for 'marketing'. Kreisky's press and media policy was a bespoke suit, which fitted only him and nobody else.

In contrast to his successors, Kreisky never had a general staff-like organized network of spokespeople and press secretaries. Apart from a single secretary or a diplomat responsible for press relations, Kreisky always relied first of all on himself, on his ability to 'feed' the mass media with genuine news, on his grasp for journalistic work and his eloquence. The observance of the deadline for the first edition of the newspaper or the TV evening news also belonged to this awareness. He was the first politician who always cared also for young journalists. Already as Foreign Minister he had, for instance, rung a very young journalist on a provincial paper with regard to a critical article and invited him to discuss controversial issues over a cup of coffee.

Although there were no mobile telephones at the time, his influence rested on his almost perpetual accessibility in person or by telephone. He was always available, and not only to the editors-in-chief of the *New York Times* or *Die Zeit*. As early as 8 o'clock over breakfast, he was just as ready to answer the questions of a young foreign editor of the *Neue Kronen Zeitung* as those of the chief correspondent of Reuters or the correspondent of the *Frankfurter Allgemeine Zeitung*. He made a habit of inviting journalists whom he regarded as important for some reason or other, or whom he found likable, for a private discussion first in his office on the Ballhausplatz and then for afternoon tea, and ultimately, as a special honour, for lunch.

It would have been at the beginning of 1962, before a trip to South Tyrol, that I was invited for the first time to lunch at the Kreiskys' rented villa in Döbling. At the time media support against Italy, especially by the British press, was clearly important for Kreisky. It was a risky decision for the new Foreign Minister Kreisky to take the South Tyrolean problem before the UN General Assembly. It was the prelude to the long-lasting Italian–Austrian negotiations, which were occasionally interrupted by terror bombings and mass arrests. In the event, they secured the best possible autonomy for the German-speaking inhabitants through the treaty later accepted by the Klaus government.

Kreisky's activities on behalf of this minority boosted his standing also in the eyes of Conservative circles, especially in Northern Tyrol. At the time I travelled to Innsbruck on Kreisky's advice. The informal background discussions held there helped me to understand better the complex South Tyrolean question. My two long interviews conducted in Bolzano (Bozen to the Austrians) with the temperamental South Tyrolean Governor Silvius Magnago and others supplied me with sufficient material for several of my articles that appeared in the *Financial Times* and the London economic weekly, The Statist (now extinct).

I met Kreisky again after my return, and reported to him about my impressions of the deep chasm between the two South Tyrolean ethnic groups. He made no bones about his motives for taking such an active part in South Tyrolean politics. Quite a few observers regarded his endeavours as exaggerated. What Kreisky intimated to me in confidence at the time, he later disclosed in his memoirs. Precisely he, the cosmopolitan-minded Socialist with Jewish roots, wanted to send a visible signal to the Austrians, Italians, as well as the international community that the solution of the South Tyrolean problem was of prime importance to him and the Foreign Ministry. The key representatives of Tyrol and South Tyrol later thanked him in cordial letters for his 'tenacious work over the years' and his 'astute and energetic' efforts. Later, as Federal Chancellor, he was particularly proud to receive the highest Tyrolean award for his hard work exerted on behalf of South Tyrol.

Exactly twenty years after that first lunch in the garden of his villa, during a special meeting which I had requested for an essay, Kreisky characterized his rule of conduct vis-à-vis the media in the following way:

'What was the reason for my relatively good relationship with the press? I told myself that if I did not tell journalists anything, I should not be surprised if they did not write anything or wrote untruths. That is why I am actually always available, I can be rung, I can be asked. The second principle: if I express myself very cryptically, I should not be surprised if journalists cannot use that. They have to receive information that is possibly unpleasant or comes across as indiscreet; but it has to have news value for the journalists, it has to be worth their while to write about it, and that is why I am perhaps not always a pleasant partner, but certainly am an indispensable one for journalists.'

What then was Kreisky's 'magic', 'narcosis' or 'opium' (expressions that both his critics and admirers used)? 'My relationship to journalists is good but reserved as far as average journalism is concerned. With knowledgeable journalists, I have a comradely relationship, because I regard them as completely equal partners.' Hugo von Hofmannsthal, the great Austrian poet, once wrote: 'Politics is magic. It obeys those who know how to invoke the Forces.' Kreisky was veritably a magician, a professional conjuror; a man constantly acting, improvising, frequently intoxicated by his own style and rhetoric, but at the same time a political player, who could keep hundreds of matters simultaneously in motion. Journalists fell easily under his spell. For him, of course, political calculation was of the essence; for us, on the other hand, it was those pieces of news and evaluations that could be of interest to our papers and readers, and later to television programmes and their viewers. To Kurt Vorhofer's question during his first press conference as Federal Chancellor, as to what emotions he felt, his reply was 'courage and delight'. Vorhofer aptly said: 'With Kreisky the journalists always get their money's worth, unlike with many other press conferences that are more often than not a waste of time for the journalist, or at best an act of piety in terms of democratic tradition.'

The fact that his private telephone number and address were always in the Viennese telephone directory, that he introduced the so-called *Pressefoyer*, a casual press forum following the weekly Tuesday Council of Ministers meetings, where even young journalists or foreign correspondents could pose direct questions without any formality in front of live TV cameras—all this was a brilliant political move. It was without doubt a successful advertising gimmick, but also a source of deep personal satisfaction for him. I was several times not only a witness, but also indirectly—as so many other of his visitors—a victim of perfect strangers ringing him, who wanted to find out something from him, but were mainly asking him for help. And on such occasions Kreisky would interrupt in midstream a conversation—usually very important to his visitor—to take notes and instruct his secretariat to look into the cases of hardship. A long-standing secretary remembered a stormy night when several assistants had been working with Kreisky on an important parliamentary speech. Around midnight an elderly woman rang unexpectedly, because her roof was damaged and the rain was pouring into the house. Kreisky interrupted the session, and to the surprise of all those present, promptly mobilized the fire brigade. In short, people felt that Kreisky was always accessible.

The 'Kokoschka episode' is also characteristic of his spontaneous and unbureaucratic willingness to help. The Nazis had deprived the famous 'decadent artist' of his Austrian citizenship, and he now wanted to get his passport back. As Kokoschka was a Swiss resident, Kreisky simply registered him at his own Vienna address. The 'lodger' Kokoschka's thank you letter is still extant and hangs in a frame next to the artist's self-portrait (which his wife has provided) on a wall in Kreisky's former residence, which now houses the Bruno Kreisky Forum for International Dialogue.

This Social Democrat had an overt soft spot not only for artists and intellectuals, but also a covert penchant for the aristocracy and tradition. During a conversation in the early sixties, while still Foreign Minister, he showed me with obvious pride the first page of a confidential report by Prince Johannes Schwarzenberg, the Austrian Ambassador to London, concerning the state of the European integration negotiations. It read verbatim: 'The day before yesterday at the hunt, the Prime Minister told me in confidence that ...' The British Prime Minister of the time, Lord Home (the former Foreign Secretary), was on friendly terms with the Austrian aristocrat. 'See what exclusive contacts this small country of ours can cultivate with a Great Power!' boasted Kreisky, only to add straight away: 'But this is confidential too!' The occasional rider: 'But you mustn't write this', could generally only be deciphered by experienced Kreisky-specialists; i.e., it was not at all certain whether he meant it seriously or whether, on the contrary, it was a go-ahead for writing it.

Otto Schulmeister, the outstanding Conservative journalist and long-standing editor-in-chief of *Die Presse*, was often reproached for being a Kreisky fan. In 1966 Schulmeister had turned down Josef Klaus's offer to assume the education portfolio in the People's Party government. This is how we wrote about Kreisky: '...it would simply be a lie to gainsay the fascination that emanated from him. ... This man is unforgettable, because he wanted more than what his own and the country's strength and resources could afford. In this respect he was a "Great Austrian", someone who measured Austria's greatness not by the country's physical size.' The special rapport between Schulmeister and Kreisky was also demonstrated at the 1986 launch of Kreisky's memoirs' first volume in the Belvedere's state hall, when the ex-Chancellor asked his 'favourite enemy', Otto Schulmeister, to introduce his book.[5]

Kreisky's 'Great Austrian'—as Schulmeister called it—or 'Austrian patriotic' approach had left its mark already during his Foreign Ministership as far as the choice and promotion of his staff was concerned. Despite opposition from his own party and to the annoyance of the CV (Catholic student associations), as well as the Freemasons, he favoured the so-called 'blood group zero' in the Ministry of Foreign Affairs, where numerous aristocrats worked, i.e. those diplomats who did not belong to any party. It was a later consequence of his era that (Count) Wolfgang Schallenberg and (Prince) Albert Rohan could be Secretaries-General of the Ministry of Foreign Affairs during the nineties. Some people saw it as a kind of 'Aristocratic Renaissance' in a country with a Social Democrat majority: Erich Bielka (von) Karltreu, a professional diplomat, became Foreign Minister, Baron Karl von Lütgendorf became Minister of Defence (he later committed suicide because of a corruption scandal) and General (Count) Emil Spannochi commander of the army. Defying intra-party resistance and in the spirit of openness—without regard to party affiliations—Kreisky appointed the practising Catholic (and former ÖVP member) Rudolf Kirchschläger in 1970 to the Foreign Ministership, and as of 1974 nominated him for the Federal Presidency which he won twice. With a stroke of genius, in 1978 he made Stephan Koren, an ÖVP faction leader (and former Finance Minister in the Klaus government), president of the National Bank.

Kreisky had an almost erotic relationship with the press. If, during our joint East European trips or at press conferences, he discovered a new face, he immediately wanted to establish contact. In the spring of 1973, when he was accompanied on the train to Budapest for a state visit to Hungary by three provincial governors and three chief whips of the parties represented in parliament, plus numerous reporters, the Chancellor suddenly wanted to talk to me. 'Who is that unfamiliar young man with that blonde woman? Why doesn't he come over here?' The young man was a Hungarian-born Austrian reporter, who simply did not dare to address Kreisky directly without an introduction. I introduced him to the Chancellor, who then chatted briefly but cheerfully with the couple. At a press conference Vorhofer once witnessed Kreisky going up to a young man he did not recognize, and asking him: 'Where do you work?' Where upon the young man politely replied: 'Inspector Sedlacek—from the security service...'

Two episodes remain memorable for me from the above-mentioned Hungarian visit; this is how I described them at the time: 'Federal Chancellor Kreisky has a special place in Hungarian history: he is the first foreigner who could leave the heavily guarded country without a passport. On his return trip at the passport control it transpired that the Chancellor's diplomatic passport had either been left behind in the government's Budapest guesthouse where the members of the Austrian delegation had stayed, or it had been lost somewhere. Even after searching his luggage, his secretaries could not find the passport...' We found out the following day that his chauffeur had put it in the inside pocket of a suit jacket. The second story is about Theodor Kery, the Governor of Burgenland, who spoke in perfect Hungarian with the hosts. Under a clear and sunny sky the relaxed Kreisky pointed out to the Hungarian President Pál Losonczi that this just proved how the Hungarian minority had made its mark in Austria...[6]

The fact that Kreisky could successfully forge a tacit coalition with the media and with intellectuals with such unmatched virtuosity was also due to his long-standing and chequered relationship with the editor-in-chief of the *Neue Kronen Zeitung*, Hans Dichand, the most powerful and most controversial publisher in Austria. Dichand, still extraordinarily active despite his eighty-eight years, spoke to me in a conciliatory tone about Kreisky, although in the third volume of his memoirs Kreisky had sharply criticized the paper:

'We went for walks several times, that's how he wanted it, on Sunday mornings up the Kahlenberg. He had rung me. So we walked, and people came towards us, hikers, who greeted him politely, and all of a sudden I overheard one of them saying, "That's Kreisky and his cop." We were on good terms. I visited him frequently. He always told me frankly both the good and the bad. But it also happened that he was a bit wrong sometimes.'

Although Kreisky was the greatest beneficiary of the Klaus government's radio reform and the 'information explosion' managed by the new Director-General, Gerd Bacher, the Chancellor and his party fought for years against Bacher and for control of the Austrian Radio and Television (ORF). Even though Kreisky managed to weaken Bacher's position and to have him removed in 1974, despite the interruptions Gerd Bacher remained the outstanding leading figure of the ORF for close on twenty years.

The fact that Kreisky was personally as closely associated with the world of the media as no other head of government had been before or since was motivated by his erstwhile aspiration for a career in journalism. He wrote so himself in the third volume of his memoirs: 'I have never wanted to be a parliamentarian or anything similar, only a journalist. It is really very appealing to be able to have one's printed opinion aired each day.' Some of his critics regarded this aspiration as already realized. Thus, for instance, a prominent Conservative editor in an extremely critical article characterized him at the time as 'an omniscient chief columnist performing around the clock'.[7]

Yet he never asked for an interview to be submitted before publication, nor to have a press officer review it. He always left it to me, as editor-in-chief, to abbreviate or edit very long and detailed discussions on sensitive foreign and domestic political topics for the quarterly *Europäische Rundschau*. Neither did Kurt Vorhofer have to show him the many Kreisky interviews made during and after his Chancellorship before they went to press. At most he would say, 'delete any-thing vulgar'.

It did happen frequently, though, that the petulant Chancellor was totally fed up with some radio and television reporters. The most fre-quently quoted case was the one when he verbally attacked a stub-bornly questioning TV journalist in front of live TV cameras by calling out: 'Study history, Mr Reporter!' The ambivalent relationship with the news magazine *Profil* fluctuated between hostility and admiration. Between 1970 and 1983 the weekly devoted its title page to him on no less than thirty occasions. Six more cover stories were added to this during the seven years until his death. A *Profil* columnist wrote about him in a touching obituary: 'He corrupted us journalists without ask-ing: he behaved towards us just as he felt like; he treated us jovially or ignored us sarcastically, inspired us or snubbed us; he could be a grandseigneur or a cantankerous grouch—but can a love—hate rela-tionship be a sin?'

12

SHADOWS OF THE NAZI PAST
KREISKY VERSUS WIESENTHAL

A dramatic and highly emotional public conflict overshadowed the dazzling Kreisky era. Due to my work as a foreign correspondent and my personal contacts, I was very close to the dramatis personae. The roots of the gripping story reach far back into the past and, directly or indirectly, still leave their mark on the image of Austria both at home and abroad.

The political bomb went off on 27 April 1970, just one day after Chancellor Kreisky's government policy statement. In a conversation with a journalist, Hans Öllinger, the new Minister for Agriculture admitted that he had been a member of the SS. When I rang Kreisky, he roundly declared that he had not known anything about the Carinthian agrarian expert's past. During the hurried government reshuffle he had relied on the advice of his Carinthian party comrades, as he had never counted on ever having to appoint a Minister for Agriculture.

I promptly sent a dispatch to my papers. After a brief account of the affair, this is what I wrote in my report to the Zurich newspaper *Die TAT*: 'It is not surprising that in Austria, where there were 567,000 registered Nazi party members, politicians with a light- or dark-brown past also play a part in the course of the generational change. ... Still, political circles have noted with dismay that by now even SS-members have become "socially acceptable". After all, 22,000 Austrians belonged at the time to the so-called Order of the Death's Head. And these were not opportunists, voluntary or forced fellow-travellers, but predominantly fanatical National Socialists.' Finally—without mentioning his name—I quoted the well-known Catholic intellectual, the historian

Friedrich Heer, according to whom this appointment went beyond the acceptable boundaries.

At the time I was not yet aware that Reinhard Kamitz, the excellent ÖVP Finance Minister (1952–60) had also been a Nazi party member and, what is more, a candidate for membership in the SS. To top it all, it was the Socialist Minister of the Interior Oskar Helmer who, as a sign of coalition harmony, had presented him on his birthday with his 'file', i.e. the documents of his Nazi past. That Helmer had rendered great services in thwarting the Communists' attempts to infiltrate the security service does not alter the fact that he was a well-known anti-Semite, and did not hide his prejudice even vis-à-vis Kreisky himself.

Rosa Jochmann was a (non-Jewish) worker and Socialist functionary who had spent six years in the Ravensbrück concentration camp, and after the war became a prominent politician. She told me that the leadership of the Social Democratic party ignored or suppressed the horrors of the Nazi era. Thus, for instance, when she once drove with Helmer to a function in Lower Austria, he asked her amicably: 'Tell me, Rosa, was it really that bad in Ravensbrück?' Jochmann was so incensed that she had the vehicle stopped that instant, jumped off, and never wanted to talk to the minister again.

But let us return to the Öllinger case, which was discussed at the time by the world press as well. Some days after the publication of the startling revelation, Kreisky held a press conference in the packed Concordia Press Club. I was the first to pose to him the crucial question of the Öllinger case: Will the controversial minister resign, and if so, when?

Kreisky, in a bad mood, gave no explicit reply at this press conference, but Öllinger resigned 'for health reasons' barely a month later. However, this did not mean the end of dealing with the murky past of the Social Democrats.

Precisely on the eve of the June party congress to be devoted to the celebration of the electoral victory, the Hamburg news magazine *Der Spiegel*—referring to Simon Wiesenthal, head of the Viennese Jewish Documentation Centre—revealed that of the eleven ministers in the first single-party Socialist government, no less than four ministers were former members of the Nazi party: including Interior Minister Otto Rösch. Incidentally Öllinger's successor, Oskar Weihs, had also been a member of the Nazi party.

However, it was not the fact that a third of the first Social Democrat government was made up of former Nazis which became the focus of the dispute, but rather the accuser, i.e. Simon Wiesenthal, the informant of *Der Spiegel*, became the focus of the dispute. At the Socialist party congress, Education Minister Leopold Gratz sharply attacked the Documentation Centre for operating like a private secret police and surveillance centre which employs informants, hunts down innocent people and pursues a campaign against social democracy. He also threatened to have the activities of the Wiesenthal Centre banned.[1]

Although I hardly knew Wiesenthal, and was aware that he was close to the People's Party, in an article I sharply criticized the grotesque alliance between the Socialists, the Polish 'anti—Zionists' (who accused Wiesenthal of spying because of his unmasking of the Polish Communist party's anti—Semitic campaign), the Austrian communist paper *Volksstimme*, and the extreme right wing. After a series of acquittals of Nazi mass murderers, Kreisky and his Minister for Justice, Christian Broda, decided in 1972—in order to avoid an international scandal—to stop any further jury trials.

In his book *Justice not Vengeance*, an embittered Wiesenthal came to two conclusions: 'The Austrian Social Democratic party has over the years become the most important advocate of the former National Socialists', and 'Christian Broda, the former Communist, the bitter enemy of the Nazis, has become the executor of the Austrian Nazi criminals' "cold amnesia".' Although these sweeping judgments were understandable in the light of later and even fiercer battles, it would still be unfair to put the entire blame on the Kreisky government for the lack of candour in dealing with the Nazi past.[2]

As far as Kreisky himself was concerned, he was time after time the butt of subtle and crass anti-Semitic attacks. Not drunk but entirely sober People's Party functionaries declared vociferously during the election campaigns of the sixties: 'If an Austrian cannot become Foreign Minister in Israel, why doesn't an Austrian become Foreign Minister in Austria instead of a Jew?' A leader of the Lower Austrian Farmers' Federation, and long-standing influential People's Party deputy, had abused Foreign Minister Kreisky at a 1966 election meeting as a 'bloody Jew', as incidentally did quite a number of Carinthian demonstrators in October 1972, who were protesting against a parliamentary decision to mount bilingual signposts in 205 Southern Carinthian communities. These invectives occurred when Kreisky refused the advice of the police to leave the building of the Klagenfurt Chamber of Labour via a side entrance: 'An Austrian Chancellor does not leave a building by the back entrance.'

As far as Wiesenthal's reproaches were concerned, ever since 1947 both great parties had endeavoured to attract the support of the 440,000 'marginally incriminated' Nazis, who would be entitled to vote in 1949. This was followed by various attempts to form a 'black–blue' or 'red–blue' small coalition by way of secret agreements: first with the League of Independents (VdU), which in one fell swoop became the third strongest party in the 1949 elections with sixteen seats, and later with its successor party, the Austrian Freedom Party (FPÖ). It is well-known that, during his secret meeting with the FPÖ Party Chairman Friedrich Peter on the night of 1 March 1970, Kreisky promised to correct the electoral law which was extremely disadvantageous for the Freedomites, and thus set the course for the toleration of a Socialist minority government by the FPÖ. Kreisky had always held the opinion that 'In Austria a National Socialist party member or a member of the SS should be able to fill any political office as long as no crime can be proved against him.' 'Coming from an emigrant and a Jew', writes President Heinz Fischer, 'this was a remarkable attitude, but he represented this standpoint sovereignly and consistently. The constitutional principles, especially the refusal of collective guilt, justified his stance. It was not fair to chalk it up to his opportunism or to an ambiguous approach toward National Socialism.'[3]

Even a pro-Socialist journalist noted that, with his understanding attitude, Kreisky 'soothed the conscience of the country'. As a Jew he could afford a frequently painful lack of sensitivity for the feelings of victims, and also verbally to break some sanctified taboos. Psychologists have from the start claimed that Kreisky actually profited from the latent anti-Semitism, from suppressed guilt complex and the fact that the broad masses regarded him as the personification of authority and reliability, precisely because he obviously did not have the attributes that anti-Semitic propaganda ascribed to Jews. As far as Kreisky was concerned, I can confirm on the basis of many personal conversations that nothing filled him with more inner satisfaction than the undeniable fact that the Austrian people had several times (what is more, on three occasions with an absolute majority) elected him, the erstwhile disenfranchised, persecuted outcast.

However, in matters of the National Socialist past, Israel and the Jews, he often showed a lack of self-control and lost all sense of proportion. Kreisky's forgiveness and relaxed attitude toward former Nazis dates from the shared sufferings of the National Socialists and

Social Democrats under the Austro-Fascist government. At any rate, he experienced the worst times only 'at second hand'. Already at the time of writing his biography we had had more than one heated argument about his uncompromising and extremely sharp stance toward the Dollfuss and Schuschnigg-type corporative state and, in contrast, about the astounding tolerance with which he treated the Nazis. In this context he always stressed that in politics everyone had the right to be wrong. In the course of one of these arguments during lunch at a holiday resort, Kreisky brought up his favourite argument: 'You know that I lost twenty-one members of my family in the Holocaust!' My counter-question was: 'Did you ask your twenty-one relatives whether you could also speak in *their* name?' Kreisky practically exploded and left the table—we were already having coffee: 'How dare you! What an outrageous impertinence!' I remained seated for a while with the secretary, and then I went for a longish walk and prepared for a premature departure.

Hardly had I got back to my room before I found a message from Kreisky asking me to return to him. In his room, as if nothing had happened, he remarked that we had to hurry to continue the book interview, as we were invited for caviar and vodka at 5.30 pm with Princess Grace of Monaco, who had just returned from Persia. 'I don't even know the Princess,' I said, nonplussed. 'What do you mean, you don't know her? Both of us have already been announced'; and with that Kreisky concluded the topic and began a long diatribe against the German and Austrian Communist exiles in Sweden.

It was this mixture of uncontrolled eruptions and subsequent periods of aloofness, self-opinionated monologues and tolerant willingness for debate, the abrupt change between sociability and rejection that belonged to the riddle of this complex personality. But at the same time—especially in the intra-party power struggles—he was also a soft, sensitive person, who at times played himself. Just as an actor needs an audience, so Kreisky too needed an echo, which, if need be, he would even extort.

Beside his disowned, disloyal crown prince, Hannes Androsch, there was only one person whom Kreisky fought with the same dogged grimness, even biblical hatred: Simon Wiesenthal.

What happened in 1970 in connection with the *Spiegel* revelations was something like a dress rehearsal for the real international scandal that erupted in the autumn of 1975. Wiesenthal wanted to thwart an allegedly 'small coalition' with the right-wing FPÖ and in this case Friedrich Peter's likely appointment to the Vice-Chancellorship. The Social Democrats gained an absolute majority, thus this plan was no longer relevant. A few days prior to the elections, however, Wiesenthal showed a sensitive report to President Rudolf Kirchschläger about Peter's wartime years, which revealed that Peter had been serving as an officer in a notorious SS infantry brigade. This unit was part of the *Einsatzgruppen*, which had massacred hundreds of thousands of Jews and other civilians in Nazi-occupied Eastern Europe in 1941–2.[4]

At a press conference after the elections, Wiesenthal distributed folders with the new documents. On 10 November, the Federation of Foreign Correspondents invited the Chancellor to a press conference. I too was present and saw a Kreisky completely beside himself with rage. In his fury he went so far as to imply by a cryptic remark that Wiesenthal had indirectly been a Gestapo collaborator, saying that he had 'an entirely different relationship [with the Gestapo] than I had'. East European experts were convinced already then that the alleged information about Wiesenthal's 'dubious past' leaked to Kreisky originated from the Polish secret service.[5]

Wiesenthal threatened Kreisky with legal action, while the latter wanted to initiate the abrogation of his own parliamentary immunity. The Social Democrat faction leader, Heinz Fischer, threatened a parliamentary inquiry against Wiesenthal and his centre. Although as a result of the discreet mediation by Jewish personalities the various threats were withdrawn, their bitter feud remained an open wound in Kreisky's relationship with Jewry inside and outside Austria until his death.

What was the reason for Kreisky's irrational outbursts against Wiesenthal and his emotional anti-Israel ardour? First and foremost, probably their entirely different personal backgrounds and their diametrically opposite political stance vis-à-vis the Jewish state. Kreisky, the scion of a totally assimilated long-established Austrian Jewish family, who regarded himself simultaneously as an Austrian, a Socialist and a Jew, with his first loyalty to the fatherland and the movement; Wiesenthal, the Galician refugee, concentration camp survivor, who was committed to the Jewish state and to hunting down and convicting those guilty of the Holocaust.

All in all, the conflict embittered Kreisky's true friends, and filled his secret enemies with joy. Four years after our argument at the holiday resort, the accumulated tensions between us regarding the Wiesenthal case erupted once again. During a memorable trip by special train to Prague in February 1976, the first visit since 1945 by an Austrian Chancellor, we had a disagreement in the dining-car. After Friedrich Peter, the FPÖ leader who was travelling with us, had left the table, I openly criticized Kreisky's choice of words and tone in his attacks on Wiesenthal in the presence of the regional governors as well as ÖVP chief whip Stephan Koren. What probably riled Kreisky was not so much my remark but the fact that it was made in front of these politicians. He reprimanded me, as if I had been an office-boy: 'How dare you talk to me like that? This will have consequences!' Dumbfounded, I left the carriage, and we did not exchange any more words for the rest of our journey.

All this was overshadowed, later during the trip, by a visit to the Theresienstadt concentration camp. The delegation made a round of the camp and the crematorium, where of the 43,000 murdered victims 6,182 were Austrian Jews, among them close relations of the Chancellor. The Freedomite leader Friedrich Peter, who, at the time that the Jews and many non-Jewish anti-Fascists (a total of 200,000) were deported to Theresienstadt, had served in the First SS Infantry Brigade, remained discreetly behind with his wife. The scene was eerie: a German cameraman was relentlessly following Peter. All this took place in the camp's courtyard. Some young Viennese colleagues relished the situation. The quiet weeping of Margit Fischer, wife of the Social Democrat faction leader, and the ever-present memory of the Austrian and Czech, German and Hungarian victims, served as a gruesome backdrop for this episode in Austrian domestic politics.

Kreisky was pale and visibly shaken as he placed the wreaths. Standing at a respectful distance from the Kreisky couple, I suddenly heard Hungarian voices behind me: Theodor Kery, the Governor of Burgenland, and Bohuslav Chňoupek, the Czechoslovak Foreign Minister, were conversing in Hungarian. The Slovak-born Chňoupek, an old KGB agent, had attended a Hungarian primary school after Southern Slovakia had been returned to Hungary in 1938 as a result of the First Vienna Award by the Axis powers.

At the reception in Prague that evening, Friedrich Peter bitterly told me: 'Your colleagues treat me like a leper, although I am the one who has led my party away from Nazism to democracy!' In his memoirs the future President, Heinz Fischer, who had been present at that time in

Theresienstadt, wrote that the visit to the concentration camp had 'deeply impressed and distressed' Friedrich Peter. 'The Friedrich Peter of 1976 is a totally different person from the Friedrich Peter of 1940 or 1945. And his distancing from that era was to me authentic.'[6] I have to confess that, at the time and after every conversation I had with Peter, I too was convinced of his genuine change into an upright democratic politician; about the details of his service in the SS unit I did not want to, nor did I, know anything...

A few more words about Kreisky's attitude in regard to Jewry and the Middle East. When I was shooting a TV documentary on the occasion of the tenth anniversary of his death, we also travelled to the Middle East. Time and again we were surprised at the sincere appreciation with which Simon Perez, Hosni Mubarak, Muhammad Gadaffi and Yasser Arafat spoke about Kreisky's person and role.

It was Uri Avnery, the heretical extreme left-wing Israeli politician, who probably summarized Kreisky's relation to Israel most succinctly: 'The Israeli Zionists could never forgive Kreisky that he was a Jew. That means that in Israel it is expected that a Jewish politician owes it to Israel to be absolutely, uncritically and unconditionally loyal to Israel. He naturally never adhered to this; he was extremely critical, and that made the relationship very difficult... Kreisky considered himself Austrian and had very little consciously in common with the Jewish community... Kreisky was a wise man, and from a distance he understood Israel's existential problems better than the Israeli politicians who were involved in those matters on a daily basis. That is why he recognized very early on something that most Israeli politicians still have difficulty in understanding, that Israel's main task is to make peace with its neighbours, the Arabian Middle East.' Despite his occasionally offensive style, Kreisky showed the way, leading to a breakthrough between Israel and its neighbours with dedication and without any ulterior motives, even when rabid fanatics on both sides wanted to block this only way out.[7]

In spite of all his outbursts of fury against Israeli politicians and his Jewish critics, Kreisky never repudiated his belonging to Jewry as a community of fate—neither inwardly, nor in his conversations with his friends. But as a politician, and thus as a result of 'tactical foresight and sober realism',[8] Kreisky chose the contentious (frequently lazy) way of compromises, the (frequently undifferentiated) way of reconciliation and the (frequently unforgivable) way of forgetting. With this background, in my opinion, it was almost logically consistent that (unfortunately too late) a non-Jewish Social Democratic Chancellor, namely Franz Vranitzky, should find those unambiguous words about Austria's responsibility for National Socialist crimes, which Kreisky—for political considerations and probably inner conflict—would not or could not express.

13

THE RIDDLE OF MINISTER RÖSCH, OR THE
BROWN STAINS OF THE SOCIALISTS

It was on 21 December 1975, a Sunday morning before Christmas, when my telephone rang. The *Financial Times* copy-editor on duty alerted me to the news that a terrorist commando had attacked the current conference of the Organization of Petroleum-Exporting Countries (OPEC) in Vienna, taking all those present hostage, including eleven oil ministers.

The *FT*'s energy expert, who was in Vienna as a special correspondent, happened to be in a nearby restaurant with other journalists, but of course there was no possibility of reporting on events taking place inside and outside the hermetically locked building opposite the university. There were no mobile telephones yet, and only one functioning telephone inside the restaurant.

That is how I became a witness, participant and reporter of the war of nerves fought for the release of hostages that lasted more than twenty-one hours. It was an unforgettable day for all those who experienced the dramatic events on the spot and at the chancellery after Chancellor Kreisky returned to his office on Ballhausplatz.

The situation changed from hour to hour. I commuted between the chancellery and my office in the nearby club for foreign correspondents. My colleague from London was practically isolated from the dramatic happenings, and therefore I had to transmit all the news for the paper's various editions.

Since I knew well not only the Chancellor but also his associates, I could exploit my advantage and send a background report to London by phone directly from the ante-room to Kreisky's office. During those hours Vienna was the centre of world attention. The attack by the six—member commando led by the Venezuelan 'Carlos' (Ilich Ramírez Sánchez) left three people dead, among them an Austrian detective. After hectic consultations with foreign governments, Kreisky reached a decision at 1.00 a.m. to let the commando leave with the foreign hostages, including the eleven oil ministers, on a chartered plane to Algiers. There the hostages were released after a few days. 'Carlos' has been serving a life sentence in France since 1994.

Already in my first report to the *FT* I had described the reproaches directed against the government for insufficient security measures. Erhard Busek, then Secretary-General of the ÖVP, sharply criticized Interior Minister Otto Rösch, who told me during the night that the Austrian authorities had acted according to the wishes of the OPEC secretariat. The terrorists could easily attack the conference because that building contained not only the office of OPEC but also the Canadian Embassy, a department of the Viennese municipal administration and several private apartments.

In the course of the almost thirty-five years that have elapsed since, and now that terrorist outrages have become ubiquitous, the governments involved have been criticized either for 'compliance' or for 'inhumane toughness'. Those, like myself, who have experienced such an incident from close by know that, at times like these, what is at stake is human life and not a popularity contest. The raid against OPEC was not the first, nor the last, terrorist action in Vienna, but it was certainly the most spectacular one so far.

The fact that Interior Minister Otto Rösch shook hands in front of the TV cameras with 'Carlos' at Vienna airport, before he flew off with his planeload of hostages at dawn, provoked sharp international criticism. Many newspapers and magazines showed photos of the gaunt Interior Minister extending his palm and shaking the hand of the chief terrorist. The most influential Austrian daily, *Die Presse*, even called for Rösch's immediate resignation.

Until that embarrassing mishap, Rösch, who held the Interior Ministerial portfolio from 1970 to 1977 and subsequently served in the government as Minister for Defence until 1983, was Kreisky's 'least conspicuous and least controversial' minister—as the newsmagazine *Profil* described him in a cover story at the beginning of 1975.[1] The Chancellor commended him once by saying: 'Perhaps Rösch can keep such a low profile because he is so tall (1.91 m) and attracts attention in any context.' Although the account leaked to *Der Spiegel* by Simon

Wiesenthal in 1970 mentions Rösch among the four former Nazi party members, the scandal around the SS member Öllinger pushed his case into the background. At any rate it was rumoured in opposition circles (and I too have heard it from some critical intellectuals) that the taciturn head of the police himself had somehow been involved in a postwar Nazi conspiracy.

Whenever this question arose—and I too put it to Kreisky once—the stock reply was that Rösch had been sent to the Nazi organization with the knowledge and even on the order of the Social Democratic party, probably by Interior Minister Helmer himself. Even the sceptical Nazi hunter, Simon Wiesenthal, tended to believe Rösch. At any rate, it seemed that he was influenced more by the minister's competence and achievements ('far exceeding his predecessor's') and his 'especially forceful actions against neo-Nazi tendencies', rather than what Rösch himself had to say about the events of 1947. According to Wiesenthal, during Rösch's ministry 'a somewhat delicate situation arose: as minister he had become the superior also of the same officials who had arrested him in 1947'.[2]

Why did two detectives of the local secret police department arrest the thirty-year-old Otto Rösch in Graz on 8 December 1947? He was suspected of being a member of the widely branching Nazi underground network organized by the Graz ironmonger, Theodor Soucek. There is a yellowed court file of 106 pages in the Austrian resistance movement's document archive, including denunciations against eighty persons, among them the names of Theodor Soucek and Otto Rösch.

This was the largest and most dangerous illegal Nazi organization in Austria with a political and a 'military' branch. Its primary function was as a rescue operation to assist the escape of top Nazis confined in the Wolfsberg and Glasenbach internment camps. Functionaries of an outfit for the assistance of discharged soldiers and prisoners of war distributed forged identity papers and financed the escape of wanted Nazi criminals, such as the ex-*Gauleiter* of Styria. Moreover, the conspirators attempted to capitalize on and foment tensions between the Allies. The 153–page interrogation record and testimonies confirmed the conspiracy of the 'unscrupulous criminals' according to the central organ of the Socialists in Vienna, the *Arbeiter-Zeitung* (4 January 1948). The local Social Democratic paper, the *Neue Zeit* in Graz, revealed (30 December 1947): 'the intention of the Nazi conspiracy was to rebuild the former Nazi organizations so that, in the case of an armed conflict between the Western powers and the Soviet Union, they would be entrusted with the special mission of creating a Greater German Empire based on Nazi ideology.'

At that time Austrian justice took the tracing and punishing of illegal Nazis seriously. Soucek and two other leading culprits were sentenced to death on the basis of the law banning neo-Nazi activities. The death sentence was later changed to life imprisonment, which lasted exactly three years—after that all three of them were pardoned. And Rösch? The extant original documents I could study in the archives of the association of Austrian resistance fighters contain the testimony of Soucek and several other prisoners. According to them, Rösch 'was entrusted with intelligence; he was supposed to take up contact with those parties, offices, the police, as well as some persons in positions of trust, who seemed suitable from an intelligence point of view. Rösch did actually receive various data from the British letter censorship and occasionally from the telephone interception office as well.' He was further accused of keeping a suitcase full of false personal identification documents, rubber stamps, blank forms, together with lists of wanted persons in his apartment since the middle of 1947. He defended himself in his testimony by stating that he had no knowledge of the locked suitcase's contents.

Rösch was chief censor in the British occupation zone in Styria, and was also active as functionary of the socialist organization which assisted former prisoners of war and returning soldiers. According to several testimonies, Soucek had earmarked him as his military adviser. While Rösch disputed that he had any knowledge of the underground movement's aims, or that he had taken part in any of their meetings, he admitted that he had met Soucek and a number of other suspects on several occasions. It seems furthermore rather odd in retrospect that, after an hour-long conversation about the possible consequences of an East—West conflict, Soucek, who allegedly had business dealings with Rösch, would have brought 'some of his associates' with him and continued the discussion on the same topic in Rösch's apartment, with the guests leaving 'fairly late'.

A few days later Rösch went to see a well-known shoemaker—who was later also arrested—'because of an urgent shoe repair job'. The same people with whom he had conversed a few days earlier were gathered in a backroom of the shoe shop. This time too they discussed political issues but, according to Rösch, only the possibility of electoral reform and by no means the election of a leader for the projected underground movement. Later, though, he remembered that Soucek and his men had talked with him also about their efforts at founding a fourth party in Austria.

On the occasion of another interrogation, Rösch admitted that he had, in fact, discussed with Soucek whether in the case of a war there could be enough time to flee to the West. He had told Soucek that, as he worked for the British, 'he would surely notice if something like that was looming'. He categorically denied that he had any knowledge of the existence of a secret Nazi underground movement. It was also a complete surprise to him that he had been slated as a military adviser.

A leaflet of 'the monarchist partisans' was found in Rösch's apartment, and allegedly also a slip of paper with data concerning the intercepted telephone conversation of one of the putative conspirators. Moreover, Rösch had promised to employ a man recommended by Soucek in the office of letter censorhip, but after their first conversation the person in question never turned up again. Soucek and two witnesses made incriminating statements about Rösch providing information gained from the British censorship of letters. Rösch's response to this was always that those topics were harmless. According to the three interrogation transcripts I read, he disputed any knowledge of a neo-Nazi organization or that he had anything to do with such an organization.

Be that as it may, Rösch was an ideal candidate for recruitment. He was not only a Nazi, but he was so trustworthy that he was engaged as teacher at a National Socialist Napola's elite school in Traiskirchen. A research associate of the Institute for Contemporary History has found out that Rösch had been a member of the Hitler Jugend as early as 1935–6, and from 1936 of the illegal National Socialist student association, and that from 1937 he had been a leading functionary of the Hitler Jugend movement in Graz. Moreover, on his personnel record card at the National Socialist Teachers' Federation, it was noted that in 1937 he was also a member of the Nazi organization, the SA staff guard. On 8 October 1938, he applied for membership of the National Socialist party, and received the card on 1 January 1940 with the membership number 8,595,796. Subsequently he became a professional officer and was awarded the German Cross in Gold. At the end of the war he carried the rank of captain.

Two things were strange in Rösch's trial. One was that on 3 June 1949 he was acquitted, though not because of his proven innocence, but on account of lack of evidence. The other was that the testimonies and a number of attendant circumstances confirm that—two and a half years after the war!—a significant number of committed Nazis were at work, and that Rösch was suspect to such an extent that he had to spend an unusually long time—eight months—on remand.

His later vindication—published only twenty-five years later, in 1970—is not convincing. Firstly, the story of his allegedly planned infiltration into the Nazi groups cannot be checked. And so far no one has clarified what Rösch or his sponsors, such as the Minister of Interior Oskar Helmer, had actually wanted. What would the Social Democratic party have gained from that infiltration? There is no reference to this in the interrogation transcripts and the testimonies. Furthermore, in that case it is hard to believe that the party would have let Rösch be imprisoned on remand for eight months!

The six-page biography written by the historian Maria Wirth, in the framework of the research programme initiated by the former SPÖ chairman Alfred Gusenbauer, supports the doubts concerning Rösch's credibility. Wirth's judgment sharply contradicts the way in which Heinz Fischer exonerated Rösch (with his 'unblemished past') in his memoirs, from which we have already quoted.[3]

Thus, for instance, the British occupying power had already noted in January 1948 that at the time of his employment Rösch had kept silent about his membership of the Hitler Jugend in 1937 and of the SA in 1938. In the course of his denazification he claimed that he had only described himself as a member of the SA on the National Socialist Teachers' Federation's personnel record card in order to receive a scholarship and a deferment of his military service. Because he was a soldier, he did not have any knowledge of receiving his National Socialist party membership, and that was why he had not reported it for the registration of Nazi party members. Although he had applied for membership, he had never paid any dues nor received a party card. He was therefore deleted from the registration list on 9 November 1949.

Already in the year of his release, his patron, the secretary of the Socialist party organization in Styria province, recommended Rösch for the post of Styrian secretary of the Socialist Municipal Representatives, and two years later he was nominated for a seat in the federal upper house. Although opposition was strong within the SPÖ, especially by the comrades in Graz who referred to Rösch's Nazi past, his nomination was approved after 'a thorough debate'.

The author of the biographical report emphasizes that on several occasions Rösch had to correct himself in public, for example, when he had to revoke his denial of the first *Spiegel* article that he had not been a party member. The Party Secretary from Graz allegedly told Kreisky after his return from Sweden about the 'daring idea' of Rösch's party assignment regarding the neo-Nazi Soucek group. At any rate, in her critical memorandum the historian stresses that there was no evidence to support Rösch's statements.[4]

The necessary question then remains: how could Rösch's fairytale career-path have been so rapid and so steep? Despite his Nazi membership number he was put in the category of 'not liable for registration'. His rise began with this denazification certificate: 1951–3 member of the Bundesrat, 1953–9 member of the provincial diet of Styria, 1959–66 state secretary at the Federal Ministry of Defence; 1966–70 member of the Lower Austrian provincial government; 1970–77 federal Minister of the Interior; 1977–83 federal Minister of Defence; 1983–91 president of the pensioners' association of the Austrian Socialist party.

What was the actual key to his rise from the ashes? The SPÖ needed clever and educated young men; and his 'Socialist pedigree' counted despite him having followed the wrong track. His grandfather had been the Socialist mayor of Stockerau, member of the regional diet of Lower Austria and member of the Upper House (1927–34). Belonging to the Socialist 'aristocracy' definitely offered a shortcut for his career. He was certainly a good organizer, a reserved politician and one of the pillars of the SPÖ's guard of grey functionaries. As one of his successors put it, there had not been much talk within the party about his Nazi past. Incidentally, Rösch is said to have told one of his comrades that, until the last day of the war, he had fought in Lower Austria at the head of a so-called rocket company and had taken out thirty-six of the Red Army's tanks.

The historian Maria Wirth justly notes that 'significant parts of Rösch's past that were definitely known inside the SPÖ ... were excluded from "the successful denazification".' In view of the convincing report by the Historical Institute's research group, it is almost impossible for me to believe in the backdated happy end to the official Otto Rösch biography.

In the pantheon of Socialist careers with shady Nazi backgrounds, the 'Rösch enigma' comes across as an albeit brilliant, but basically almost normal Social Democratic career. Six former National Socialist party members in the Kreisky governments, a provincial governor and several deputy governors, as well as numerous high-ranking officials, members of provincial governments and managing directors, forty-three national and federal parliamentary deputies had all belonged to the National Socialist party (fifty-one of the People's Party).[5]

Credit is due to the former Party Chairman Alfred Gusenbauer for the critical public reappraisal of the Social Democratic party's long-hidden 'brown stains'. Although numerous old-guard Social Democrats have criticized this step, for many it has meant a salutary shock after the decades of self-inflicted amnesia. Nevertheless it may have been an additional reason for his ultimate fall from grace, which we discuss in our final chapter.

14

POWER STRUGGLE IN THE
'COURT OF THE SUN KING'

On 21 August 1980, a special session took place in parliament at the request of the opposition People's Party. This was the starting point of a tax case which, after years of covert and overt power struggles, spelled the sudden end of one of the most unusual political careers in post-war Austria.

Hannes Androsch, the forty-two-year-old Vice-Chancellor, Finance Minister and Deputy Chairman of the Social Democratic party, was in the symbolic dock. In hindsight, in view of the consequences, it became clear that what came to pass on this memorable day was a political execution. The executioner was the People's Party member of parliament Heribert Steinbauer.

The ÖVP put an urgent question to the Chancellor regarding the dismissal of Finance Minister Hannes Androsch. Press reports stated that he was allegedly involved in a scandal concerning the building of the General Hospital (AKH) in Vienna; that his chartered accountant firm, Consultatio, had highly profitable business connections with companies embroiled in the AKH scandal; and furthermore that he had misled the public. In his powerful speech the Chairman of the ÖVP, Alois Mock, referred to the frequent critical remarks which Kreisky himself had made concerning his Vice-Chancellor's private business interests, and called on the Chancellor to act at last.

It was at this stage that the first bombshell was dropped during the session held in the hot and humid summer atmosphere. Kreisky's fifty-four-second-long response consisted of just one sentence: he had no intention of suggesting the Finance Minister's dismissal to the President of the republic, as Androsch would personally set right the relevant press reports. The opposition speakers naturally exploited the Chancellor's demonstrative detachment from his beleaguered deputy. In his lengthy speech, the latter immediately 'solemnly and resolutely rejected the untrue assertions, assumptions and slanders'.

After a few more speeches, Alois Mock asked without any explanation to have the session suspended for twenty to thirty minutes. Meanwhile rumours were afloat among the surprised deputies about new exposures concerning the financing of the much-discussed Androsch villa in Vienna. Continuing the interrupted session, Heribert Steinbauer put the 'smoking gun' (in the parlance of thrillers) on the table. In a short but astute speech he presented a highly compromising document, which was obtained—clearly in violation the rules about bank secrecy—from the Zentralsparkasse, the Viennese central savings bank. It was a bank account slip, sent as an attachment to an anonymous letter dated July 15, which confirmed the suspicion that Androsch had financed the construction of his house in 1975 with black money. The anonymous letter was sent to the Chancellor at the same time as a denunciation to the Viennese Public Prosecutor's Department. This letter constituted the basis for the future decision of the tax authorities.

The 'endless saga'[1] of the tax proceedings against Androsch lasted in all another sixteen years! After the dramatic session, two opposition politicians pressed charges against him on suspicion of tax evasion. In connection with the pending criminal proceedings, Androsch was interviewed in March 1981 by the parliamentary subcommittee investigating the hospital scandal. He had resigned as Finance Minister on 1 January 1981 and become Director-General of Austria's largest bank, Creditanstalt-Bankverein. He asserted that the money for purchasing the house had been put at his disposal by a 'step-uncle' (his mother's partner). Androsch has since been convicted of tax evasion, and eventually in 1996 a panel of two professional judges and two lay judges imposed a fine of 1.5 million schillings (about larger 110,000) on him.

In January 1986, not long after a Viennese court had concluded that the Androsch villa was acquired from his own untaxed funds (not from the 'step-uncle's' money), an ÖVP deputy pressed charges against him on suspicion of having made false statements as a witness at the hearing before the parliamentary subcommittee. In January 1988 his past caught up with Androsch, then Director-General of the Creditanstalt: the court pronounced a verdict of guilty for having made false statements before the subcommittee investigating the hospital case and imposed a fine of 3,000 schillings per day for 360 days.[2] Two days after the sentence he resigned as Secretary-General of the Creditanstalt bank. (Since then, and especially lately, Androsch appears frequently in public as a successful entrepreneur and an acknowledged economic expert.)

How and why did the Androsch family's bank account balances get into the hands of the People's Party and eventually to public notice? Contrary to the various conspiracy theories, a 'lone operator' was responsible for the document presented in parliament. In the course of my research for this book, a well-known ÖVP politician—who asked me not to reveal his identity—told me the following. The document originating from the Zentralsparkasse was handed personally by Josef Bandion, then administrative director of Vienna's Socialist city administration, to Erhard Busek, who was at the time Vienna's deputy mayor and head of the People's Party's organization in the capital, with the request to bring it to public notice in an appropriate manner. Bandion did not have any doubts about the document's authenticity, since he had allegedly received it from a close family member who worked at the Zentralsparkasse.

Why did Bandion, a life-long Socialist and the highest ranking civil servant in the city administration, ignite the fuse of this explosive charge?

No one could give an explanation for Bandion's initiative. He was definitely not a close confidant of Kreisky. The prominent People's Party politician Erhard Busek, whom the high-ranking official must have trusted implicitly, recalls after almost three decades how much repugnance the hard-core Socialist Bandion felt toward the network of the Androsch family's anonymous bank accounts and the Finance Minister's lifestyle. Be that as it may, Busek did not waste any time, and handed the extremely sensitive document to the then Party Chairman, Alois Mock. The party leadership eventually appointed Steinbauer as executioner, because in one of his earlier parliamentary speeches he had already infuriated the Social Democrats by comparing the Vienna hospital scandal to Watergate.

This time, too, things were coming to a boil after the Steinbauer address. The emotional eruption of the generally restrained leader of the Socialist parliamentary group, Heinz Fischer, is still remembered today. He flung his pen down on the marble floor of the old meeting room and screamed at Steinbauer: 'You swine!' Fischer apologized at the end of the session, but even today, as federal President, he told me: 'I was terribly angry that someone would use an anonymous letter to demand an extraordinary meeting of parliament, and to attack the person to whom that anonymous writing refers, when in my understanding of political culture only facts and not anonymous letters can be used to attack someone.'[3]

Despite Heinz Fischer's lasting resentment, when it comes down to it, the leak from the Zentralsparkasse was a well-calculated political move—the beginning of the end of a first-class political talent. Androsch can be seen as possibly the best Chancellor Austria never had, somewhat along the lines of the British politician Rab Butler, who, although the most outstanding personality of his time, was bypassed by his party in favour of Harold Macmillan in 1957 and Lord Home in 1963.

Two more dramatic episodes belong to the 'endless saga' of the taxation case. Finance Minister Herbert Salcher, who succeeded Androsch at the beginning of 1981, received further important documents in the summer of 1984 from a director of the savings bank, relating to the Androsch family's various anonymous securities accounts. The Finance Minister passed this information on to the head of the Viennese Department of Public Prosecution. This set in motion the preliminary inquiry against Hannes Androsch.

Prior to his startling action, Salcher, previously Socialist Party Chairman in the province of Tyrol, had consulted with outstanding jurists and tax experts. He acted in defiance of many of the party's leaders. In our conversations he still stressed that Bruno Kreisky had never asked for his opinion on the Androsch case, nor did he inform Kreisky about the course of the inquiries.[4] The die was cast at the beginning of September 1984, when in the course of a government reshuffle Chancellor Sinowatz replaced Salcher with Franz Vranitzky as Finance Minister. Subsequently, Sinowatz declared at an informal meeting of the cabinet that he hoped this would spell the end of the fuss about the Androsch case.[5]

However, running the gauntlet of tax fraud investigations was by no means over yet for Hannes Androsch. A few days before Christmas of 1985, his former secretary and by now Finance Minister, Franz Vranitzky, had to make a decision whether to let Androsch's tax fraud case lapse or not. The authorization for this would only have been possible with a written ministerial directive. Since three of the Finance Ministry's high-ranking officials declared that such a ministerial directive would violate the law, Vranitzky did not go ahead with it.[6]

To this day Androsch still sees himself as the victim of a conspiracy by Kreisky and Salcher, Vranitzky and Lacina, the People's Party and the hostile media. To my question as to why Vranitzky should have sent the head of the local tax office on Christmas Eve 1985 to the Androsch villa to deliver the income tax assessment, Androsch replied: 'Because it was in his interest to please Kreisky, and to get rid of me as a rival. And from that time on I was angry with Vranitzky...'[7] This went on till at least 1988, when Vranitzky, by then Chancellor, approved Androsch's dismissal (for perjury) from his managing directorship of the then still state-owned Creditanstalt.

To this day Androsch cannot forgive Vranitzky, his erstwhile assistant who later became Federal Chancellor. In a long conversation, he did not mince his words. For legal reasons it is impossible to reproduce here his diatribe against his 'cowardly, brutal and money-grubbing' ex-secretary, and the rest of the slanderous recriminations. As an interesting psychiatric study puts it: 'Envy is an aggressive, more or less lasting emotion, which begrudges another person's positively appraised, highly visible success; the envious person deeply desires and aspires to that success, but at the same time realizes it is unattainable.' In addition, envy can escalate to unforgiving hatred, and attempts at moral discreditation of the opponent.[8] In spite of the differences due to their circumstances, their age and the events, for almost twenty years Androsch has now been behaving toward Vranitzky in the same way as Kreisky had once behaved toward him.[9]

What was the background to the Kreisky–Androsch conflict and the ensuing power struggle? These clashes had increasingly disturbed, even thwarted governmental activities already before open confrontation broke out in 1980. On the surface it was a power struggle between an ageing, ailing 'Sun King' and his ambitious, impatient, twenty-seven-years-younger 'crown prince'. However, those cleverly and unscrupulously disseminated leaks, which tried to present Androsch pretty much as the 'sacrificial lamb of the wicked old man', who, out of envy and other complexes, disowned his crown prince and threw him to the wolves, have nothing to do with the truth.

During that period of internal battles in the governing party I not only met Kreisky frequently, but also all the other protagonists. Above all, as already mentioned, a relationship of mutual trust developed between me, the foreign correspondent, and the Chancellor while Kreisky was still Foreign Minister,[10] during the joint East European trips, and later during many confidential conversations in the course of the election campaigns and my work on his biography. During our long walks in the Vienna woods, accompanied by Titus or Bianca, his two boxer dogs, or sitting in his garden on Sunday afternoons talking about topical foreign policy or economic issues, he would time and again return to his depressing personal problems.

In 1978, the power struggles and intrigues in the party were already in full swing. Due to the impending 1979 parliamentary elections, the governing party tried to avoid the impression of inner conflict. In the early afternoon of a mid-September day in 1978, we were sitting together in the Chancellor's Ballhausplatz office. As usual, Kreisky was short of time. Our conversation on the Eastern European situation was constantly interrupted by telephone calls and his secretary's tactful reminder notes. The time was obviously too short for the planned in-depth interview for an Austria supplement of the *Financial Times* on the extent and limitations of change in the Eastern Bloc.

The Chancellor suddenly put a surprising question to me: 'Tell me, how are things between you and the Hungarians at the moment?' I had no idea why he had asked this, but I replied without hesitation: 'My relationship with them is more or less normal now. I have not been on their blacklist for years. I can travel there freely and, although I am being tailed, there are no special problems...' Kreisky interrupted me: 'Well, then everything is alright. Next week I am travelling to Budapest on a working visit. Come along as my personal guest, and then we shall have plenty of opportunities to talk about this topic!'

Kreisky's idea of course exasperated the protocol officials on both sides of the iron curtain: to take along on an 'unofficial working visit' a journalist, on top of it a native Hungarian 'expert', was an unusual and 'an extremely awkward matter' (as the Austrian protocol chief remarked with a deep sigh to one of Kreisky's assistants). Yet neither his own officials nor the mistrustful Hungarians dared to say anything to the Chancellor.

Kreisky was a far more dangerous opponent of the Communist dictatorships than many who wore their anti—Communism on their sleeve, because he was a believer in the policy of offensive détente. Early on he recognized the character of the transformation processes in the Communist world, and became a trailblazer of that imaginative policy, always aware of the limits as well as the possibilities of Western influence.

Although, apart from his wife, only the head of the department for nationalized industries, a secretary and a bodyguard accompanied him, the prominent guest was received by a large delegation led by the then Prime Minister, György Lázár, escorted by numerous officials and a contingent of secret police. Actually, even the working visit upset thousands of Hungarians—directly or indirectly—as quite a number of main roads and bridges in Budapest were closed for normal passage during the Friday afternoon peak traffic. The same process was repeated on the route of the special train from Budapest to Debrecen, Hungary's third largest city, and on its return. Hungarian police and soldiers, ready for every eventuality, were guarding the viaducts and crossings. Although, as Kreisky's guest, I was still present on the plane to Budapest, I could not witness this vigilance personally. I was separated from the little group already at Budapest airport, and could not even say goodbye to the Kreiskys. To my question as to why I could not travel by rail to Debrecen, the reply of my escort was short and to the point: 'There is not enough room on the special train!' I was taken by car to Debrecen in the company of a Foreign Ministry official, who was very close to the State Security Service.

However, to the annoyance of the Hungarian organizers and my escort, Bruno Kreisky did not forget about his 'guest', and the following day invited me for breakfast. During the course of a walk in the nearby woods, discreetly followed by a whole cohort of security men, a doctor and a protocol official, the Chancellor resumed our conversation that had been interrupted in Vienna. Soon he changed tack, however, and turned to his favourite topic, the supposed advantages and disadvantages of the potential crown princes and other leading party officials. At that time, compared to his later outbursts, he was still relatively restrained in public, but with his confidants, or in a small circle of people whom he trusted, he made no bones about his profound disappointment with Androsch and not least with the latter's 'legal adviser', the Minister for Justice, Christian Broda. 'One can trust only very few people, my friend,' he said poignantly when he said goodbye to me at Vienna airport.

The roots of party intrigues against the Chancellor reached back to the time of the Olah crisis, when Kreisky defended the controversial union leader, subsequently Interior Minister, thereby provoking the revenge of his mighty opponents. Franz Olah (1910–2009) was one of the greatest talents of the Socialist movement. He had spent almost seven years in the Nazi concentration camp of Dachau, and was Kreisky's close friend from their early youth. Basically they both fought for the same political goals: opening of social democracy toward the church, youth and the bourgeoisie in the spirit of a modernizing offensive. However, Olah's boundless ambition, and his uncontrolled handling of trade union funds for newspaper financing and subsidies in favour of the right-wing Freedom Party, eventually caused his downfall. More than once he had contributed to Kreisky's career, for example in 1962–3, when he saved the post of Foreign Minister for Kreisky by his tough negotiating tactics. So, when Olah got into trouble, Kreisky stood by his friend and supported him in the party. However, the anti-Olah coalition was in the majority, with Kreisky stranded on the side of the losers. Seething with revenge, Olah founded his own splinter party, whose initial success in Vienna contributed to the defeat of the SPÖ in 1966.

What seemed at the time to be Kreisky's personal loss of face turned out to be extremely helpful to him in 1966, when he was chosen as leader of the Lower Austrian regional organization of the SPÖ. This served as a stepping stone to his election as Chairman of the entire party. Irrespective of Olah's later, most probably politically motivated, conviction in a criminal case,[11] Kreisky's loyalty to the popular Olah considerably strengthened his position within the party, since it proved that, if convinced of something, Kreisky stuck to his position disregarding any risk.

In the vindictive campaign against Olah, the Socialist Minister for Justice, Christian Broda, played first fiddle. Already as a youth activist he had taken part in the interwar Communist movement. In 1960 Franz Olah had opposed Broda's appointment to the justice portfolio because of the latter's suspicious activities after 1945 and his tardy break with the Communists.[12] He was undoubtedly the 'head and central planner' of the anti-Olah front.[13]

The relationship between the Social Democratic party's two most outstanding personalities, Bruno Kreisky and the great legal reformer, Christian Broda, was destroyed by the internal power struggles of the 1960s. At that time I met Justice Minister Broda fairly frequently, as he was extremely interested in the developments in Yugoslavia, Poland and Hungary. It was incidentally Kreisky who acquainted me with both Olah and Broda. In the foreword of his book *Democracy, Law, Society*, published in the summer of 1962, Broda still emphasized that 'the strongest personal and political friendship' bound him to Kreisky. He presented me later with the book and a warm personal dedication.

At the time I had no idea yet about the deep split caused by the Olah conflict between Kreisky and Broda, since the two of them had known each other already during the 1930s and in illegal affairs. I also interviewed Broda for my Kreisky biography. He confirmed from 'his own experience' that Kreisky 'had never quite moved to the extreme left, for he was always a Social Democrat'. The young Broda, who at sixteen was the leader of a small Communist youth group ('at the best of times there were about twenty of us') in a Viennese district, tried—albeit quite unsuccessfully—to lure away the members of Kreisky's much larger youth group during meetings and discussions in front of a pub. When talking to friends later, Kreisky formulated it much more strongly: 'I was always in the mainstream of the Austrian labour movement, while Broda was a sectarian, together with his Communists. And I recall—I was in the young labour movement—that I had a marvellous gathering, and then Broda came with his Communist fellas and wanted to disrupt the meeting. Well, they sure got it in the neck.'

Apart from stupidity, the only thing that irked Kreisky was the long-term and demonstrative disloyalty of his closest collaborators. Of course it was true of him too, as of other great personalities who were in power for a long time, that in the end he did not quite trust anyone. In his case, especially from the mid-seventies, his distrust was justified. All those who admired Bruno Kreisky, not only as a politician but also as a human being, were repeatedly appalled at the resentment, not to say hatred, of those disappointed members of his cabinet who did not, or did not immediately, make the great career that they had expected from the 'Sun King'.

One of the secretaries made secret diary entries about Kreisky's alleged weak points; a second transmitted useful information to the Androsch-Broda-Benya group; while a third one openly changed sides to Androsch after the Chancellor's resignation. Contrary to Androsch, Kreisky neither had the talent nor the interest to forge a totally devoted network. When someone called him 'the most professional politician' at the start of his Chancellorship, Kreisky replied: 'What nonsense. I am the only amateur among these so-called professional politicians.' In his memoirs he quotes his wife, who has always said that he was too

117

gullible. In contrast to his ambitious deputy, he did not demand unconditional commitment. In Olah's words: 'Kreisky was not a hater; he
could get on with everybody.' Both Federal President Rudolf Kirchschläger, who worked with him for a long while, and Franz Cardinal
König told me in almost identical terms that Kreisky 'was simply a
good man'.[14]

Max Weber wrote in his famous 'Politics as a Vocation' essay that
one of the pre-eminent qualities for a politician was passion, a passionate commitment to a 'cause'. Naturally Kreisky the politician also
aspired to power, and even at seventy-two—blind in one eye and
undergoing thrice-weekly four-hour dialyses for his serious kidney
disease—he still wanted to cling to power. But the question is not
whether a politician seeks power; what matters is the way he uses that
power, and what he wants to achieve by it. From his earliest youth,
power for Kreisky had not only meant the sensation of power, but
from the outset it implied in the Weberian sense 'a passionate commitment to a cause', and service and responsibility toward that 'cause'.
The 'cause', which the young Kreisky made 'the fundamental lodestar
of action', was the Social Democratic movement, the honest belief in
the profoundly humanistic goals of his party in the historical sense; in
a movement that, despite all the aberrations and alterations, Kreisky
regarded as a movement of solidarity and openness, and not a gathering of cliques, of cowardly careerists and risk-averse, self-righteous
paragons of virtue.

Three episodes that became known only several decades later reveal
how passionately rancorous the battles for the top party positions were
in 1966–7, and how they led to the conflict that would erupt later
around Androsch. This is how Kreisky describes the dramatic clashes
in his memoirs: 'I held off, as I was of the opinion that my election
would mean a burden to the party. Although I had always identified
with the Austrian people, I was aware of some anti-Semitic tendencies
and did not want to stand in the way of my party. ... When I posed the
question to Christian Broda, whom I had recommended for some functions including the Justice Ministership, whether he could explain to
me why he regarded one of the candidates—I do not want to name
him—better than me, Broda just shrugged his shoulders and said that
for some highly influential functionaries anyone would be better than
me. I knew where I stood.' That is how his 'closest personal and political friend' behaved in a decisive situation.

Only in his memoirs did Kreisky reveal another painful case. Although by then he was already deputy leader of the party, the leadership had in effect forbidden him to use any office space in the central party building. Kreisky had to move with his secretary to the nearby Vienna office of the Lower Austrian provincial party organization, whose chairmanship he was about to take over within a few weeks. That is where I visited him before his election to the Chairmanship of the Social Democratic party.[15]

The third, and in hindsight almost unbelievable, episode was the decision by 'party heavyweights' to set up Hans Czettel, the forty-four-year-old Lower Austrian party functionary and successor to Interior Minister Olah, as a man of the 'new generation' in the battle for the Party Chairmanship against Kreisky—who was supported by the provinces. Who was then this candidate recommended in a vicious anti—Kreisky speech by trade union president Benya? The study published in 2005 (mentioned already in a previous chapter) about the Social Democratic party's 'brown stains' reports that the long-standing deputy governor of Lower Austria was not only a member of the Hitler Jugend between 1938 and 1942, but was also admitted to the German National Socialist party on 1 September 1941 with membership number 8,551,326. Referring to the serious injuries suffered in the battle for Stalingrad, he repeatedly applied for a salaried job in the Nazi party. In his file the local leader praised him for his 'flawless character and ideological attitude'. There is no proof of his registration as a former Nazi, nor of the denazification process. A Socialist Party Chairman, possibly even a Chancellor burdened by a Nazi past, would probably have sparked off an unprecedented international scandal. Luckily, as we know, Kreisky won the election and became the Party Chairman.[16]

These facts, mostly unknown to the general public, shed light on the personal and political background of the Kreisky–Androsch conflict. Hannes Androsch, the youngest member of parliament, then youngest Finance Minister and Deputy Chancellor, was undoubtedly in every respect an extraordinary talent. During the first half of the seventies, Kreisky promoted his career without reservations. Their cooperation in the economic field, albeit in a different direction, recalled the halcyon days of the Raab–Kamitz era back in the 1950s. That Androsch became Deputy Chairman of the party at 36, and two years later even Deputy Chancellor, vexed of course the older top functionaries.

The first crack appeared soon after the death of Federal President Franz Jonas in the spring of 1974, when Hannes Androsch and

Leopold Gratz, the mayor of Vienna, supported also by the union boss Anton Benya, tried to pitch the Federal Presidency to Kreisky. Kreisky regarded this offer as insulting, since the position offered far fewer political possibilities for him. That was when he first began to suspect that Androsch wanted to displace him with the help of the former anti-Olah coalition. Sometime later Kreisky happened to see a joint entry by Androsch and Gratz in the guest book of a Viennese restaurant, and considered this as proof of a conspiracy in the offing against him.

Hidden behind the failed attempt to convince Kreisky to accept the candidature for the state Presidency was indeed the plan to promote the then thirty-six-year-old Androsch to the post of Prime Minister. At the time attending an international summer conference at Alpbach, Franz Vranitzky, then Androsch's secretary, asked me whether I was willing to travel back to Vienna with the Finance Minister. My relationship with Androsch had been good from the start, and I regularly reported on his successful fiscal policy in the *Financial Times*. On the return trip to Vienna, and during a short lunch-break in an inn, Androsch made it clear self-confidently and eloquently that he would be capable of filling the post of Chancellor, and that especially union leader Benya, and other unnamed persons in the party leadership as well, would be ready fully to support him.

Meanwhile Kreisky threw his 'party friends' off their guard with an ingenious move: he proposed Rudolf Kirchschläger, a Catholic without party affiliations, who had already been a successful Foreign Minister, as his candidate for the Federal Presidency. Many in the SPÖ executive agreed only grudgingly to break with the tradition of always nominating a Social Democrat for the Federal Presidency. Kreisky's calculation paid off. Not only did Kirchschläger win the election by a mile, but in his second term of office the People's Party nominated him as well, and he filled the office of Federal President for twelve years to everyone's satisfaction.

During this period until the second electoral victory, with an absolute majority in October 1975, the reform programme was carried out with full vigour: reform of the criminal law, equality of the sexes in marriage, social improvements in the education sphere (free travel for students, introduction of free textbooks), commencement of construction of the UNO-City, steel merger, liberalization of trade regulations, a law permitting abortion in the first trimester, maternity benefits, the labour constitution act, introduction of community instead of military service.

The increasingly self-confident and independent-minded activities of the young Vice-Chancellor, and above all his unconditional hard currency policy through maintaining the exchange rate of the schilling, led to the first open confrontation with Kreisky in 1977. When in those days I occasionally met Androsch on weekends at Kreisky's home, his behaviour reflected his growing self-assurance. The real shock for Kreisky came less than a year after he had made him Deputy Chancellor, when Androsch asked him whether he could take the post of president of the National Bank that had just become vacant (at that time by far the best-paid job in Austria). Yet again the Chancellor found a risky but brilliant solution: in order to preserve the power of the SPÖ, in 1978 he arranged the appointment of Stephan Koren, a former Finance Minister and chief whip of the ÖVP in parliament, as head of the National Bank. Thus the People's Party lost one of its most talented politicians, while Kreisky avoided losing Androsch, his undoubtedly ablest minister.

At first only subtle hints, but with time sarcastic remarks dropped by the Chancellor, indicated that Kreisky's former affection for the capable but overly self-assured young man was slowly but surely turning into growing mistrust. Of course, press leaks by jealous rivals of Androsch also contributed to the estrangement. It was above all the never-ending spate of front-page stories and reports in the media about the booming business of his Consultatio chartered accountancy and tax consulting firm, as well as the gossip about the private enrichment of Androsch and his friends, that continued to inflame the underlying tensions.

Kreisky's eye injury suffered in December 1978 at the occasion of the opening of the Arlberg tunnel, and the defeat in the referendum for the commissioning of Austria's first nuclear power plant, boosted the efforts within the party to oust him. But to the greatest consternation of his opponents in the party, at the May 1979 general elections he managed once again to score a resounding victory: the number of Socialist votes rose, and the party, enjoying already an absolute majority, gained two more seats. However, despite this unprecedented success, Kreisky still did not succeed in forcing Androsch to detach himself from the tax—consulting firm or in removing him from the cabinet.

It must have been sometime in the summer of 1980, sharing a cup of tea with me in his home one Sunday afternoon, when the Chancellor got suddenly enraged and said: 'They are conspiring against me. Well, isn't it a conspiracy if half the government or even more get together behind my back and plot against me? They want to defeat me, but they won't succeed; the party, the people, are with me...' When I asked him who these so-called 'conspirators' were, the furious Chancellor named Androsch, Broda, Hertha Firnberg (Minister of Research and chief of the Socialist Women's Organization) and several other senior ministers. Despite his outwardly good relationship with union leader Anton Benya on a number of questions, and their weekly meetings, he entertained a growing mistrust of the so-called 'Androsch–Broda–Benya axis'.

The political scientist Norbert Leser suspects that 'feelings of envy, malevolence and jealousy, even the fear of prematurely losing his power, played an important role' in the Chancellor's resentment of Androsch.[17] It certainly cannot be denied that his profound disappointment with the young politician, whom he had initially so steadfastly supported, changed into hatred, and after his retirement in 1983 into virtual paranoid persecution mania.

Still, considering later developments, despite all his exaggerations Kreisky proved to have been very far-sighted. His letters written to the Social Democratic party's archive and only released after his death, as well as the numerous hints dropped during interviews, suggest the following: it was not only a matter of Androsch, but of the whole complex of power and ethics, the incorruptibility of the Socialist leaders, a return to the puritanical principles of interwar Social Democracy, or as Federal President Kirchschläger put it, 'drying out the morass of corruption'.

But if really such weighty factual and ethical reasons motivated Kreisky in his conflict with Androsch, then one has to reproach him (as did the political scientist Norbert Leser in his study quoted earlier) for tacking about, manoeuvring and shying away from the necessary consequences. What fascinated the unbiased domestic and foreign observers was that, in spite of the daily disclosures and after the memorable special parliamentary session, described at the beginning of this chapter, the party executive did not stand behind Kreisky, but produced only 'pathetic horse-trading' (Norbert Leser). They justly regarded the phoney compromise in the matter of the tax—consulting firm owned by his deputy as a defeat for Kreisky.

As far as the secret ambitions of the young 'crown prince' are concerned, one can quote a totally reliable witness, Gerd Bacher, then

Director-General of the Austrian Broadcasting Corporation and a friend of Androsch, who told me the following: 'I was on a skiing holiday with him in France, and we were going up on the lift. I said to him: "Hannes, you have to make up your mind at last: what do you want, power or money?" He replied: "Both; power *and* money." That was around 1980.'

It was only on 11 December 1980 that the executive of the SPÖ accepted Androsch's resignation, and appointed the man whom the head of government was accusing of corruption to be in charge of the Creditanstalt, then the largest (and mainly nationalized) bank. As already mentioned, the seemingly never-ending battle for the political future of the Kreisky era's greatest talent lasted until January 1988, when the court pronounced him guilty of tax evasion and false testimony.

One might well ask why it was so hard for Kreisky to topple—and then only partly—his rebellious 'crown prince'. The reason was the balance of power within the party. All the important members of the top party bodies (Presidium and executive board), including several provincial governors as well as Heinz Fischer and Leopold Gratz, supported, and on 9 September 1980 actually induced, the stalemate between Kreisky and Androsch. When two months later Kreisky still hesitated to pay 'the exorbitant and morally unjustifiable price', namely shifting and appointing Abdrosch to head the Creditanstalt Bankverein, union boss Benya gave him a de facto ultimatum: 'Listen, my dear friend, I shan't let you send him away just like that. That's not in the deal.' Peter Kreisky, the Chancellor's son, and Karl Blecha both confirm that Benya had threatened the Chancellor with a 'split in the party'.

According to all available information, just as in the Olah case so this time too, Christian Broda, the long-standing Minister of Justice, was 'the actual head and the centre' of the anti-Kreisky opposition and the pro-Androsch camp. Once, when he was very angry at Kreisky, he said the following verbatim to one of his closest associates: 'He would never have become Party Chairman if I had not removed Olah for him', only to add that he was the great reformer, while Kreisky only ploughed the sea…

Broda was also ready to use people with murky pasts. His closest adviser in the matter of the criminal law reform was a university professor of law who had acted as prosecutor during Nazi times in cases that resulted in death sentences. After the publication of the incriminating documents, Broda not only defended the Nazi jurists, but even went to great lengths to cut off the dispute over the 'judiciary scandal'.[18] As far as Otto Rösch, who had been involved in the erstwhile neo-Nazi case, was concerned, Broda's associate, quoted earlier, told me: 'Rösch was for him the ideal Interior Minister. He consulted him about everything. Under Rösch, Broda was to all intents and purposes also running the Interior Ministry.'

Every day, very early in the morning, Broda chatted with Benya on the telephone, and almost as frequently with Heinz Fischer, Hertha Firnberg and other leading functionaries. Broda's commitment was not only due to his unconcealed admiration for the talent and accomplishments of the young Finance Minister, but also to the sneaking apprehension that Kreisky might sooner or later replace him as minister with a legal expert without party affiliations.

Even if Kreisky's unbridled fits of rage and severe illnesses towards the end of his life sometimes overshadowed his enormous achievements for Austria, the Kreisky era was in fact an extraordinary period. What has he left behind? To the question put by Kurt Vorhofer during a lengthy conversation sometime before the loss of the Social Democratic party's absolute majority and his resignation, as to whether Kreisky would like to have a statue erected to him on the Viennese Ringstrasse, he replied: 'My vanity does not involve such things. I do not want a place, nor a house named after me, I don't want anything. What I would really like is for the people to remember me: well, yes, those were the good old times when we fought our way out of the quagmire of ordinariness and gave our country a bit of an image.'[19]

Bruno Kreisky died on 29 July 1990 at the age of seventy-nine. On 7 August, the day of the funeral, at the invitation of his children (his wife, Vera, had passed away a year and a half earlier), friends and guests gathered in the evening in his house where everything was still the way the deceased had left it. With the final farewell to this grumbling, half-blind and powerless pensioner, part of our life also disappeared irrevocably. Without Bruno Kreisky, Austria became smaller, greyer and more boring.

15

THE WALDHEIM AFFAIR AND THE MISFORTUNE
OF A SUCCESSOR

There is hardly any other Austrian politician who had so little luck at the apex of his career as Fred Sinowatz, who was Kreisky's successor as Chancellor (1983–6) and as Chairman of the Social Democratic party. At the same time, there is hardly any politician of whom even his political opponents have nothing but the best to say.

Jörg Haider, the erstwhile Governor of Carinthia, told me: 'Sinowatz was certainly very important for Kreisky as his number two man. However, as a leader he was not up to the challenges of his position. But as a person he was a very likable guy, whom I respected very much.' Here is Heinrich Neisser, the former Minister of Science and second President of the National Assembly: 'I already admired him when he was secretary of the SPÖ in Burgenland. Sinowatz was a very upright and decent personality.' Then Josef Cap, the chief whip of the Social Democrats: 'Many people were exceedingly unfair to him. Sinowatz was an extremely honest, intelligent and quite outstanding Education Minister. He was one of the best Education Ministers since 1945. He was also very much underrated as Chancellor.' Ferdinand Lacina (whom Sinowatz appointed as Minister for Transport and Public Economy in September 1984), regarded him similarly: 'He was completely underestimated. His problem was his hang-up about the media. During confidential conversations, without the presence of cameras, he could talk far more sophisticatedly and more openly. ... He took a weight on his shoulders, which he did not really want to carry, and if someone really does not want to be the Number One— and I believe he never wanted it—then he cannot become a good Number One.'[1]

At the beginning of January 2007 I spoke at length with Fred Sinowatz (he died in August 2008) about the time of his Chancellorship. A few weeks later Sinowatz was once again the main topic of my interview with the star reporter Alfred Worm, whom Sinowatz had sued for libel in April 1986 because of an article of his. Worm, who died suddenly just four days after our conversation, told me the following, word for word: 'I have always admired this truly cultured, very congenial and intelligent person. Sinowatz was a tragic figure: the right man in the wrong place—without punch and without the will to succeed.' Memorable words from the mouth of the dreaded investigative reporter about the man for whose personal and political tragedy he too was at least partly, if unintentionally, responsible.

Until his recent death this erudite, profoundly decent politician, who had been ailing much of his adult life, was held in low esteem and discredited as a laughing stock with out-of-context quotes from his speeches. In stark contrast to his successful decade as Education and Sports Minister, a streak of bad luck led relatively fast and inexorably to his disfavour in the public eye.

Sinowatz was born in 1929 in the Burgenland region of Eastern Austria, into a working-class family of Croatian descent. After completing his studies at Vienna University, he joined the Social Democratic party. His political career took off with his election as member of the regional parliament and secretary of the Burgenland SPÖ. He soon became the number two man after the Burgenland Governor, Theodor Kery (before 1945 member of both the SA and the National Socialist party). His strategy was responsible for the party's successful election campaign in 1968, which ensured it an absolute majority in the province. The small, corpulent man with the large nose became familiar and popular from 1971 as the Kreisky government's Education Minister, and from 1981, succeeding Androsch, as Deputy Chancellor. Amid the power struggles within the SPÖ, Kreisky saw in him the only possible successor able to win at the next election.

After the loss of the absolute majority it is easy to forget that, even though the SPÖ had been in power for thirteen years and headed lately by an ailing leader, it still gained 47.8 per cent of the votes and ninety seats out of 183 in April 1983. With his retirement, Kreisky set the stage for Sinowatz as his successor at the helm of a 'small coalition' with the Freedom Party. The entire party leadership accepted Kreisky's conception for splitting the People's Party. The fact that at the May

1983 party congress all in all only fifteen votes were cast against this risky experiment provides ample proof that the putative advantages of a coalition with a weak partner, permeated by Nazi nostalgia, carried more weight than the party's much-vaunted anti-Fascist tradition.

I got to know and to respect Chancellor Fred Sinowatz in my capacity as editor-in-chief of the Austrian Broadcasting Corporation (ORF) responsible for Eastern Europe. Like Kreisky, as well as Foreign Ministers Gratz and Mock, he too defended the free and uncensored coverage of the Communist world, and sharply rebuffed domestic and foreign attacks. I should like to mention only one example: because of a 'provocative indiscretion' I was blacklisted by the Moscow and Prague party leadership.

In November 1982 I conducted a television interview for ORF with Gustav Husák, the head of the Czechoslovak Communist party and State President. During our conversation Husák confirmed that 'Comrade Brezhnev' would be taking part in the forthcoming Warsaw Pact summit to be held in Prague, although at the time we recorded the interview Brezhnev had already been dead for quite a while. In a brief TV commentary from Prague I hinted that the Soviets had kept Brezhnev's death secret not only from their own people and world opinion, but even from the other party leaders. The vain and rigid Husák was enraged that, because of the Kremlin's secretiveness, he had been made a laughing stock 'in front of the whole world'. He protested sharply to Moscow. Although the Soviets could not revive Brezhnev, they decided as a small consolation for Husák at least to punish the 'hostile specialist' with an entry ban.

The ice was broken by the new Chancellor, Sinowatz's first official visit to Moscow in November 1984. Chancellor Sinowatz declared that he would travel to Moscow only if all the Austrian journalists registered for the trip could travel with him. I received my visa at the last minute. Nothing demonstrates the absurdity of the Communist approach more than the fact that they could not and would not give an explanation either before or after for the entry ban and the Soviet media's attacks against me and the ORF East European desk.

In April 1986—on the occasion of the second official visit for the opening of the Austrian exhibition in Moscow—we could even organize a 'Club 2' discussion with the Chancellor's support. *Le Monde* from Paris, the *Neue Zürcher Zeitung*, the *Frankfurter Allgemeine* and other international papers reported on the first Moscow live telecast of a debate programme.

Meanwhile, even before the first Moscow trip, a government reshuffle caused an estrangement between Sinowatz and Kreisky, who had been elected Honorary Chairman of the SPÖ in October 1983. The replacement of Kreisky's confidants—Finance Minister Herbert Salcher by Franz Vranitzky and Foreign Minister Erwin Lanc by Leopold Gratz—signalled the emancipation of his successor. At the same time, political, economic and international complications cast a shadow over the Sinowatz government.

Late in 1984 he faced a crisis over the clashes between the trade unions, the police and thousands of environmentalists supported by the mass circulation daily *Kronen Zeitung*, campaigning against the building of a power station on the Danube. That was actually the birth in Austria of the Green movement. Sinowatz eventually decided to reduce the tension by announcing a 'Christmas peace', which meant in effect that he stopped the entire construction work.

At the end of 1985 the flagship of nationalized industry, the VOEST-ALPINE concern, found itself in a dramatic crisis situation due to the disastrous oil speculations of one of its subsidiaries. The entire VOEST board was to step down collectively. But this was only the tip of the iceberg. Worse was to follow when it came to light that the massive long-range heavy artillery (the reputedly superb GHN 45 model) had been sold by the company's arms subsidiary 'Noricum' to Iraq and Iran, both sides in the First Gulf War. This was in flagrant contravention of Austrian laws on neutrality and arms exports, and discredited Chancellor Sinowatz and the Ministers of the Interior and Foreign Affairs. The three, by then long retired, politicians were acquitted of the charges only in June 1993.

The arms exports played a very great role both at VOEST and the Creditanstalt-owned Steyr-Daimler-Puch concern. The much publicized affair was followed by a series of mysterious deaths: the suicide of a Defence Minister in 1981; the sudden death of the Austrian Ambassador to Athens (whose reports had provoked the entire investigation), and the suspiciously sudden fatal heart attack of the discharged director-general of VOEST. At any rate it is quite remarkable that several former cabinet ministers and ex—managing directors of the respective companies hinted in off-the-record conversations to me that they do not believe to this day that the above individuals died of natural causes.

The thirteen years of single-party government undoubtedly engendered the moral erosion of the victorious Social Democratic party.

The dimensions of the arms and other scandals became evident only during the time of the Vranitzky government (of which more in the next chapter).

The manner in which the leadership of the Social Democratic party had at the time hushed up the scandals about hospital financing, the Androsch affair and the shady VOEST arms deals, as well as the forced resignation of a Minister of Construction and trade union leader because of corruption, once again proved the accuracy of the German sociologist Robert Michels' 1911 warning of the 'iron law of oligarchy', of the inevitable emergence of cliques in the Social Democratic parties only interested in maintaining their power.[2]

However, all this was far surpassed by the international outrage provoked by the person of Kurt Waldheim, the People's Party candidate for Federal President. At the 1986 presidential elections the SPÖ nominated Dr Kurt Steyrer, a Viennese doctor and Minister of Health, as its candidate; the ÖVP's candidate was Kurt Waldheim, the non-party diplomat, former Foreign Minister (1968–70) and two-term UN Secretary-General.

I had known Waldheim personally since the first half of the sixties, when he was political director of the Foreign Ministry at a time when Kreisky was Foreign Minister. We met on official occasions, and once at Kreisky's behest he even 'smuggled' me into the Paris session of the Council of Europe as a member of the Austrian delegation, so that I could observe at first hand the atmosphere and the event. I had interviewed him repeatedly during his steep career path, rising from UN Ambassador to Foreign Minister and finally to UN Secretary-General during two terms of office. I also knew that Kreisky and Waldheim as well as their wives were on friendly terms. Kreisky actively supported Waldheim for UN Secretary-General as well as his re-election in order to boost the prestige of Austria. I knew of course just as little of his wartime past as did the Austrian journalist who, acting as his ghost-writer, penned his controversial memoirs with its famous omissions.

Election posters proudly proclaimed 'A man trusted by the whole world' with Waldheim's photo in front of the UNO glass palace in New York. Just as most independent observers, I too counted on the probable victory of the highly respected if colourless diplomat. It is still a contentious issue who actually played the 'Nazi card', and where (in Vienna or New York). Hardly had the election campaign commenced when Waldheim's Wehrmacht history sheet, with entries about his membership of the National Socialist German Students' Association and an SA cavalry company, was leaked to the media and the World Jewish Congress in New York.

The man who for ten years had symbolized the conscience of the world became overnight directly or indirectly linked with Nazi war crimes. And not only he, but Austria too, became identified with the accusations brought against him that had never been proved.

The best, most proficient and at the same time most objective description of the sad Waldheim affair can strangely be found in the memoirs of Simon Wiesenthal.[3] His account confirms the suspicion that the 'Waldheim bomb' was ignited partly by the election strategists of the Austrian Social Democrats and their close journalistic friends as well as by the top functionaries of the World Jewish Congress, Israel Singer and Elan Steinberg, who were blinded by the arrogance of ignorance. Simon Wiesenthal, who, with all the authority of the world's leading Nazi hunter, asserted from the very beginning that Waldheim had neither been a Nazi nor a war criminal, was consciously ignored by the manipulators of the campaign. He was later the target of scurrilous attacks, even the insinuation of being an accomplice of Waldheim and the Austrian People's Party.

The two American organizers of the witch-hunt (discharged in the meantime for financial irregularities) gave an unbelievably provocative interview to a Viennese weekly and to Austrian television, which had an enormous influence. 'Steinberg and Singer had the audacity to make the most grotesque threats, not only against Waldheim, but against all Austrians: if Waldheim were to be elected President, everyone with an Austrian passport would be made to feel it abroad, and be enveloped in a cloud of distrust' (Simon Wiesenthal).

The foreign attacks elicited the solidarity not only of the ÖVP voters, but of the entire population. Unfortunately they also provoked an ominous anti-Semitic backlash. The event confirmed the words of Karl Renner, who remarked in his study *State und Parlament*, published under the pen name Rudolf Springer more than eight decades earlier: 'Crises awaken the spirits, but in Austria only ... the demons.'[4] These demons were the 'Jewish conspiracy' and 'international Zionism', cultivated once by the Nazis and ever since by right and left extremists. It is also a fact that the People's Party, and particularly its Secretary-General Michael Graff, used the slogan 'We Austrians elect whomever we want' without any reservation as the central message of the pro-

Waldheim campaign. Graff (who died in 2009) insisted to me in an interview that there was no attempt at all at any cheap anti-Semitic propaganda. Looking back, Erhard Busek sees it entirely differently: 'Graff played a key role with his slogan. It was a consistent line. He knew what game he was playing. He was flirting with certain deeply ingrained basic attitudes.'[5]

The SPÖ was helpless against the campaign, as it had lost its own credibility through its ambivalent stance toward the Nazi period displayed before and during the Kreisky era. In the first ballot at the beginning of May 1986, Waldheim received 49.6 per cent, Steyrer only 43.7 per cent, the Green candidate 5.5 per cent and a right-extremist figure 1.2 per cent. Then in the second round the Social Democratic party suffered its first crushing defeat since 1966: Kurt Waldheim came out the clear winner with 53.9 per cent to Steyrer's 46.1 per cent, and was elected as the first 'black' Federal President since 1945 with an 87 per cent voter participation. Straight after the election Fred Sinowatz resigned the Chancellorship (and in May 1988 also the Party Chairmanship), and proposed Finance Minister Franz Vranitzky as his successor.

An international commission of historians established by the Austrian government announced in February 1988 that it had failed to find any evidence implicating Waldheim in Nazism or war crimes, but that he had known what he denied having known.

Nevertheless Kurt Waldheim remained on the watch list on which he had been placed by the US Government in 1987 without any proof. Even as a private person, until his death on 14 June 2007 he was banned from entry into the United States. This was undoubtedly a political decision that had been reached because of fierce debates in the American public, kindled by Waldheim's unfortunately framed and later regretted statement of 'fulfilment of duty' in the German army and by his persistent claims of ignorance—professed to the very last but disbelieved by everybody—of the horrors committed in the Balkans during the Second World War (for example the mass deportations of the Jews of Saloniki although he had been stationed there). At the ceremony marking the end of Waldheim's six-year term, Heinz Fischer, in his capacity as President of the National Assembly, said that '... an injustice has been perpetrated against Kurt Waldheim the man and the Federal President, when he was accused of ... actions that, according to every historical evidence, he had not committed...' Waldheim's last will and testament, which was made public on 15 June 2007, one day after his death, contains the following: 'I am profoundly sorry that I have ... much too late stated my position comprehensively and unambiguously about the National Socialist crimes.'[6]

Neither as editor-in-chief of Austrian TV, nor later as director of Radio Österreich International (RÖI), was I involved directly or indirectly in the debates surrounding Kurt Waldheim's Presidency. However, in view of the campaign's international dimensions, I did not and could not remain idle. For me it was a matter of the reputation of Austria, the country where I had found a new home, and I felt that I had to stand up for her especially in difficult times.

I had experienced a kind of dress rehearsal for such a commitment thirteen years earlier, in the autumn of 1973 after the Marchegg hostage drama, during a four-week tour of the United States at the State Department's invitation. As a result of a translation error during the first few days after the terrorist attack, the fatally wrong impression was created abroad that the Austrian government would not only close down the Schönau transit camp, but would also stop the transit of Soviet Jews to Israel through Austria.[7] US newspapers castigated the 'capitulation to terror' (*New York Times*) often in a self-righteous tone, and accused the Kreisky government of 'cowardice and lack of principles'. In the course of my discussions with American journalists and scientists, diplomats and bank managers, the topic of the latest events in and about Austria cropped up inevitably. 'Austria has probably not dominated our headlines as much since the *Anschluss*.' This was said to me in Boston by a professor of history from Harvard during the time of the furious reactions against the Austrian government's decision.

Together with the Austrian diplomats, I too endeavoured to rebut the excessive and unjustified criticism of Austria with arguments, particularly with evidence relating to Austria's refugee policy. We even managed to receive a definite promise that a guest commentary of mine would appear on the op-ed page of the *New York Times*.

While I was still in the States, and before my commentary was published, a new Middle East War broke out on 6 October 1973. Austria disappeared from the headlines, and with it my already typeset article from the paper. However, I cautioned both in my report and in my conversations with government officials after my return that it would be wrong to believe that with the war the entire Austrian affair had been forgotten: 'The Austrian government, the diplomatic missions, as well as official and private forums have painstakingly to repair the damage and re-establish Austria's prestige. ... International reliability is the foremost imperative for a small country without an effective army, which itself is dependent on international solidarity. ... Let us not deceive ourselves: Austria's reputation is at stake!'[8]

The international media echo was, of course, much worse in the Waldheim case than after the closing down of the Schönau camp: partly because after his ten years as UN Secretary-General he was known worldwide, partly because an incessant flood of real or alleged new revelations came to light. Eleven days after the elections I wrote a memorandum in which, seeing the 'dramatic deterioration of Austria's image', I urged that day-to-day political debates be put aside in order to mobilize all available abilities and resources in the spirit of a nation-wide effort.[9] Neither short-term knee-jerk reactions nor alibi actions would suffice. What was needed was a comprehensive conception: a preferably small commission, comprising recognized and independent personalities, should work out quickly and unbureaucratically a confidential report and a set of measures. In the following days I handed the memorandum to Federal Chancellor Franz Vranitzky, his predecessor Fred Sinowatz, then still Chairman of the Social Democrats, Alois Mock, People's Party leader (and future Foreign Minister), Foreign Minister Peter Jankowitsch, as well as to Cardinal Franz König and the banker Karl Vak, president of the Foreign Policy Association.

In my confidential report I observed that the deterioration of Austria's image was by no means limited to the East Coast or the Jewish organizations. There was no chance of repairing President Waldheim's image, but the untrue and unfair, biased and superficial reporting about Austria could be corrected self-confidently but also self-critically by objective arguments: 'Every attempt to present the distorted image of Austria in a proper light again is doomed to failure, unless the preconditions in Austria itself are given. The prerequisites include the outright and persuasive rejection of anti-Semitism and xenophobia, and the condemnation without fail by political functionaries of anti—Semitic and racist comments.'

Independently from the state organs, we organized a small, informal group with President Karl Vak—at the time chief executive of the Zentralsparkasse—as host, for the exchange of ideas and the coordination of concrete steps. Some of the participants at the four meetings between the summer of 1986 and the spring of 1987 were Cardinal König, Simon Wiesenthal, plus well-known journalists, industrialists, managers and scientists. With the help of Prince Schwarzenberg and the manager of the Hôtel de France, we invited the leading editors of the *Financial Times* and *Le Monde*, and the deputy editor-in-chief of the *Boston Globe*. They met a number of important personalities in Vienna, and wrote several critical, but basically informative articles about Austria.

During this time an embarrassing misunderstanding occurred. Foreign Minister Mock met Daniel Vernet, director of *Le Monde*, at my apartment. Mock spoke excellent French, and the meeting was obviously a success. Vernet's long report about Austria appeared subsequently. It was during these days or somewhat sooner that a scandal erupted, because Michael Graff, the Secretary-General of the People's Party, gave an interview to the reporter of the Paris weekly *L'Express*, and to her question whether and when Waldheim would resign, he replied: yes, if they can produce proof of his personal guilt. To the additional question as to what personal guilt that would be, his response was: if Waldheim had strangled six Jews with his own hands! As a result of furious domestic and foreign protests, Graff had to resign.

Unfortunately Daniel Vernet mixed up Mock with Graff, and in his article attributed the assertion to the Foreign Minister. Since Mock was one of the few regular readers of *Le Monde* in Vienna, I immediately pulled every string to get a quick correction. It was promptly published, and Mock made peace with me and Vernet. During my interview for this book with Graff almost twenty years later, he himself brought up the interview that had raised so much dust at the time: 'I replied stupidly. It was only idiotic, but not anti-Semitic.'

Still, the most important thing was to counteract Austria's loss of face in the United States, but this time more comprehensively and with better organization than during my coincidental presence in 1973 after the closing of the transit camp. Thus in the second half of October I went on a two-week lecture and information tour to Los Angeles, Chicago, Boston, New York and Washington. I had occasion to talk to, among others, Senator Glenn, Zbigniew Brzezinski, the national security adviser, and Congressman Tom Lantos, the influential Holocaust survivor from Hungary, who passed away recently. The fact that for me as an Austrian speaker no lecture hall was available at New York's Columbia University, and it was only due to the help of Professor István Deák (originally also from Budapest) that I could speak to professors and students in his institute on contemporary Austrian history, says everything about the prevailing anti–Austrian atmosphere.

Two weeks after my return home, I succeeded with the help of Robert Kaiser, then managing editor of the *Washington Post*, to have an oped guest commentary published in his paper under the title 'The smearing of Austria' (18 November 1987). In it—as in my lecture in the State Department before an audience of American and foreign diplomats—I rejected the blanket and stereotyped accusations against the entire Austrian people. I cited Professor Shlomo Avineri, the noted Israeli political scientist and former Director-General of the Israeli Foreign Ministry, who condemned the 'vindictive, badly prepared and sensation-seeking campaign by the World Jewish Congress' in extraordinarily sharp terms. I also referred to the fact that 270,000 Jews had migrated via Austria from the Soviet Union, and tens of thousands from other Eastern European countries, to Israel and the United States.

Having read all the available reports, I was and am convinced that Kurt Waldheim did not do anything wrong in a criminal sense. However, his selective memory and attempts at manipulating the truth, which he later regretted, cannot be denied. I met him several times during his Presidency in the Hofburg. He explained to me his strategy for defence and always showed me different new documents. I shall never forget how in his beautifully furnished office in the Hofburg palace this sad, haggard, tall and already stooping old man repeatedly tried to convince me of his complete innocence.

Waldheim's successor was Thomas Klestil, the third professional diplomat in this high office. Only insiders were aware that Klestil had judiciously and indirectly, through background interviews, thwarted Waldheim's second nomination for the Presidency, arguing that it would prolong Austria's international isolation. Incidentally, of these three heads of state I had the closest relationship with Klestil and was therefore able to follow his career closely, up to his tragic early death.

As already mentioned, Fred Sinowatz too was indirectly a victim of the Waldheim affair—both politically and humanly. His quick resignation benefited not only the party, but also the country. But the fact that he sued Alfred Worm of *Profil* for libel was viewed as a grave mistake by all observers and friends. Quoting a high-ranking Burgenland ex-functionary, who was estranged from the party, Worm reported that already at the meeting of the regional party leadership in November 1985 Sinowatz had indicated the plan to bring up Waldheim's 'brown past' during the election campaign. Although all thirty-nine members of the party body denied the crown witnesses' allegations, Worm was acquitted on the strength of that one witness's written notes. Alfred Worm later told me in detail how the most prominent German hand-writing experts had certified the authenticity of those minutes. He then added: 'Sinowatz had a well-known lawyer, but he gave him bad advice. I would gladly have reached a settlement with him.' Sinowatz himself was convicted of perjury by a right-wing judge, and the convic-tion was upheld by a Court of Appeal in 1991. A former high-ranking Social Democratic functionary says today: 'The story is terrible, because it is doubly wrong. Firstly, if I had made such a statement, I would not risk a court case. Secondly, it would have actually been better for him to say: I admit having said this, it was my right to say such a thing; after all, one of the candidates was tainted with "brown stains".'

Until the end, Sinowatz always averred during personal conversa-tions that he had never said such a thing about Waldheim's past. In any case, it is a pity that the long and successful career of a politician who had done so much for the people, first in the Burgenland region and later in Austria, had to end in such sad circumstances.

16

THE VRANITZKY DECADE
OF RELATIVE STABILITY

Who would ever have imagined that Franz Vranitzky—son of a Communist foundry worker and one of the secretaries of Austria's youngest ever Finance Minister—would govern Austria as Federal Chancellor (June 1986–January1997) and Chairman of the Social Democratic party (1988–97) for over ten years? Four People's Party Deputy Chancellors alternated in his coalition government. It was a time of relative stability, an era without lustre and without crises. At the same time, four important initiatives are associated with Vranitzky's name: the break with Haider's Freedom Party (FPÖ) and the return to the grand coalition with the People's Party (1986); trend-setting speeches that gave impetus to facing up at last to Austria's Nazi past (1991); entry to the European Union (1994); and reform of the state-owned industrial sector.

Ever since I was appointed in April 1987 as head of Radio Austria International—this state-financed but, in terms of editorial personal policy, totally independent institution—I had ample opportunities to meet the Chancellor, whom I had already fleetingly known as secretary of Androsch. Still, this was not the same kind of close personal relationship that I had with Kreisky and some of the other leading politicians. Whatever the reason, this tall, successful basketball player (forty-two times in the national team) of impeccable working-class origins was always friendly yet reserved, and not only toward his political opponents or the representatives of the press but with very few exceptions also toward his party friends. Although he had worked his way up by his talent and diligence from the poorest of backgrounds, with his elegance and manners he gave the impression of a conservative London banker.

He passed his first trial of strength after taking office with flying colours. When the right-populist Jörg Haider overthrew the relatively liberal Deputy Chancellor from his own party at the Innsbruck congress of the Freedom Party, Vranitzky reacted immediately by cutting the ties to the FPÖ under its new leader and forcing a new parliamentary election in November 1986. Together with his long-standing Finance Minister, Ferdinand Lacina, the Chancellor, brought up in an anti-Fascist home, was not willing to make any concessions to the far right. A straight path led from the breach with Haider's FPÖ to his famous speeches on the country's National Socialist past. During the course of a parliamentary debate on the Yugoslav war on 8 July 1991, the Chancellor cautiously but explicitly declared that Austria had to own up to the dark side of its history, 'to shared responsibility for the suffering that was drawn over other human beings and peoples, if not by Austria as a state, then by citizens of this country'. Vranitzky was even more specific on a visit to Israel in a speech made at the Hebrew University in Jerusalem on 9 June 1993: 'We acknowledge all the facts of our history and the deeds of all parts of our population, the good as well as the bad. Just as we claim credit for our good deeds, we must beg forgiveness for the evil ones.' Well-known personalities, with the publicist Hugo Portisch in the lead, had for years urged such an unambiguous declaration, had even suggested appropriate wording on several occasions to the initially hesitant head of government. Nonetheless, no one can deny that Franz Vranitzky was the first Austrian Federal Chancellor ever publicly and sincerely to acknowledge the past.[1]

Soon after his election I went to see him about my memorandum on the effects of the Waldheim affair, and subsequently, as head of Radio Austria International, I informed him from time to time about our plans and of course about our budgetary problems. We talked about politics also when Vranitzky risked the premature elections in the autumn of 1986. I recall how the otherwise cautious man suddenly remarked bitterly that everyone was regarding him only from the sidelines. What seemed to have weighed on Vranitzky's mind was the subjective feeling that by shattering the small coalition he alone had to bear responsibility for the risks of the first election in the post-Kreisky era. The new face and the telegenic appearance, together with a clever advertising campaign, were decisive: although the SPÖ lost ten seats, it won 43.12 per cent of the votes, thus preserving its leading role. The ÖVP also lost out, even if only four seats (from eighty-one to seventy-seven), and received 41.29 per cent of votes. By doubling the total popular vote of his Freedom Party and increasing its seats from twelve to eighteen, Haider, 'the Carinthian Robin Hood', began his dizzying ascent. The Greens moved into parliament for the first time with eight mandates.

Two topics emerged as the main subjects of interest and media speculation in the wake of the elections: Alois Mock, Chairman of the ÖVP, who three years earlier had been riding high after breaking the Social Democrats' absolute majority, not only looked gravely disappointed on election evening, but with his absent-minded expression seemed to be physically afflicted as well; the three other leaders almost had to support him in front of the TV cameras. The other main subject of interest was whether this time the People's Party would form a small coalition with the Freedom Party. On the basis of electoral mathematics, the People's Party and the Freedom Party, with their ninety-five seats out of 183, would have had a possibility of doing so against the Social Democratic party and the Greens, with only a total of eighty-eight seats. However, Alois Mock could not get this favoured option of his accepted by the leadership of the People's Party. The party's economic spokesman opposed this with all his might, and with the support of other exponents of the economy, managed to thwart Mock's intention.

After lengthy negotiations, the two major parties decided to form once again a grand coalition. Vranitzky remained Chancellor, and Alois Mock became Vice-Chancellor and Foreign Minister. Vranitzky's giving the Foreign Ministry portfolio to the ÖVP, and especially to Alois Mock, was responsible for Bruno Kreisky's public split with his party. He resigned in protest as Honorary Chairman of the SPÖ. In his long letter written for the archives of the Social Democratic party, which was made public only much later, Kreisky warned: 'Giving up the Foreign Ministry is patently a catastrophe. The question remains, whether we can exist abroad with a Federal President like Waldheim, and with a Foreign Minister who is Chairman of the party that had nominated and completely supported him...'[2] Still, in his last years Bruno Kreisky made peace with the SPÖ and also personally with Franz Vranitzky, who then visited him several times at his home.[3]

Contrary to Kreisky's apprehensions, the ailing Mock did not play as big a role in foreign affairs as Vranitzky, who as a kind of 'substitute President' distinguished himself abroad as well. In the meantime Waldheim's international standing and credibility had sunk to such a low that not much effort was needed for Vranitzky to grow into this temporary part. Vranitzky was so successful at it that in 1992 the union leader Anton Benya, speaking 'in the name of friends', tried to talk him into accepting the Presidential nomination after Waldheim's retirement. In his memoirs Vranitzky wrote this enigmatic sentence: Benya 'did not name any name, and I did not want to know about names'. To his question, as to who he and his 'friends' thought should be his successor as Chancellor, Benya named Rudolf Streicher, Minister for Nationalized Industries and Transport. 'And who should be Party Chairman? To that he had no answer.'

Surprised and somewhat alarmed, Vranitzky promptly and subtly turned the tables on Benya: he pushed Streicher's nomination for the Federal Presidency through the Social Democratic party, and forced him to accept it. Fifteen years later I tried—almost by a kind of detective work—to clear up this story and track down the 'friends', i.e. the nameless wire-pullers. In a long and very frank conversation, Streicher insisted that originally he had 'no idea' about the suggestion that he should be made Chancellor and Vranitzky President. As his chances against the diplomat Thomas Klestil, who had meanwhile been chosen as the candidate of the People's Party (his advantage was 12 per cent), were excellent, after some hesitation he accepted the SPÖ's nomination.[4] Although neither Vranitzky nor Streicher would name the actual initiator of this abortive idea, insider sources believe that it could not have been anybody else but Hannes Androsch.

Streicher, who had risen from toolmaker to star manager and minister with a key portfolio (1986–91), was—to everyone's surprise—thoroughly defeated in the second round (57 per cent to 43 per cent) of the Presidential election by the diplomat Thomas Klestil, who had been underestimated by the SPÖ. After his defeat, Streicher once again took over as managing director of Steyr-Daimler-Puch, Austria's third largest industrial enterprise, involved also in arms production. Later there were unverifiable rumours afloat, according to which the owner of the Steyr concern, the Creditanstalt, had sold it too cheaply to the Austro-Canadian multimillionaire Frank Stronach.

Thomas Klestil's unexpected victory in 1992 signalled the end of Vranitzky's pleasant double role, and sparked off a rivalry between Vranitzky and the new President. Although Klestil had started his career in Chancellor Klaus's cabinet and was a member of the CV student fraternity organization (mentioned earlier), he did not really belong to the inner circle of the People's Party. He had spent practically his entire professional life serving as a diplomat in the United States.

I first met Klestil in 1971, when he was Austria's Consul-General in Los Angeles, and after 1989, when he was already Secretary-General of the Foreign Ministry at the time of the Waldheim turmoil, we had a close relationship. The vain and ambitious Klestil would have liked to become Foreign Minister in place of the ailing Alois Mock. Paradoxically it was the independent-minded Social Democratic mayor of Vienna, Helmut Zilk, who had originally suggested Klestil's nomination. Since the ailing Alois Mock could not stand as candidate on behalf of the People's Party, the then Party Chairman Erhard Busek accepted Zilk's idea and pushed Klestil's nomination through the party leadership. At a lunch with several leading journalists Klestil had already openly stood up against Waldheim's renomination. This, along with Busek's convincing arguments behind the scenes, finally led to President Waldheim informing the Chancellor by telephone as early as the summer of 1991 that he would not seek a second term of office. Six years later it was Helmut Zilk again who persuaded the SPÖ's leadership to accept Thomas Klestil as the two coalition partners' joint candidate.

The jealousies between Klestil and Vranitzky led in the meantime to embarrassing scenes in 1994 during the signing in Corfu of the Treaty of Accession to the European Union, because, to the surprise of the hosts, President Klestil also appeared beside Vranitzky, and a place at the 'head table' had to be secured for him at the last minute. Despite their squabbles, though, both of them acted in concert as far as the opening toward the EU was concerned. To this day, even the Conservatives credit Vranitzky with having freed his party, whose Chairmanship he took over in May 1988, from its ideological fetters stemming from its dogmatic past. The fact that on 12 June 1994 two-thirds of Austrians voted for joining the European Union was for Vranitzky, and arguably also for his Deputy Chancellor Erhard Busek, the pinnacle of their political careers. At the same time, the criticism was justified that Chancellor Vranitzky and the Austrian Social Democrats in general behaved passively at the time of the political changes in Central and Eastern Europe, especially compared to the one-man-diplomacy of Erhard Busek, who had for years built up important contacts with the region's oppositional intellectuals.[5]

Vranitzky's Party Chairmanship was not only criticized because he had changed the party's name from Socialist to Social Democrats, but also because the membership had dropped by a third. Surprisingly many, otherwise left-oriented, observers agree with Androsch's harsh judgment: 'Because it did not interest him, Vranitzky has ruined the party in terms of content, ethics and finances.' A contributing factor to the animosity inside the party was that Vranitzky was not loyal enough to his colleagues who got into tight spots or who were attacked. And here it was not, or not only, a matter of Androsch, Blecha or Gratz who were implicated in various corruption scandals. It was also a question of the manner in which he acted: Vranitzky had two central secretaries promptly fired, who had been attacked for alleged 'financial irregularities', although it subsequently turned out that the accusations were totally baseless. One of their successors, Josef Cap (at present chief whip of the parliamentary SPÖ faction), found out from the radio at the time that he had been sacked from his executive director's post before Vranitzky 'had personally spoken to him about it'.[6]

A strange episode was also the reason for Ferdinand Lacina, the long-time Finance Minister, to resign; he was accused by a vociferous union leader, who has since faded into well-deserved oblivion, of 'lacking a social conscience'. Eventually within a relatively short time hardly anyone survived from the Kreisky team (apart from Heinz Fischer, at the time parliamentary faction leader). When in the course of the state-owned industry's reorganization Rudolf Streicher sketched the first privatization of 25 per cent of the ÖMV's share capital before the Social Democratic party's leadership, Fischer bitterly observed: 'Rudolf, as I'm listening to you, it makes my stomach turn.' Incidentally, on the occasion of Fischer's election to President in 2004, ex-minister Streicher commented openly and somewhat spitefully: 'Unlike Hannes Androsch, he is a political slalom champion, who has never made a mistake on the slopes and never upset a gate...'

At any rate one has also to admit that such critical minds, as for example the philosopher Rudolf Burger, still rate Vranitzky's style very positively, and his modernization of the country's political thinking, as well as the transformation of the SPÖ into a European-style party and the decisive achievement of joining the European Union. Burger acknowledges Vranitzky's speeches of 1991 and 1993 relating to the Nazi past, which, according to the philosopher, were not approved by the majority of his own party. In his essay 'Farewell from a statesman'—which he wrote well before the 'political turn' of 2000 and their personal estrangement caused by the black-blue government—he praised Vranitzky's determination. At his last press conference as Federal Chancellor, Vranitzky said that the aim of his last ten years in office was the return to 'a normality that could be taken for granted'. According to Burger, he had largely achieved that goal.[7] The journalist Peter Pelinka also writes aptly about Vranitzky in his portrait collection, 'Austria's Chancellors': 'Ten years without lustre and glory, but filled with that calm continuity which the majority of Austrians obviously wished for themselves, particularly in times of upheaval.'

Vranitzky's period of governing was indirectly linked from beginning to end with a politician who, in his rhetoric, political style, negation of social consensus, and last but not least in his ambiguous stance vis-à-vis the Nazi past, symbolized the diametric opposite to Franz Vranitzky's person, politics and ethos: that politician was Jörg Haider. Although I had met him already during the 1980s at various conferences and receptions, I only got to know him more closely in October 1990 as a guest at my round-table TV programme at Klagenfurt. At the time he was Governor of Carinthia for the first time. Officially the topic was the seventieth anniversary of the Carinthian plebiscite. Incidentally, this referendum turned out favourably for Austria only because the majority of Carinthia's Slovenes opted for staying with Austria rather than joining the new state of Yugoslavia.

Ten years later, on the eightieth anniversary of the plebiscite, I once again conducted a political discussion programme on television, again with Governor Haider. This time too it was difficult to find qualified participants from Slovenia, as everyone who had been approached found some pretext for declining a joint appearance with Haider. Eventually I managed to recruit Katja Boh, a sociologist from Ljubljana who was a former cabinet minister and a close acquaintance since her years as Slovenian Ambassador to Vienna; in addition we also had a German and an Austrian journalist. In both telecasts Haider tried, albeit in different styles, to justify the Carinthians' 'primal fear' of Slovenia, castigated Slavic and Slovenian 'imperialism', and stressed at the same time his affirmative actions on behalf of the Slovenian minority in Carinthia. Contrary to the Austrian State Treaty of 1955 and the rulings of the Austrian Constitutional Court, Haider, as Governor, thwarted the erection of sufficient bilingual town signposts, although the latest ruling stipulates that such signs need to be put up in all localities where the share of the ethnic Slovenian population has exceeded 10 per cent in recent history.

Between these two dates of 1990 and 2000, the triumphal rise of the Haider party at the polls marked a turning point in Austrian politics.

Born in 1950 in Bad Goisern (Upper Austria), Jörg Haider was elected as leader of the Freedom Party in the autumn of 1986. He ranked as a kind of honorary Carinthian with a large inherited estate in the province (acquired by his great-uncle in the Nazi period on favourable terms from a Jewish owner). From the very first, this charismatic figure conducted an aggressive and uncompromising oppositional policy, and with his unbridled energy, brilliant rhetoric and unscrupulous turncoat ability managed to capture progressively more and more of the Social Democratic party's core voters.

As a 'virtuoso of foul play', Haider recognized that the so-called 'foreigner problem' was a time bomb. Simultaneously he ceaselessly attacked the abuses of the fossilized electoral system, the mendacity of the party and union functionaries, and their failure to face up to the growing migrant problem. He succeeded in increasing his support at the polls from election to election: from 9.73 per cent in 1986 to 16.63 per cent in 1990, to 22.5 per cent in 1994, and finally to the record figure of 26.91 per cent of the popular vote in 1999. Many observers viewed with alarm the unprecedented rise of a right-wing populist party, moreover one that was internationally discredited because of its extreme right-wing line and its hankering toward National Socialist nostalgia.

Vranitzky's anti-Haider battle, and his policy of 'ostracism' of the Freedom Party, were initially generally approved, but given Haider's political successes, this turned with time into criticism. The point of the matter was not the aim of the battle against right-wing populism, but its method and substance, as Haider's party—if needed—could easily masquerade as a socially committed left-wing movement. Of course, the clear dissociation from Haider was unavoidable and sensible, particularly where 'this postmodern Robin Hood' (Rudolf Burger)[8] served the shrinking group of veteran Nazis or the ever-growing number of radical xenophobes with his irresponsible and only too meaningful 'verbal excesses'.

Haider, who grew up in a Nazi family and was educated in a right-radical secondary school and university atmosphere, had scored an assortment of so-called 'blunders', from commending 'the Third Reich's orderly employment policy' to his speech in Krumpendorf before Waffen-SS veterans, whom he addressed as 'honest people, people with character', going so far as to reduce the severity of the Nazi extermination camps, calling them 'punishment camps'. Characteristic of his unscrupulous xenophobic agitation was the 'referendum initiative against immigrants' (1993). However, only 13 per cent (413,000) of those entitled to vote signed it.

All this led to anxious questions and enquiries for us at the short-wave broadcasting service, but also addressed to Austrian businessmen and diplomats abroad. Yet at the same time I shall never forget when a quarter of a million people with candles in their hands held an anti— xenophobic demonstration on the Ringstraße and the Heldenplatz ('sea of light'). It was the largest political demonstration in the history of the Second Republic.

Why did the voters not support Vranitzky's uncompromising stance? Why did even firmly anti—Freedom Party journalists conclude that it was his strategy that helped Haider to gain strength in 1999?[9] Of course, in his heyday Haider was a charismatic figure, sporty and elegant, quick-witted and charming with an inimitable political instinct, the most aggressive and most talented opposition politician in the history of the Second Republic. In politics he was the best actor since Kreisky (in his youth he had been an aspiring actor), with a smirk on his face, unscrupulously interrupting his opponent or interviewer, consciously duplicitous or sarcastic.

Above all, with his brilliant rhetoric and always perfectly prepared with facts and figures on his opponent's weak points, Haider could make use of the live telecast's potentials.[10] Like a rabbit caught in the headlights, Vranitzky froze during a live TV debate in 1990, when Haider presented his sensational 'table' act: he placed small cardboard labels on the studio table, which showed to the viewers the figures about the various salaries and the staggering total income of a union functionary from Styria, who belonged to the SPÖ. He was chairman of the central works council of the Vereinigte Edelstahlwerke AG, member of parliament, president of the Styrian Chamber of Labour, president of the Styrian Ironworkers Union, etc., and drew salaries or incomes from all these functions. This incident was a real technical knockout and launched the Freedom Party's successful campaign against the Socialists as a 'party of scandals'.

In the course of Haider's 'hysterical demonization' (Rudolf Burger) at home and abroad, it was forgotten or ignored that his attacks against the various SPÖ-backed hair-raising privileges and aberrations, such as their political influence in schools, the high number of social insurance institutions, the multiple salaries of chamber and union functionaries, and the abuses of pensions in the state-owned industry, were often well-founded. The deficient or belated reactions of the Social Democratic party and the grand coalition's governments to the Haider party's astute and unscrupulous propaganda paved the way for the defeat of the large parties. By 1999, Haider had conquered the majority of workers and almost half of voters under the age of thirty. Despite repeatedly proven unreliability, his triumphal advance was unstoppable, because the *Proporz* system (proportional representation of the two big parties according to electoral strength at all levels; see the chapter on Joseph Klaus) and the institutions of social partnership had become fossilized and marked by a mixture of mendacity and moral corruption.

Extremely important roles were also played by various investigative journalists. Let us look briefly at the much reported case of the freighter *Lucona*'s disappearance in the Indian Ocean in January 1977—due to an explosion in which half a dozen crew members perished—which was part of a huge insurance fraud.[11] The mastermind of the affair, Udo Proksch, whom I had never met personally, was the owner of the most famous café–patisserie in downtown Vienna and founder of the notorious Club 45 on the café's upper floors. The exclusive club attracted some of the highest-level civil servants and members of the Socialist party bureaucracy, including several current and former cabinet ministers. There were also rumours afloat about alleged sex parties organized occasionally by Proksch. It took fifteen years (!) from the *Lucona*'s disappearance to Proksch's conviction (he died later in prison). Two friends of his, Leopold Gratz, formerly Foreign Minister and then Speaker of Parliament, and Interior Minister Karl Blecha, finally had to face court and to resign all their political offices.

One must not forget that the road to the 1999 political turnaround had started at the time of the ÖVP's entry into the grand coalition. It was through this that the monopoly of exposures dropped into Haider's lap. The accusation by the political magazine *Profil* that Vranitzky was the 'Haider-maker' is doubly fallacious: the system, hence also the grand coalition, offered the chance to the Freedom Party, and the dozens of cover stories written by left-liberal journalists and editors also in *Profil* and later in other magazines helped him to capitalize on that chance to the maximum.

During the years characterized by deadly dullness in domestic politics, the cover stories about the Carinthian politician were certain bestsellers. The bitter truth, often indignantly rejected by those concerned, is that it was not the much-maligned mass circulation tabloid *Kronen Zeitung* but, as an astute observer put it, the 'political magazines, which at that time even more than during the previous years—on the pretext of wanting to hinder the further rise of Jörg Haider and the FPÖ—provoked a self-fulfilling prophecy with their regular weekly writings'.[12] I have to agree with the judgment of my colleague, and therefore reject the charge against Vranitzky as the 'Haider-maker'.

According to journalist Trautl Brandsteller, the ten years of Vranitzky's government was a lost decade.[13] I do not share this blanket criticism. However, by now Vranitzky himself admits in private conversation that by choosing Viktor Klima as his successor to lead the government and the Social Democratic party, he probably committed a fatal error. In the opinion voiced by another observer, Klima will not even go down as a footnote in the history of the Second Republic.[14] This also is too harsh a judgment. Klima was rather the involuntary grave-digger of thirty years of Social Democratic and union hegemony. He paved the way for that turnaround whose emblematic personality—contrary to domestic and foreign hysterical reactions—was not Jörg Haider, but rather Wolfgang Schüssel, the most talented centre-right political operator.

17

SCHÜSSEL, RISE AND FALL OF A PLAYER

After a spectacular turning point at the end of January/early February 2000, politics in Austria again became exciting. The old categories of 'right' and 'left' were no longer applicable. Disagreements over the best responses to international and national challenges split the traditional political camps more than once, and even divided families. The unexpected events and bewildering U-turns in Austrian politics confirm the great German political scientist Max Weber's statement: 'The fundamental fact of all history is that the final result of political action often, no, even regularly, stands in completely inadequate and often even paradoxical relation to its original meaning.'[1]

One of the world's most stable and flourishing countries, where strikes, demonstrations and clashes were a rarity, suddenly became a deeply polarized society after the formation of the so-called 'black-blue' coalition government of the right-wing FPÖ and the conservative ÖVP on 4 February 2000. About 200,000 people crowded onto Vienna's Heldenplatz for a mass protest demonstration. 'Resistance' became the slogan of the regular 'Thursday demonstrations' against the government. For the first time in history, members of the new government had to make use of the underground corridor leading to the President's office in the Hofburg. President Thomas Klestil conducted the swearing-in ceremony with a stony face and noticeable reluctance.

As a matter of fact, the way this government was formed was most unusual for Austrian conditions. It happened for the first time that the Chancellor was not nominated by the party with the most mandates and votes, namely the SPÖ, but the one in third place, the ÖVP, which had been outstripped even by the FPÖ with 415 votes. With Wolfgang Schüssel, the People's Party once again after a gap of thirty years conquered the Chancellorship. Schüssel had possibly prevented an even more serious defeat by threatening before the elections to take the People's Party into opposition if it were to slip to third place. What however provoked an unparalleled storm of protest both inside and outside Austria was the participation of the FPÖ in the government, although Jörg Haider himself, the internationally ill-famed symbol of the party, did not join the government, but remained Governor of Carinthia. Nevertheless, he led the coalition negotiations on behalf of his party, and he was the one who stepped side by side with Schüssel in front of the representatives of the international media—not Susanne Riess-Passer, the designated Vice-Chancellor—to inform them on 2 February 2000 of the coalition agreement.

The decision of the other fourteen EU members on 31 January 2000 to impose diplomatic sanctions if the Freedom Party were to participate in the government hit the country as a bolt from the blue. In a vain attempt to prevent the formation of an ÖVP–FPÖ government, the governments of the 'EU-14s' officially announced that they would not have any bilateral contacts with the Austrian government, would not support any Austrian candidates for international organizations, and would receive Austrian ambassadors to the capitals only on a 'technical level'.

Looking back on my fifty years spent in Austria, I can state without exaggeration that living through that year was personally also perhaps the most difficult, even if in some respects the most exciting, period ever. In a cloak-and-dagger operation, contravening all EU regulations, Austria was to be made Europe's pariah or bogeyman: the very country that had voted in June 1994 for entry into the European Union with the highest ratio (66.5 per cent) of all the other countries. Fourteen states decided about the fifteenth without listening to it.

I was asked in the ORF newsreel's late night edition about the international consequences.[2] Then, as well as in my commentary during the following night's TV news, I categorically rejected Austria's international ostracism as a high degree of hypocrisy and as a mixture of ignorance and arrogance. To illustrate the double standard, I referred to the fact that the same European Union politicians had not even considered such measures against the right-wing populist and ex-Fascist Fini's and Bossi's participation in the Italian government, nor against the presence of the subsequently convicted war criminal Maurice Papon and Communists loyal to Moscow in the French government.

To the indignation of some (or many?) Socialists, I also recalled the fact that Bruno Kreisky had four former Nazi party members in his first government.

Even though references to Haider's pro-Nazi 'gaffes' have never been absent from my commentaries and later interviews, nor how carelessly his party had dealt with its sad past; even though I had always stressed that the unconditional rejection and combating of xenophobia and anti-Semitism were the preconditions of an all-Austrian and non-partisan action against the branding of Austria as 'Haider-country'; even though I had signed a resolution against the Viennese Freedom Party's xenophobic posters, and Haider had therefore described me as 'the lifelong loyal follower of the imperial Left'; yet practically overnight I was regarded as an advocate of the black-blue coalition government. This labelling was, of course, also due to the fact that many Austrian Social Democrats and Greens welcomed the tough stance vis-à-vis Austria by the fourteen EU states of which eleven at that time were governed by Social Democrats.

I was always a supporter of the great coalition or of a majority government, and was never in favour of an experiment with the Haider party. But, together with such important and sober-minded foreign observers as, for instance, Hugo Bütler then editor-in-chief of the *Neue Zürcher Zeitung*, Walter Laqueur the American political scientist, and Lord Weidenfeld the British publisher (both of them refugees from the Third Reich), I rejected the attempts to project this virtuoso of right-wing populist demagoguery as a dramatic threat to Austrian or even European democracy, despite his unacceptable statements about the Nazi era. Criticizing the hectic EU measures, we stressed that blanket judgements and exaggerated responses against one of Europe's most stable democracies could turn out to be counterproductive.

In the course of press polemics I refuted among others the assertion by a German historian in a Munich paper that Haider had won the 1999 elections by anti-Semitic statements, and in conclusion I wrote: 'I was not willing during the Waldheim crisis, nor am I today when Haider is being demonized, to take part in the rabid campaign against Austria, the country that has given shelter to hundreds of thousands of refugees and enabled 270,000 Jews to leave the Soviet Union.' I likewise raised my voice during a live telecast international debate against the 'brazen self-righteousness' with which one person wanted to lecture Austria and the Austrian politicians. Referring to the threat of a boycott against Austrian artists and scientists (voiced in France or Belgium), as well as the bitter experiences of Austrian students in Strasbourg, I emphasized that: 'Experiences show that it is the population and not the politicians who are hit by a boycott.'[3]

The international media, with a few exceptions (*Neue Zürcher Zeitung, Frankfurter Allgemeine*), during those days lost all sense of proportion. It was not surprising therefore that at that time 64 per cent of French and 54 per cent of Britons believed that the participation of Haider's Freedom Party in the government constituted a danger for European democracy. The chasm between the negative stereotypical image of Austria and Austria's self-image has perhaps never been as deep as in the spring of 2000. In any case, the country lost face even more than at the time of the Waldheim affair. Yet at the same time, according to public opinion polls, more than two-thirds of Austrians believed that the sanctions were not imposed as a defence against right-extremism and racism, but for reasons of power politics and competition. The bias in Brussels, and elsewhere too, to judge the big and the small countries, the left and the right by double standards, justifiably aroused astonishment and indignation in Austria. Karl Lamers, the CDU–CSU foreign policy spokesman in the German Bundestag, voiced the bitter truth: 'Such a step would never have been taken against Italy.'[4]

Within a few days a provincial politician with the gift of the gab became a European media star and immutable villain in the international media. Yet the content of the much-discussed sanctions was 'actually ridiculous', as put by the former Vice-Chancellor Erhard Busek. The restrictions on the various contacts led merely to media titbits about who did not shake hands with whom, who invited whom to a meeting, who was seated at the end of the table at working lunches, whose expression on the EU family photos indicated what. All this also unmasked the critics, since simultaneously with the 'Austria blockade', representatives of Middle Eastern and Asian dictatorships beat a path to the diplomatic doorsteps of Paris and Berlin, Madrid and Rome.

The courageous and incorruptible critic of Haider's 'hysterical demonization', Rudolf Burger the Austrian philosopher, aptly stated: 'And precisely because one cannot accuse him of any actions, only foolish statements, these appear in the minds of the half- or totally uninformed international public as genuine horror stories.' Jean-Claude

Juncker, the long-serving Prime Minister of Luxembourg, was the only head of government publicly to question the course of action taken against Austria, indirectly confirming Burger's thesis: 'I doubt whether we have acted correctly in every detail. I also doubt that we have given sufficient attention to Austria's domestic sensibilities. ... Austrians too have to realize that the reaction of the fourteen was not so far-fetched. The European Union's other states took the Freedom Party's election campaign statements seriously and thought: deeds will now follow the words.'[5] But nothing happened, nothing at all: no xenophobic or anti-Semitic incidents, no acts of violence, no arson, no aggression.

Despite the bleak warnings, Austrian democracy passed the historic test of smooth transition from the 'classic' grand coalition to the first centre-right coalition government; just as smoothly as the birth in 1966 of the ÖVP single-party government, and in 1970 Kreisky's minority and later majority government, not to mention the by now forgotten 'red–blue' small coalition in 1983.

Thus it was quite natural—though of course hardly noticed by world opinion—that on the advice of its own special international commission, the European Union lifted the sanctions on 12 September 2000 without any further ado.

Of course, the debates about the new government continued. In a lengthy article published in the *Frankfurter Allgemeine*,[6] which later appeared in a somewhat abridged form in *Le Monde*, I broke the same taboo as the distinguished philosopher Rudolf Burger. I wrote that 'what has almost been forgotten by now is that it was Kreisky who, through a new electoral reform, saved the Freedom Party, which at the time was led by the former Waffen-SS officer Friedrich Peter. The support of the Freedomites ensured the survival of the Social Democratic minority government for eighteen months. Somewhat exaggeratedly one can say: without Kreisky perhaps there would be no Haider today.'

In this article, as at several meetings of the German–Jewish Dialogue in Berlin organized by the Bertelsmann Foundation, I tried to explain the 'Haider phenomenon'. I stressed that Haider's 1,244,087–strong voter block (almost 27 per cent of the electorate) was primarily due to his criticism of the abuses of the disliked bipartisan 'back room' deals (*Proporz*) and the resentment of the post-war system built on historical lies, as well as to the genuine and alleged abuses of the asylum policy which Haider of course cleverly exploited.

Leading German politicians, prominent representatives of world Jewry as well as historians, journalists and scholars from various countries took part in the above-mentioned conferences of the Bertels-mann Foundation. Twice I had occasion—in the autumn of 1999 and in July 2000—to put forward my views in that circle regarding the danger of the Austrian extreme right. At the July meeting in Berlin, Tony Judt, the well-known British historian, called the EU's policy vis-à-vis Austria 'hypocritical and damaging'. Others, however, such as Shlomo Avineri, the Israeli historian, stood up for the sanctions.

Despite our disagreements regarding the Haider question, it was my friend Avineri who gave me the opportunity to state my case in Jerusa-lem as well. I was asked to give a paper on the topic of 'Austria and the European Union' at the Hebrew University, where I had partici-pated at an international meeting on national tensions in and about Kosovo. In the presence of three former Israeli Ambassadors to Austria (the government had recalled its Ambassador from Vienna following the formation of the black–blue coalition) I labelled the sanctions a 'crucial political mistake'.

How did this black–blue coalition government actually come into being, and who from the Austrian side encouraged a stand in favour of the sanctions? Many media and political observers, and first and fore-most the political opponents, were and still are convinced that the two party leaders, Wolfgang Schüssel and Jörg Haider, had already pre-pared and concluded their agreement immediately after the elections in the autumn of 1999, and at least well before the official end of the almost four months long coalition negotiations. That is why they were able to present a finished programme at lightning speed, within five days after the negotiations had broken down between the ÖVP and the SPÖ. In their long conversations with me, both Schüssel and Haider have rejected this widely-held thesis.

Haider told me point blank that no negotiations had taken place in the interim between the ÖVP and the FPÖ. He had only one conversa-tion with Schüssel soon after the elections, still in October: 'At the time I told Schüssel that if nothing came of his negotiations with the Social Democratic party, I could imagine that the People's Party would enter into a coalition with us. I noticed then that the penny had dropped for Schüssel. Now he practically had an ace up his sleeve.'[7] Schüssel insists to this day that he had negotiated earnestly with the SPÖ from the beginning to the end. He claims that these negotiations broke down finally because the trade unions vetoed the pension reform that the two parties had already agreed on, and because Chancellor Viktor Klima's power base within his party was too weak. Schüssel maintains that, as a compromise solution, he had even suggested the appointment of an independent expert for the finance portfolio instead of someone from the People's Party.

An insider from the SPÖ, the only one from that side, in an off-the-record talk with me confirmed Schüssel's version. It is his opinion that his party left Klima in the lurch. Everyone knew that the pension reform was unavoidable, and Klima ought to have acted in line with the positive decision of the party executive and also accepted the trade-off proposed by the ÖVP-Economics Minister for Finance Minister. But the Social Democrat Finance Minister wanted to stay by hook or by crook. His crude saying is still remembered: 'I would rather set the fox to watch the geese than the ÖVP to watch the taxpayers' money.' The decisive factor was Klima's weakness and ultimately his break-down: he had to spend a week in hospital before the elections.[8]

It is clear in retrospect that the entire leadership of the ÖVP supported Wolfgang Schüssel's pact with the FPÖ. That is why all six ÖVP provincial governors appeared with Schüssel already at dawn—after the SPÖ broke off negotiations during the night—at the Federal Presidency to persuade him to swear in the black–blue government as soon as possible. President Klestil made one more attempt to form an SPÖ minority government with Klima, supported by the FPÖ. However, Haider was not satisfied with vague promises. So during that period the Federal President got together several times with Haider, with whom he had already been on friendly terms earlier.

Schüssel and Haider had signed the much-discussed preamble to the government programme already before the black–blue cabinet was sworn in. Schüssel claims that it was actually he who had recommended the preamble during a discussion with Klestil and Haider, and not the President as is generally believed. Obviously as a reassurance for the outside world, the three and a half page text expressed the coalition partners' 'commitment to the intellectual and moral values that are the common heritage of the peoples of Europe'. In keeping with this heritage, the government pledged itself to strive for 'an Austria in which xenophobia, anti-Semitism and racism have no place'.

As far as the true course of the Schüssel–Haider negotiations and the secret ambitions of these completely different professional politicians are concerned, we can only rely on conjectures. The various Austrian conspiracy theories have also to be handled with caution.

Most probably the deal was produced by an accidental amalgam of various elements.

The final phase of the failed ÖVP–SPÖ negotiations coincided with the much-publicized international Holocaust Conference in Stockholm, attended by twenty prime ministers and heads of state, as well as high-ranking delegates from forty-five countries and 800 journalists. Observers saw the physically and psychologically drained Viktor Klima's appearing in Stockholm as a man crying out for help. The Scandinavian press reported that at a confidential meeting of the Foreign Affairs Committee of the Danish parliament Rasmussen, the Danish Prime Minister, allegedly spoke of 'a distress call from Vienna' and of 'the active role played by Klestil and Klima'. Both of them rejected these and similar reports emanating from Paris. Contrary to rumours spread by the ÖVP and FPÖ, the anti-Austrian sanctions were definitely not decided by the Socialist International, even though António Guterres, the Socialist Prime Minister of Portugal, who happened to represent the Presidency of the European Council at the time, was also the President of the Socialist International.

The most active opponents of the Freedom Party's participation in the government were first and foremost Jacques Chirac, the conservative French President, and Guy Verhofstadt, the conservative-liberal Belgian Prime Minister. In France it was a matter of marginalizing Le Pen's right-radical party, and in Belgium the xenophobic and anti-EU Vlaams Blok. They were worried in both countries about a potential magnet effect of an extreme-right government party in Austria. They regarded the Freedom Party as just that, especially because in no other European country did a right-wing party get as many votes as Haider's.

At a reception celebrating the Carinthian Governor's 50th birthday, Austrian television reported live Haider's vehement attacks against the 'corrupt Belgian government' and Jacques Chirac, the 'pocket Napoleon'. French and German TV stations of course lost no time in informing their viewers of these outbursts. This obviously hardened the negative attitude in Brussels. The German government, and Chancellor Schröder's foreign policy adviser in particular, also played a key role in composing the text of the sanctions and coordinating it with Paris and Brussels. President Thomas Klestil and the leading politicians of the Social Democratic party, while perhaps not asking for it, must certainly have welcomed the EU countries' stance as a support for their attempts to prevent the black–blue government experiment.[9]

But back to our original question: what did Wolfgang Schüssel actually want? His aspiration was no secret. Already on 22 April 1995, as the newly elected Party Chairman of the ÖVP, the fifty-year-old ex-Economics Minister declared in a firm voice in the ballroom of the Viennese Hofburg before 600 party delegates: 'I want to become Chancellor with your help!' The brilliant orator received 95.5 per cent of the votes. The wearer of flamboyant bow ties, a talented drawer, soccer player and mountaineer, piano, guitar and cello player, became Chairman of a party embroiled in identity and leadership crises for a quarter of a century, ever since the fall of the Klaus government. The leading bodies of this disparate party, which is made up of nine provincial party organizations, each composed of six *Bünde* or federations (Workers and Salaried Employees, Farmers, Business, Young People, Senior Citizens and Women's Movement), time and again confirmed Churchill's adage: 'There is no friendship in politics, particularly at the top.' In this sense the history of this Christian party is also the un-Christian history of covert and overt intrigues and battles for top positions within the party.

Only later emerged the details of what was probably the most dramatic decision in the history of the People's Party when choosing a new leader. In order to appreciate its explosive nature, one should briefly recall the history of internal party conflicts.

Schüssel's career had always been closely linked to that of Erhard Busek, his predecessor at the top of the party. Similarly to Schüssel, Busek did not come from the circle of Catholic Student Fraternities (CV), but from the more liberal and somewhat unconventional Catholic University Youth movement. Despite his successes in Viennese politics, and the great esteem in which he was held by the intelligentsia, he was elected Chairman with only a small majority (56 per cent) at the 1991 congress of the People's Party, against a colourless candidate supported by the hardliners. As in the case of most of his predecessors, no sooner was he elected than his opponents began to undermine his position. After the defeat in the 1994 autumn elections (the ÖVP lost eight, the SPÖ fifteen mandates; the SPÖ's percentage of votes fell from 42.8 per cent to 38.9 per cent, that of the ÖVP from 32.1 per cent to 27.7 per cent), and the FPÖ's simultaneous success (it won nine additional seats and increased its share of the popular vote by 6 per cent), Busek's opponents sounded the alarm. A veritable witch-hunt was launched in the media and behind the scenes against this liberal politician who was at that time Vice-Chancellor in the coalition government, and ÖVP Chairman.

Wolfgang Schüssel, as Minister for Economic Affairs heading a business delegation, travelled to China over Easter 1995. While he was attending a deeply touching celebration on Easter Sunday in Beijing's Catholic Cathedral, the battle was raging back in Vienna within the party leadership about the succession to Chairman Busek. The latter was willing to resign, but wanted by all possible means to prevent a victory by the extreme Conservative chief whip of the parliamentary group. In the fifteen-member electoral committee, Busek, together with two governors, put forward Schüssel's name. Meanwhile the chief whip, rejected by the majority ('too Conservative and overambitious'), was so sure of victory that he presented a full list of ÖVP ministers to President Klestil. Klestil, who could never take the ambitious man, promptly informed Busek.

Schüssel, regarded as a 'Busek friend', was neither mentioned on the above list nor did his name figure in any of the other combinations. Consequently complete confusion reigned at the start of the 'kingmakers' meeting on Easter Monday. This gave rise to a bizarre story concerning an obscure university professor of constitutional law from Linz, who up to that time had played no role at all in politics. Allegedly Erwin Pröll, the powerful Governor of Lower Austria, had suggested him as the future party chief. During our conversation Pröll energetically denied this otherwise widely disseminated version, and named the chairman of the party's business league as the 'inventor' of the scholar from Linz. In any case, the naïve academic, whoever was to contact him, was already sitting in the nearby Café Landtmann vainly awaiting the expected call by the ÖVP. To add insult to injury, millions of viewers could watch the pathetic episode live, since the TV reporters of the main evening newscast were all along present with their cameras and even gave an interview with the embarrassed scholar.

Meanwhile on that Monday Schüssel was sitting on the Beijing to Vienna flight, with next to him a famous mountaineer who had interesting experiences to relate about Tibet. Schüssel told me: 'I decided there and then that I would definitely go to Tibet, which I then managed to do three years later as the first of the European Union Foreign Ministers. But I never dreamt that I would ever become Party Chairman. For me it was already certain that someone else would be chosen, but oddly enough I actually dreamt about it on the way home. I slept for quite a while, and I had a very peculiar dream: that it could happen to me after all. I had not thought about that at all, but as frequently happens, such a dream reveals that one is still toying with the idea—subconsciously.'

While Schüssel was dozing on the plane, the power struggle for the leadership of the party was in full swing. Although Governor Pröll himself declined the nomination, he wanted to thwart the chief whip's election. The first roll-call ballot showed a clear majority—eight votes—in favour of Schüssel. When Schüssel arrived at Schwechat airport around 9.00 p.m.–because of the time difference it was 4.00 a.m. for him—a leading party functionary was waiting for him with the news that he was wanted immediately at party headquarters. Schüssel asked for time for reflection; he wanted to talk it over with his wife, he had to freshen up, etc. 'So I went home and then back to party headquarters, and then finally I accepted it. It was quite a strange, almost somnambulistic situation, which I believe an outsider cannot really imagine,' Schüssel told me, looking back almost exactly twelve years later.

When he eventually accepted the nomination late at night, he was unanimously elected. Actually this decision was the only chance for Schüssel's political survival, says a cynical insider, since otherwise his rivals would have removed him from the coalition government and every other leading position. This was then the beginning of his 'rebirth' as a master of survival. His take-off was ideal; the first public opinion polls and the media echo were excellent. Soon, however, Schüssel as Vice-Chancellor, and in the meantime Foreign Minister, committed his first major blunder. He called new elections in December 1995. The Social Democrats won an unexpected victory, increasing their share of the popular vote by 3.4 per cent while the ÖVP, hoping for a breakthrough, stagnated with a mere half per cent increase.

To this day, Schüssel still vigorously rejects the view held almost unanimously by observers that he deliberately provoked the elections. Be that as it may, he effortlessly survived the consequences. Then, at the first elections to the European Parliament in October 1996, Schüssel chose a well-known female TV journalist as top candidate on the list. Due to her popularity, the ÖVP managed to attain the first place—after many years—at a nationwide election. The right-wing FPÖ, however, increased its share to a record high of 27.5 per cent and captured 50 per cent of the workers' vote: alarm signals for Chancellor Vranitzky, who resigned a few months later.

One of the reasons why the Conservatives three years later opted for a partnership with the right-wing FPÖ was their anger over the takeover of the 'black' (i.e. belonging to the ÖVP sphere of influence) Creditanstalt Bankverein by the 'red' Bank of Austria (dominated by the Socialists). The deal between the basically state-owned banks was adroitly planned and brilliantly executed by the bankers close to the SPÖ. At that time and even now, Schüssel believes that the coalition partner had 'taken him for a ride'. Subsequently in 2000 the Bank of Austria became part of a Munich-based banking group, which in turn in 2005 was taken over by the Italian UniCredit bank. Schüssel regards the sell-out of the prestigious Creditanstalt as 'the greatest catastrophe of economic policy' in the history of post-war Austria. The political defeat of the ÖVP in the battle over the control of the Creditanstalt was seen later by independent observers as the prelude to the clinical death of the Great Coalition due to the gradual destruction of any kind of trust between the two major coalition parties.

If we want to analyze Schüssel's brilliant tactics during the crucial period between 2000 and 2002, it is worthwhile recalling a statement made by Kreisky in a lengthy interview in the autumn of 1982: '... looking back now, it is actually rather odd that my greatest political fiasco—in the Olah case [in 1964]—and at the same time my greatest personal defeat was the beginning of my success.'[10] Whatever one might say about the outcome of the parliamentary elections of 3 October 1999, it was doubtless the worst result for the People's Party since 1945, but at the same time it paved the way to Wolfgang Schüssel's triumph.

In the seemingly hopeless post-election situation, Schüssel proved his nerves of steel, as possibly the most astute political tactician in his party's history. Against the combined opposition of the SPÖ, still the number one party in terms of seats, the extremely active President Klestil, the mass circulation popular daily *Neue Kronen Zeitung* and a worried European Union, Schüssel finally achieved something that had seemed hitherto impossible: as leader of by now only the third largest party, he neither went into opposition (as promised prior to the election in case of a defeat) nor did he enter into a grand coalition with the SPÖ as a humiliated junior partner; instead he succeeded in forcing a weak and inconsistent head of state to swear him in as Chancellor of a small coalition. For the first time in the history of the Second Republic, Schüssel formed a coalition government with the FPÖ without a mandate from the Federal President. It was a particularly bitter defeat for Thomas Klestil, whose health was on the rocks, as was his reputation in wider Catholic circles due to his divorce and his long affair with a diplomat, whom he subsequently married.

During his second term in office after 2000—he was re-elected in 1998 as the joint Presidential candidate of the coalition partners—Klestil's relationship with Schüssel and with the government remained tense, and was marked by mutual resentment. Once at a ceremony in the Hofburg I virtually had to plead with him to exchange at least a few words with Foreign Minister Benita Ferrero-Walder. In particular the various spoken jibes as well as the malicious press reports concerning his private life deeply offended the ailing Klestil. More than once he agitatedly showed me insignificant provincial papers or low-circulation publications by ÖVP women's organizations containing spiteful remarks or news items mainly about his wife but also about himself. All this sounds banal in retrospect, but at the time the petty jealousies and small-minded 'boycott measures' between the Ballhausplatz and the Hofburg certainly did not contribute to the esteem of the republic abroad.

That both of Schüssel's 'master strokes' succeeded—setting up a government in February 2000 and the resounding election victory of November 2002—was not only due to his tactical finesse and strong nerves. The only chance for him to survive the worst electoral defeat was the Chancellorship. But the man who made that success possible at all was in fact Jörg Haider, the Governor of Carinthia: 'Schüssel could thank his rise first and foremost to the fact that Haider misjudged the situation and his personality', believes Josef Taus, the astute former ÖVP chairman. 'Haider underestimated Schüssel; had Haider remained in opposition for one more term, he would have received maybe 35 per cent at the next elections. The only chance for Schüssel at the time was a coalition with the FPÖ.'

The philosopher Rudolf Burger has a similar opinion of the situation: 'It is a moot question whether Schüssel wanted this from the beginning, or whether he failed because of the trade unions. The decision was basically right, and for the country the absolutely correct one. Had Schüssel not entered into this coalition, Haider would have received 34 or 35 per cent at the next election, or at the latest in 2003. This was the only chance to thwart Haider's landslide, even if that was not Schüssel's intention.' In a subsequently released exchange of letters with the former

161

INSIDE AUSTRIA

Chancellor Franz Vranitzky, Burger wrote the following: 'I consider the coalition unfortunate, but totally legitimate. After all, one cannot blame Schüssel for being more intelligent than his present opponents.'[11]

There are, however, a handful of high-ranking ÖVP politicians, as for instance Heinrich Neisser, the ex—Minister of Science, who categorically disapprove of the Schüssel course even today: 'Any collaboration with Haider is like an infectious disease; it makes you sick. I am convinced that the People's Party was damaged, and this 2000–2006 period was not a success. The People's Party shifted to the right, something I cannot endorse at all; it has in part adopted Haider's political manners, and I have to say, despite all of his successes, Haider has harmed this country tremendously. I have seen the way he attacked and ruined people, systematically. He was one of the most unscrupulous power politicians ever.'[12]

In our interview Jörg Haider regarded the forming of the black—blue coalition as undoubtedly the greatest success of his political life; he became stronger than the ÖVP, and he managed from a position of strength to enter government. He rejected the thesis that by remaining in opposition the Freedom Party might have achieved a larger percentage at a later date. According to him, after thirteen years in opposition that would have been impossible: 'If one does not want to govern, one should not vie for the voters. As far as the sanctions are concerned, it is certain that I was the reason for them. Still, I am not at fault. To impose sanctions on a democratically elected government is an out-and-out breach of the European Union Treaty. There is no problem with Berlusconi and the Poles.'[13]

Why then did Jörg Haider and his party suffer the greatest defeat in Austria's history only two and a half years after his 'greatest victory'? In November 2002 the Freedom Party slumped from 27 per cent to just 10 per cent, thereby losing two-thirds of its 1999 voters. In contrast, the People's Party scored its greatest and at the same time most unexpected electoral triumph: its percentage jumped from twenty-seven to forty-two, and it gained 800,000 more votes. For the first time since 1966 it once again became the strongest party and increased its seats from fifty-two to seventy-nine, while the Freedom Party's seats crashed from fifty-two to eighteen. Never before had any party gained proportionally as much in an election as the ÖVP, and never has any party lost as much as the FPÖ.

The architect of the defeat was in fact the same politician who had brought about the earlier turnaround: Jörg Haider. He, of course, saw the decisive mistake simply as stepping down as party leader on 1 May 2000 in favour of Vice-Chancellor Susanne Riess-Passer. In retrospect he claimed, with seemingly undiminished self-confidence, that he does not regret anything, not even on the subject of his famous 'gaffes'. Besides, 'he was always ahead of his time' as regards the immigrant question and the European Union.

All independent observers, and even more so Schüssel and Riess-Passer, are convinced that the morbid jealousy and hysterical reactions of this unpredictable and psychologically unstable politician shattered the same coalition that he initially extolled so effusively. The Governorship of Carinthia was not enough for him. Six months after setting up the government he began to hassle and to show on every possible occasion who had the last word in the Freedom Party. Susanne Riess-Passer had proved to be a capable, calm and trustworthy politician, and the young Finance Minister Karl-Heinz Grasser soon became very popular. Public opinion polls showed that, while Grasser and Riess-Passer ranked high on the popularity list, Haider's rating was slipping ever lower. 'The tragic part of the story was that the better we did in government, the harder it was to get on with him,' says Riess-Passer, and adds that Haider 'was an ingenious opposition politician'. For him polarization was a decisive element and provocation was an end in itself.

The fundamental rupture occurred when, without any prior notice to Riess-Passer, Haider flew to Baghdad on Shrove Monday of 2002 to meet with Saddam Hussein precisely when Riess-Passer was on her first official visit in Washington. The tension within the FPÖ reached its peak on a Saturday, 7 September 2002, when, prompted by Haider's loyalists, delegates of the fundamentalist wing of the party held an informal meeting in Knittelfeld, a small town in Styria. They passed a vote of no confidence in the FPÖ members of the government, and a close Haider associate demonstratively tore up the draft compromise signed the previous evening by both Haider and Riess-Passer. The following Sunday night in front of the TV cameras Susanne Riess-Passer announced her resignation, along with Finance Minister Karl-Heinz Grasser and the chief whip of the FPÖ parliamentary faction.

The next day Schüssel seized the initiative: instead of the compromise proposal expected by Haider, the Chancellor terminated the coalition and announced snap elections. Schüssel still insists that it was never his intention to kill his partner: 'The implosion of the FPÖ happened from the inside; until the Knittelfeld episode the Haider party had never slipped below 20 per cent.' Riess-Passer, who has left politics in the meantime, believes in retrospect that the black–blue coalition could have stayed in power for even three terms. And Haider? Riess-Passer was convinced that deep down Haider himself realized that he had essentially destroyed his own life's work, and what chances he could still have had...[14]

Is Schüssel then an ice-cold technician of power? A Social Democrat observer told me: 'Schüssel is the most intelligent power politician Austria ever had. He has an uncannily quick grasp of matters and he is cultured; there is only one thing that can be brought against him: he does not have a great political agenda, he has only his own right-conservative value concept.' According to Riess-Passer: 'He is by far the greatest professional, the best negotiator, who always thinks ten steps ahead.' In the words of Schüssel's formerly closest political friend: 'He is a gambler, a political survivor, but unquestionably also the cleverest power politician.' Haider thought likewise: 'Schüssel is the best, the most consistent negotiator, but if one knows him, it is not difficult to handle him.' Josef Taus also regards Schüssel in an unemotional manner: 'Schüssel was never popular. People as intelligent as he is are never popular. His problem is that anyone can convince him—and perhaps he can convince himself—that he is popular, but he isn't.' As a twice unsuccessful candidate for the Chancellorship, Taus was probably speaking from his own experience.

I first met Wolfgang Schüssel sometime during the seventies at a reception organized by the Economic Union of the ÖVP, and afterwards on several occasions when he was Minister for Economic Affairs. When he took over the Foreign Ministry together with the Vice-Chancellorship after Busek's retirement, our association, partly because I was then director of Radio Austria International, became considerably closer. I was always deeply impressed by his curiosity, openness and flexibility. In contrast to his predecessors and successors, he was always interested in the opinion of others, for example regarding East European politics.

Even after he became Chancellor in the black–blue coalition government, Schüssel remained just as relaxed, informal and open as he had been. He was the most intellectual and well-read Chancellor since Kreisky. His occasional 'philosopher lunches' in the Federal Chancellery for a maximum of twenty guests, including writers and philosophers, political scientists and artists, were always inspiring and challenging. He always kept a low profile as far as his private life and family were concerned. 'Offended, but not worn down', was how one of his best friends described the Chancellor's mood at the time of the fiercest attacks. A devout Catholic, Schüssel finds a sense of security and gains strength at the Benedictine monastery in Seckau in Styria where he withdraws for a weekend each year at the end of August with a dozen or so friends for meditation and discussion.

Wolfgang Schüssel is a modern politician with an excellent memory and a facility to speak freely before any audience without a manuscript or a teleprompter. I have frequently observed him reacting to speeches by visiting statesmen not with stock phrases but with improvised witty remarks. He always took a tremendous amount of time to prepare himself thoroughly for TV discussions and debates, and was one of the few people who could defeat Haider in a TV debate.

Even after his brilliant electoral victory in 2002 he remained the brunt of the media and the favourite target of many intellectuals. The profound aversion of the media, not only of the tabloids but also of the quality papers, is due not only to the fact that it was he who catapulted the Freedom Party to power. Schüssel does not let himself be appropriated; he refuses any 'back-scratching' with newspaper magnates and editors-in-chief. During his Chancellorship he abstained from any back-room deals with the mighty owners of magazines and tabloids. In brief, far from the case of Kreisky, there is not, nor was there any complicity between him and the media.

Schüssel's cool aloofness and authority, which sometimes spills over into arrogance, harmed him inside the small world of the Austrian media also during the four years of the second coalition with the FPÖ. Not only Erwin Pröll, the Governor of Lower Austria, who voted against the renewal of the black–blue coalition in the People's Party executive, but many other observers would have preferred a black–green experiment in 2003, i.e. a coalition with the (naturally also unpredictable) Green party.

The economic and social record of the much criticized first post-war centre-right government was mixed. Here I want to mention merely that the pension reform and budget consolidation, the privatizations and company tax reductions, the sponsorship of apprentice training and other measures had undoubtedly encouraged the economic upturn. On the basis of the figures for unemployment and inflation, balanced budget and likely growth, such independent sources as the respected *Frankfurter Allgemeine Zeitung* and influential economists spoke about Austria's 'golden years'.[15] A German futurologist and analyst living in Vienna even wrote an entire book on 'happy Austria', about the 'search for the Austrian secret'. He asked how this country could function so well 'despite all the Haiders and BAWAG scandals'? Why is Vienna rated the city with one of the highest standards of living (third in 2007 and equal second with Geneva in 2008) by an international survey?[16] The combination of economic upswing, social stability and industrial peace provided the indirect answer to these questions.

Yet despite these internationally acknowledged positive trends, at the elections in October 2006 the People's Party with Schüssel at the helm lost thirteen seats and 8 per cent of the vote. This result was a debacle both for the party and its leader. Schüssel resigned as Party Chairman and became subsequently chief whip of the ÖVP in parliament until 2009. The previous losses of the Governorships of Styria and Salzburg had already been early warning signs. Even though the Socialists also lost a few votes and one seat, they again captured the relative majority. Thus there was no other alternative than a grand coalition, now with the Social Democrat leader Alfred Gusenbauer as the next Chancellor.

This forty-seven-year-old professional politician has always regarded Bruno Kreisky as his political and human model ever since he was a leading socialist youth functionary. In the course of a two-hour-long conversation he told me the poignant story of how the frail Kreisky, whom he had frequently met for evening talks in his house, appeared at Gusenbauer's graduation ceremony at the University of Vienna. The position of the Chancellor in his party, however, came under fire soon after the victory, both by the media and more importantly by prominent party functionaries; Gusenbauer managed to gain only 75 per cent of the executive committee for the coalition agreement, under which the most important cabinet posts (foreign and interior affairs, finance, economy, justice) went to the weaker partner.

Why did Schüssel and his party lose the general election despite the scandals affecting BAWAG (the union bank) and the Trade Union Federation, both dominated by the Social Democrats? It is assumed that Schüssel and his party, particularly the regional organizations, were resting on their laurels. Schüssel himself told me: 'We were not fighting hard enough and—this is my fault—we forgot to make concrete proposals to the new voters whom we had won over in 2002; some

200,000 to 300,000 of them stayed at home.' It cannot be denied that arrogance and the presumption of certain victory played an important part. But Schüssel's image of social aloofness and human frigidity noted by many observers could also have contributed to the defeat. The shortcomings of the education and social policies as well as the unresolved problem of the private and public nursing systems for the elderly and sick certainly were further important negative factors.

Furthermore, from the very beginning and especially since 2002, most of the Freedom Party ministers of the coalition government were characterized by a bizarre mixture of dilettantism in their work and effrontery in squandering millions of public funds. The republic had to pay a high price for the favourites chosen by Haider and his sister, who for years was Minister of Social Affairs, and then in quick succession wrought havoc in the transport and economic portfolios.[17] One must add to all this the right-radical statements by some FPÖ functionaries and their contacts with groups accused of neo-Nazi tendencies. Between 2000 and 2002, a third of the FPÖ members of parliament belonged to extreme right-wing organizations.[18]

Nonetheless, the remarkable black–blue coalition leaves behind a legacy which was described by Friedrich von Schiller in his inaugural address as a professor of history at Jena in 1789—albeit in an entirely different context—as follows: 'Although the self-seeking man might pursue base goals, he unconsciously promotes excellent ones.'[19] Without this right of centre ÖVP–FPÖ government, parliament would probably not have voted unanimously in 2000–2001 for the belated yet highly significant international agreement on the compensation for former forced labourers and Holocaust victims. The first step had already been taken in 1995 when the Vranitzky government set up a National Fund (29,884 Austrian victims of the Nazi regime received 5,087 euros per capita as a symbolic payment for injustices suffered). Nevertheless the long overdue decision about restitution payments to forced labourers and persecuted Jews was approved by all members of parliament only at the initiative of the Schüssel government.

Following the July 2000 legislation establishing the Austrian Reconciliation Fund, 352 million euros were disbursed to 132,000 claimants from sixty-one countries, and the substantial residue was spent on various humanitarian projects. Many Austrians do not know that in 1944 there were 1 million forced labourers in Austria in addition to the 1.7 million 'free' employed persons. Chancellor Schüssel appointed

Maria Schaumayer, former president of the Austrian National Bank, as the government's representative for the negotiations with the US Special Representative for Holocaust Issues, Ambassador Stuart E. Eizenstat, who held top positions in the State Department and the Treasury during the Clinton administrations, as well as with other states and victims' organizations. The late Austrian Ambassador Ernst Sucharipa (later Director of the Diplomatic Academy) conducted the negotiations on restitution, but it was Wolfgang Schüssel whose leadership and personal commitment, according to the American diplomat, were indispensable. On a dozen occasions Schüssel personally met Eizenstat or the delegations. After seven hours of intensive preparatory negotiations, constantly interrupted by telephone conversations with representatives of various Jewish organizations in Washington and New York, the two of them achieved breakthrough in Schüssel's office on 5 October 2000.

In his book about the restitution negotiations in Switzerland, Germany and Austria, published in 2003, Eizenstat pays tribute to the two special representatives, Schaumayer and Sucharipa, but especially to Schüssel. According to Eizenstat's own admission, the fact that in the end a 1.1 milliard dollar package was agreed, not including the Viennese Jewish community's stolen artworks and other assets, was the outcome of exceedingly generous calculations. That is how they wanted at long last to 'pacify' the US lawyers and Ariel Muzicant, the Viennese Jewish community's extremely 'difficult' president, and to induce him to sign the agreement in Washington on 17 January 2001, just three days before the end of the Clinton administration.

Eizenstat wrote verbatim: 'Although Schüssel was a very tough negotiator who held his cards close to his chest, I would soon come to trust him as a person of his word ... his energy, intelligence, and intensity made him a significant presence... He believed he could reinforce the Freedom Party's moderates by giving them a taste of power and thus isolate them from their radical wing. (Time has proven him correct.)' Eizenstat's tête-à-tête talks with Schüssel were 'my most intensive negotiations with a head of government during all the years of my Holocaust pursuits... I believed that he truly wanted a solution and that he was acting with courage in a political environment that was far more difficult than Schröder's in Germany.'

The agreement regulates compensation for property, including those of Jewish organizations, leaseholds, personal valuables, insurance policies, real estate property, the increase of additional social benefits (health and pensions), prescribes the investigation of the provenance of art objects, as well as the various compensations to the Jewish community. The American top diplomat wrote his book of 400–odd pages with no-holds-barred frankness, including the chapters about Austria.

At this point, I must confess that I am not a dispassionate chronicler as far as the matter of the forced labourers is concerned. Maria Schaumayer told Eizenstat that, as a young girl living in the province of Burgenland near the Hungarian border, one haunting image stuck with her more than any: one day in the bitterly cold winter of 1944–5 she saw a procession of wretched figures pass by, guarded by armed soldiers. As she later discovered, they were Hungarian Jews, seized and commandeered by the SS and the Hungarian Nazis to build the so-called 'South Eastern Defence Wall' in Eastern Austria. The earlier restitution regulation had not covered this group of victims. She was proud, Maria Schaumayer stated, that Austria was able to identify and compensate this group through the Reconciliation Fund. Incidentally, as she confided to Eizenstat, it was not until she heard a historian's lecture on the plight of Hungarian Jews more than half a century later that she realized what she had seen as a child.[20]

As a fifteen-year-old, on 20 October 1944 I too was deported from Budapest by the Arrow Cross and herded from one place to another.[21] The death march toward the Austrian border began in icy wind and rain. Totally exhausted men and women were lying in the ditches. Shots rang out from time to time. In November, I managed to flee with an older mate in the vicinity of Budapest. Otherwise I might have been among the thousands of doomed people Maria Schaumayer saw somewhere near the Hungarian border in Austria. Many, very many, completely worn-out forced labourers were shot or beaten to death at the time in Western Hungary or in nearby Austria by Waffen-SS henchmen or rabid Hitler Jugend activists.

As president of the Austrian National Bank, Maria Schaumayer was for many years chairperson—and a very helpful one at that—of the *Europäische Rundschau*'s board of trustees. In my capacity as editor-in-chief and co-publisher we had frequent conversations, but never about the Second World War. That is why I was so touched by her personal story, which I found out only from Eizenstat's book.

Max Born, the physicist, said once that in some cases a catastrophe produces also something good as 'there is nothing more beneficial and refreshing for a person than when he loses his roots and puts down new roots in an entirely different environment.' In view of all the crimes that I had seen and personally experienced under the brown and red dictatorships, I have always felt it my obligation, consciously or unconsciously, to protect the country where I have struck new roots over fifty years, both from internal and external dangers. In the Waldheim case and later in regard to sanctions I not only stood up for Austria out of gratitude for her giving me a home, but also because hysteria and demonization as a reaction to the various versions of right-wing radicalism are just as dangerous as the repression and minimization of these phenomena.

The philosopher Rudolf Burger coined the expression 'dragon slayer' for Schüssel in 2002, because his sweeping victory seemed to herald the end of Jörg Haider's political career as a national figure, even though he carried on as Governor of Carinthia. Schüssel at that time may have destroyed Haider's dream of ever becoming Federal Chancellor, but this did not mean the disappearance of the so-called 'third camp'. It split into two factions, but even at the 2006 general elections the 'new' Freedom Party (minus Haider and headed by the young Heinz-Christian Strache) and its rival, the orange-coloured BZÖ (set up by the disgruntled Haider and based primarily in his Carinthia), jointly received 15 per cent of the votes.

18

BATTLE FOR POWER: THREAT TO STABILITY

There have been phenomenal twists and turns in Austrian politics since the Schüssel era: above all the surprisingly quick downfall of the new Chancellor and Social Democratic Party Chairman, Alfred Gusenbauer; the snap election provoked by the Vice-Chancellor and People's Party leader, Wilhelm Molterer, and his subsequent fall; combined with the re-emergence of a powerful, even if for the time being split, radical right-wing bloc in the newly elected parliament; all these events have opened a new phase of uncertainty. With the increasingly unpopular 'grand coalition', and lacking any acceptable parliamentary alternatives, the country is for the time being back to the routine of two scorpions in a bottle.

What happened in the years 2007–8 could have been taken from the script of a political thriller. Chancellor Gusenbauer was of humble origins (his father was a bricklayer, his mother a char), born in a small town, but generally regarded as a brilliant intellectual, equally at ease in English and French, Spanish and Italian; he was well read and a man of the world. However, despite his long career in the socialist youth movement, he failed to win the hearts of the party members and of the Austrians in general. Regarded as conceited and aloof, with blunders in internal communication and slipping in the popularity polls, Gusenbauer also alienated the powerful trade union officials. After the Social Democrats lost several regional elections, the party leaders, above all the powerful mayor and Party Chairman in Vienna, decided to get rid of the Chancellor, who had become an electoral liability. Fighting for his survival, Gusenbauer in June 2008 pushed through the election of Werner Faymann, Minister of Infrastructure and Transport, as executive Party Chairman. He told the press, however, that he was determined to remain as Chancellor and would lead the SPÖ at the next election. A few days later Gusenbauer and Faymann wrote a joint letter to Hans Dichand, the publisher of the *Kronen Zeitung* and a sharp critic of the European Union, in which they pledged to call for an immediate referendum about any major changes in the union. The letter was generally regarded as a demeaning capitulation before the eighty-seven-year-old powerful media mogul.

However the situation completely changed on 7 July. Seeing the disarray in the Socialist ranks, the dramatic decline of Gusenbauer's authority and popularity, and relying on internal opinion polls predicting a relative majority for his party, the ÖVP leader and Vice-Chancellor Molterer attacked the turnaround in the policy of his coalition partner towards the EU and forced snap elections. The SPÖ reacted immediately: Gusenbauer announced his resignation from all his positions and the party executive nominated Werner Faymann as the top candidate; four weeks later, at a hastily convened SPÖ congress, he was duly elected by 98 per cent of the delegates as new Party Chairman.

It soon became evident that Vice-Chancellor Wilhelm Molterer, the amiable ÖVP politician, had committed one of the most fateful blunders in modern Austrian history. His own party was not prepared at all for the campaign, the posters came late and were of poor quality, the long-winded slogans and his colourless appearances failed to stir interest let alone enthusiasm, even among the party faithful. Several powerful regional chieftains were for reasons of finance and interest against the idea of the snap election.

The political initiative was immediately seized by the Social Democrats, who had engaged the country's most formidable advertising agency, and quickly presented in mid-summer a series of popular proposals for tax cuts, greater welfare benefits and the elimination of university fees. The letter to the *Kronen-Zeitung* publisher helped to win the total support of a daily which in terms of per capita comparisons ranks as the newspaper with the largest circulation in the world: in a country with 6.3 million eligible voters it can boast of 3.8 million readers and a circulation of 800,000 copies. Almost every fifth potential voter reads daily only this paper. Publisher Dichand publicly reckoned that his support for Faymann and thus for the SPÖ must have meant more than an additional 3 per cent support, as estimated by a well-known polling expert.

As a result of its quick reaction and the disciplined silence of Gusenbauer, despite his shabby treatment by his comrades, the SPÖ managed to retain the number one position. However, it was a Pyrrhic victory: despite the cult of Faymann in the *Kronen-Zeitung* and his better popularity ratings than those of his main rival, the Social Democrats lost ten seats in parliament and their share of the votes fell by more than 6 per cent to just over 29 per cent, their lowest ever poll since 1945. It was a meagre consolation that the People's Party led by the hapless Molterer fared even worse: it lost 8.2 per cent and sixteen seats, the worst ever performance of the Conservatives since 1945. No wonder that Molterer almost immediately resigned and was replaced by the hitherto Minister of Agriculture, Josef Pröll (nephew of the Lower Austrian Governor Erwin Pröll, who in March 2008 scored his biggest ever triumph with 53 per cent at the local elections).

To sum up, the real losers were the two coalition parties, who for the first time since 1945 also lost their two-thirds majority, which is an essential condition for passing important laws.[1] The real winners of the unexpected poll were the two right-wing parties: the FPÖ led by Heinz-Christian Strache, which received 17.5 per cent, up by a third from 2006, and gained fourteen additional seats; even more surprisingly Haider's BZÖ jumped from 4.1 per cent to almost 11 per cent and also trebled the number of its seats to twenty-one. The surge in right-wing votes meant in fact that the two parties together were as strong as the two coalition parties. These also paid a high price for their hasty decision to reduce voting age from eighteen to sixteen years. As a result, almost every second voter in this group voted for the FPÖ, and in the group of young voters under thirty the two right-wing parties captured 36 per cent. Thus the reduction in age limit proved to have been a boomerang. It was particularly the young and dashing Strache, almost twenty years Haider's junior, who profited from this move. The Social Democrats were also faced with the fact that the Freedomites and the BZÖ gained more votes among the male and female workers than the SPÖ. All these trends became even more pronounced in the traditionally Socialist districts in Vienna at the June 2009 elections to the European Parliament.

It must also be stressed that the September 2008 election was Jörg Haider's personal success story. With unparalleled energy the Governor of Carinthia (at the same time Chairman and top candidate of the BZÖ) addressed innumerable meetings and thus managed to treble the number of BZÖ seats in parliament. His triumph was particularly impressive in Carinthia where his BZÖ polled 38.5 per cent of the votes, almost 50 per cent more than two years earlier.

During the campaign he was more restrained and more subtle in his attacks against the coalition government and in setting the right-wing agenda with regard to immigration and schools than his younger rival Heinz-Christian Strache. In the TV duels he was the only top candidate who gained higher ratings by the viewers than the percentage his BZÖ achieved at the election. At fifty-eight he projected once again a different image on the screen: almost statesmanlike and not recklessly aggressive, a mature politician concerned about the low income groups, and not a radical right-wing populist attacking the coalition.

At 1.15 a.m. on Saturday 11 October, Jörg Haider was driving alone, drunk, at a speed of 142 k.p.h., twice as fast as was allowed on this stretch in the outskirts of Klagenfurt, the provincial capital. After overtaking a small car, he lost control of the large official limousine, which hit a concrete pillar and then overturned. He died immediately. The tragedy of this controversial figure shocked the country, and above all Carinthia. His state funeral, transmitted live by the Austrian television network and also covered by the international media, was attended by the Federal President and all the political dignitaries.

Subsequent events, including the European elections, indicate the return to the pattern of the late 1990s, when the coalition was gridlocked due to disagreements between the parties, and Haider's FPÖ became the second strongest political group with 26.9 per cent of the votes. Now the two right-wing parties could claim the support of 28.2 per cent of the national electorate. It is likely that they will eventually merge again, paving the way whether they will eventually merge again, paving the way for the emergence of 'Haiderism without Haider'. The far right is undoubtedly on the rise again, profiting from the resentment of immigrants and fear of rising crime attributed to the influx of foreigners and job losses.

The global financial crisis of course affects the state of affairs and the national mood, even in the fourth most prosperous member state in the European Union. The very fact that Austria has been a highly successful pace maker in the European openings to the East, involving massive investments by banks and industries in Central and Eastern Europe, has lately engendered concern about the economic outlook. However, all financial and economic data indicate that in terms of the real economy (GDP, unemployment, exports, employment etc.) Austria is still doing comparatively better than most other European countries. Since 2000, the economy consistently expanded faster than the Eurozone average.

Bearing in mind the economic success story since 1945, and the underlying strength of small- and medium-sized businesses, as well as the still functioning partnership between the two sides of industry, one should not dramatize the temporary economic setbacks. In view of the (controversial) extension of the term of the legislature from four to five years, the grand coalition could still have time to learn from past mistakes and to tackle the pressing unresolved issues. Nevertheless, the ability of the coalition government to maintain stability has come so far at the cost of shirking crucial long-term problems, such as pensions, health and education.

All in all, Austria is still the model of a successful political and economic experiment after the disintegration of the empire and the harrowing experiences of wars and dictatorship. This is why the gap between Austria and its post-Communist neighbours, in terms of living and social standards and of political stability, is still as large as ever.

Unfortunately the latest election results and all the opinion surveys indicate a continued forward march of the extreme xenophobic right-wing, mainly in Vienna and other urban centres. The general decline of European social democracy is particularly pronounced in Austria, and the right-wing populist FPÖ, led by the telegenic and recklessly provocative Hans-Christian Strache, has managed to score impressive successes in the working-class districts of Vienna. The weak performance of the Faymann–Pröll coalition government and new successes of the Freedomites, who could sooner than expected swallow up the remnants of the Haider BZÖ party outside Carinthia, create optimal conditions for growing political instability. Despite the impressive post World War Two balance sheet of the Second Republic, anti-Moslem and anti-Semitic outbursts and coded messages indicate the possible return of the old demons. The mixture of rising anti-foreign sentiment and the fear of growing unemployment, combined with the fall-out from the recession, remains a classic breeding ground for far-right extremist and populist groups. One must not forget that since 1918 independent Austria provided ample proof for stranger reversals of fortune than those experienced in most other European countries. Once again this small, independent, neutral country—despite an unparalleled level of social stability and economic prosperity—will have to walk, as so often in the past, along a political knife-edge.

NOTES

1. INTRODUCTION: WHY DID I WRITE THIS BOOK?

1. For my adventures in Hungary and the road to freedom, see Paul Lendvai, *Blacklisted*, London: I. B. Tauris, 1999.
2. Cf. for details Paul Lendvai, trans. Ann Major, *One Day that Shook the Communist World*, Princeton, 2008, esp. pp. 195–210.
3. In *Europäische Rundschau*, Wien, 1995/2, p. 9.

2. AUSTRIAN CLICHÉS: THE MEDIA CURTAIN

1. Bruno Kreisky, *Zwischen den Zeiten*, Wien, 1986, p. 292; cf. also *Süddeutsche Zeitung*, München, 19.2.1988.
2. E. H. Carr, *What is History?*, London: 1961, revised edn ed. R.W. Davies, Harmondsworth: Penguin, 1986, p. 30.
3. Ernst Bruckmüller in the exhibition catalogue 'Das neue Österreich', Wien, 2005, pp. 241–54; cf. also his book *Nation Österreich*, 2nd enl. edn, Wien, 1996.
4. Erwin Ringel, 'Neue Rede über Österreich' in H. Rauscher (ed.), *Das Buch Österreich*, Wien, 2005, pp. 46–69.
5. Carl Zuckmayer, *Als wär's ein Stück von mir*, Frankfurt am Main, 1966, pp. 70–78.
6. Cf. Oliver Rathkolb, *Die paradoxe Republik*, Wien, 2005, pp. 357–98.
7. For the quotes of Bischof see *Europäische Rundschau*, Wien, 2005/2, pp. 3–21. Heinz Fischer, *Überzeugungen*, Wien, 2006, pp. 63, 74–5.
8. Ernst Hanisch in A. Pelinka and E. Weinzierl (eds), *Das Große Tabu*, Wien, 1987.

3. THE VICTIM MYTH AND 'ZERO HOUR' 1945

1. For the murder of thousands of Hungarian Jews, see Szabolcs Szita, *Verschleppt, verhungert, vernichtet: die Deportation von ungarischen Juden auf*

das Gebiet des annektierten Österreich 1944–45, Wien, 1999. I evaded the death march to the Austrian—Hungarian border by my escape in November 1944; cf. Paul Lendvai, *Blacklisted*.

2. Dieter Stiefel, 'Entnazifizierung in Österreich' in Henk/Woller (eds), *Politische Säuberung in Eurioa*, München, 1991.
3. For the text of the Declaration of Independence see H. Rauscher (ed.), *Das Buch Österreich*, pp. 431–4. For the full text of the Federal President's speeches cf. Heinz Fischer, *Überzeugungen*, pp. 73–55, 83–6.
4. For the atmosphere and the course of events cf. Ernst Trost, *Figl von Österreich*, Wien, 1972, pp. 11–14.
5. Rudolf Burger in *Merkur*, München, 1995, pp. 59–67.
6. Stourzh, op. cit., pp. 60–61. The author also deplored the 'lack of moral insight of feeling shame for the crimes committed by one's countrymen even by those who were not personally to blame for them.' (ibid.).

4. FOUNDING FATHER OF MANY FACES

1. Ramin Jahanbegloo, *Conversations with Isaiah Berlin*, London: Orion, 1992.
2. Cf. Bruno Kreisky's Memoirs, *Zwischen den Zeiten*, pp. 220–22.
3. Cf. Viktor Reimann, *Zu groß für Österreich, Seipel und Bauer im Kampf um die Erste Republik*, Wien, 1968.
4. Jacques Hannak, *Karl Renner und seine Zeit*, Wien, 1965, pp. 650–53.
5. Kreisky, op. cit., p. 46. Renner's Jewish son-in-law, his two sons and his daughter were also at risk as 'half-Jews' and had to emigrate to Britain; Hannak, op. cit., p. 653.
6. For the exchange of letters and the conjectures about the background cf. Hannak, op. cit., pp. 671–7; for Renner's and Scheltov's roles, see Ernst Trost, *Figl von Österreich*, pp. 66–71, 169.
7. *Observer*, October 1949, quoted in Hannak, op. cit., p. 671.

5. THE ROLE OF A FOREIGN CORRESPONDENT

1. Theodor-Herzl lecture, Vienna, 2005.
2. There are today 17 dailies in Austria; in 1959 there were 35 daily papers, 6 Monday papers, and 124 weeklies; cf. *Medienpioniere erzählen* (Media pioneers tell), Wien, 2004, pp. 9–11.

6. COMPROMISE: THE BASIC PRINCIPLE OF SOCIAL PARTNERSHIP

1. cf. Georg Simmel, *Soziologie*, Collected works, Vol. 2, 4th edn, Berlin, 1958, p. 250.
2. Hermann Withalm, cf. *Aufzeichnungen* (Notes), Wien, 1973, pp. 41–3.
3. Josef Taus in *Europäische Rundschau*, Wien, 2005/1, pp. 65–80.

4. Cf. Alfred Klose, in *Europäische Rundschau*, Wien, 1977/3, pp. 79–85.
5. Cf. Egon Matzner, in *Europäische Rundschau*, Wien, 1983/1, pp. 141–6.
6. Taus, ibid.
7. The other two were the *Arbeiter-und Angestelltenbund* and the *Bauern-bund* (Federation of Employees and Workers and the Peasant League). Since that time three more part-organizations were established for women, youth and senior citizens.
8. In 1986, 21 of the 76 ÖVP deputies belonged to the *Wirtschaftsbund*.
9. All quotations of Busek and Schüssel are from tape-recorded conversations conducted from February to April 2007.
10. Interview in *Europäische Rundschau*, Wien, 1980/2, p. 20.

7. THE ECONOMIC MIRACLE

1. Hans Weigel in *Europäische Rundschau*, Wien, 1977/2, pp. 85–9.
2. Ernst Trost, *Figl*, op. cit., p. 49.
3. Hans Seidel, *Österreichs Wirtschaft und Wirtschaftspolitik nach dem Zweiten Weltkrieg*, Wien, 2005.
4. Herbert Krejci in *Europäische Rundschau*, Wien, 1983/1, p. 137.
5. Karl Aiginger in H. Androsch, H. Krejci, P. Weiser (eds), *Das neue Öster-reich*, Wien, 2006, p. 26. For Switzerland cf. *Neue Züricher Zeitung am Sonntag*, 7.1.2007.
6. Aiginger, op. cit., pp. 25–8.

8. THE CRISIS YEARS OF THE COALITION

1. Cf. Karl Pisa, 1945, *Geburt der Zukunft*, Wien, 2005, pp. 125–30.
2. Barbara Tóth, *Karl von Schwarzenberg, Die Biografie*, Vienna, 2005, pp. 87–90. In conversations with me, ex Vice-Chancellor Erhard Busek and the former Styrian Governor Josef Krainer jun. described their futile endeavours to have him appointed as Austrian Foreign Minister or State Secretary; see also Tóth, ibid., pp. 101–2.
3. Cf. Pisa, op. cit., pp. 124–30.
4. Fischer, *Überzeugungen*, p. 12.

9. THE REFORMER JOSEF KLAUS

1. Quotations about and by Klaus in this and the following chapter are from his memoirs, *Macht und Ohnmacht in Österreich*, Wien, 1971; from inter-views in R. Kriechbaumer (ed), *Die Ära Josef Klaus*, Vol. 2, Wien, 1999; as well as from conversations I had with political and media personalities in January-April 2007.
2. For the full text cf. *Die TAT*, Zurich, 25.2.1964; see also *Financial Times*, London, 26.2.1964, 'Men and Matters'.

3. Although Gorbach would have been an ideal candidate by virtue of his concentration camp past and his conciliatory disposition, at the time the notion of a balance of powers still shaped the attitude of many voters: red Federal President and black Federal Chancellor.

10. THE SPLENDOUR AND MISERY OF THE ÖVP GOVERNMENT

1. Cf. Beatrice Weinmann, *A Biography of Josef Klaus, Ein großer Österreicher*, Wien, 2000, pp. 110–11.
2. Cf. interview with Lujo Tončić-Sorinj in Kriechbaumer, op.cit., pp. 11–22.
3. Klaus, op. cit., p. 234.
4. Extract from the speech: 'An die Slowenen in Kärnten' in W. Ettmayer, E. Thurnher (eds), *Josef Klaus, Führung und Auftrag—Ausgewählte Reden und Aufsätze*, Graz/Vienna /Cologne, 1985, pp. 45–9.
5. Friedrich Nietzsche, *Menschliches, Allzumenschliches*, München, 1994, p. 258.
6. See his foreword in Weinmann, *Klaus*, pp. 17–22.
7. Bacher, op. cit., p. 22.
8. Weinmann, *Klaus*, pp. 185–7; for Hanisch cf. *Transformation*, ibid., pp. 21–2; for Bacher see Weinmann, ibid., Preface.
9. Interviews with Erwin Pröll and Josef Taus; cf. also Karl Pisa, op.cit., pp. 159–62 and Weinmann, op. cit., p. 313.
10. Cf. my interviews.
11. Quotes from Weinmann, op. cit., pp. 349–56.
12. Interview with me on 5.2.2007.

11. KREISKY'S SECRET POWER BASE

1. For Thurnher cf. *Das Trauma, ein Leben—Österreichische Einzelheiten*, Wien, 2000, p. 48; for Leser, *Salz der Gesellschaft*, Wien, 1988, pp. 187–240; Vorhofer in W. Gatty, G. Schmid, M. Steiner, D. Wiesinger (eds), *Die Ära Kreisky*, Innsbruck/Wien, 1997, pp. 150–61.
2. The reflexions about Kreisky's personality and politics also contain partly updated versions of my memoirs, *Blacklisted*.
3. The term 'greatest communicator' was coined by the political scientist Christine Teuber-Weckersdorf, in *Die Ära Kreisky*, p. 123.
4. Cf. Heribert Prantl, *Süddeutsche Zeitung*, München, 21.3.2007.
5. Cf. my interview of 10 January 2000 for the TV documentary 'Kreisky— Licht und Schatten einer Ära' (with Helene Maimann); Kreisky obituary, *Die Presse*, Wien, 20 July 1990.
6. See *Kleine Zeitung*, Graz /Klagenfurt, 1 April 1973.
7. *Europäische Rundschau*, Wien, 1981/1.

12. SHADOWS OF THE NAZI PAST: KREISKY VERSUS WIESENTHAL

1. For details cf. Simon Wiesenthal, *Recht, nicht Rache*, Berlin, 1988, pp. 354–60.
2. Cf. Paul Lendvai, 'Unbewältigtes in Österreich' in *Der Monat*, Berlin, Sept. 1967, pp. 15–30.
3. Heinz Fischer, *Reflexionen*, Wien, 1998, pp. 167–8.
4. Wiesenthal, op. cit., pp. 360–73.
5. Cf. Paul Lendvai, *Antisemitism without Jews*, New York, 1972.
6. Fischer, op. cit., pp. 171–2; see also his *Die Kreisky-Jahre*.
7. See in W. Gatty, G. Schmid, M. Steiner, D. Wiesinger (eds), *Die Ära Kreisky*, pp. 139–43.
8. Wolfgang Petritsch, *Bruno Kreisky*, Wien/Zürich/München, 2000, p. 118.

13. THE RIDDLE OF MINISTER RÖSCH, OR THE BROWN STAINS OF THE SOCIALISTS

1. *Profil*, Wien, 2 Jan. 1975, 'Polizeiakte Rösch', pp. 13–19.
2. Cf. Simon Wiesenthal, *Recht, nicht Rache*, Berlin, pp. 69–71.
3. Maria Wirth on Otto Rösch in M. Mesner (ed.), *Entnazifizierung zwischen politischem Anspruch, Parteienkonkurrenz und Kaltem Krieg—Das Beispiel der SPÖ* Wien, 2005, pp. 320–25. Heinz Fischer attacks *Der Spiegel* and Wiesenthal, and acquits Rösch without any qualification. In *Reflexionen*, op. cit., p. 218.
4. She quotes Kreisky in *Profil*, op. cit. 'When I returned from the Swedish emigration to Austria, I was aghast that I was surrounded by people like Rösch. I simply could not understand it. The then Styrian Provincial Party Secretary Taurer ... convinced me after a nightlong discussion that Rösch was alright. After all, he had been sent there with the party's knowledge and on its behalf. Naturally it was a bold idea. Whether Taurer or Rösch himself had thought of it, I do not know.' In this context we have to remember also the warning by the member of parliament, Karl Mark: 'When Kreisky returned from Sweden, he once said: "You are treating the Nazis far too well, with kid gloves." When someone comes home from abroad, he can be certain he does not know what has happened here. He cannot know it, but we could observe it. After all, we saw that there was a difference between one Nazi and another, and they should not be tarred with the same brush.' Quoted in Neugebauer and Schwartz, *Der Wille zum aufrechten Gang*, op. cit., pp. 307–8.
5. Cf. M. Mesner, *Entnazifizierung*, pp. 277–9.

14. POWER STRUGGLE IN THE 'COURT OF THE SUN KING'

1. Cf. Liselotte Palme, *Androsch—Ein Leben zwischen Geld und Macht*, Wien, 1999.

2. In March 1989 an appeals court confirmed the guilty verdict and the fine. An appeal against the 26 May 1996 verdict of the panel of judges in the matter of the tax evasion charge was rejected by the High Court.
3. From my interview with the Federal President on 22 March 2007.
4. Telephone conversation with Herbert Salcher on 5 June 2007. In an account of his tax case, Hannes Androsch accused Herbert Lugmayer, the manager of the Zentralsparkasse, and Erwin Lanc, the former minister and an employee of the Zentralsparkasse, of having made information on his bank account public 'in violation of banking privacy'.
5. Heinz Fischer, op. cit., p. 363.
6. From my interview with Franz Vranitzky on 29 January 2007.
7. From my interview with Hannes Androsch on 16 January 2007.
8. Rainer Paris, 'Neid' in *Merkur*, München, 2006/11.
9. Barbara Liegl and Anton Pelinka, *Chronos und Ödipus. Der Kreisky—Androsch-Konflikt*, Wien, 2004, p. 175.
10. As early as February 1968, when he was Chairman of the Social Democratic party and leader of the opposition, he asked me to take part in his stead at the very important international Bilderberg Conference held that year at Mont Tremblant in Canada. Cf. regarding details Paul Lendvai, *Blacklisted*.
11. Cf. Norbert Leser, *Salz der Gesellschaft*, pp. 147–85.
12. In his memoirs Olah refers to some unresolved circumstances ('dark stains') in Broda's life during the war and in 1945, and hints that these unanswered questions might explain Broda's opposition to his appointment to Interior Minister; ibid., pp. 252–60. According to verbal information by the Communist scientist and resistance fighter, Eduard Rabofsky (1911–94), Broda did not break with the Austrian Communist party fully and in writing until 1949, and not in 1945.
13. Leser, ibid., pp. 150–51.
14. Interviews for my television documentary, 10 and 11 January 2000.
15. Bruno Kreisky, *Im Sturm der Politik*, Berlin /Wien, 1988, pp. 391–3.
16. M. Mesner (ed.), *Entnazifizierung*, op. cit., pp. 286–7.
17. Leser, ibid., pp. 230–31.
18. Neugebauer and Schwartz, *Der Wille zum aufrechten Gang*, pp. 193–7.
19. *Kleine Zeitung*, Graz/Klagenfurt, 24 July 1982.

15. THE WALDHEIM AFFAIR AND THE MISFORTUNE OF A SUCCESSOR

1. From my interviews with Haider (14 February 2007), with Neisser (5 February 2007), with Cap (5 February 2007) and Lacina (15 January 2007).
2. On Michels see his book *Zur Soziologie des Parteiwesens in der Modernen Demokratie*, Leipzig, 1911; 2nd edn, Stuttgart, 1957
3. Wiesenthal, *Recht, nicht Rache*, pp. 380–94. This chapter, balanced and rich in facts, as indeed is the whole 468-page book, is ignored by important

NOTES pp. [130–147]

historical writings about the period; cf. the bibliographies in Peter Pelinka, op. cit., and Oliver Rathkolb, op. cit.
4. Quoted in Leser, *Salz der Gesellschaft*, p. 253.
5. Interview with Graff on 18 January 2007 and with Busek on 2 February 2007.
6. Waldheim himself later admitted the regrettable formulation: 'The sentence about fulfilment of duty ... was probably not a fortunate expression, but a mistake!' He stated that 'in the heat of the debate I probably did not show enough compassion for the victims of National Socialism.' *Profil*, Wien, 6 April 1998. On the extracts from Fischer's speech see his *Reflexionen*, pp. 454–5.
7. On 28 September 1973 Arab terrorists attacked a train at Marchegg and took three Soviet Jews and an Austrian customs officer hostage. They demanded the closing of the Schönau transit camp. After the relevant promise of the Austrian government, they freed the hostages, and the three terrorists were allowed to fly out on 29 September.
8. Cf. 'Österreich im Zerrspiegel', *Kleine Zeitung*, Graz/Klagenfurt, 28 October 1973.
9. My relevant efforts can be found in part in *Blacklisted*.

16. THE VRANITZKY DECADE OF RELATIVE STABILITY

1. Cf. Franz Vranitzky, *Politische Erinnerungen*, Wien, 2004, pp. 185–93.
2. O. Rathkolb, J. Kunz, M. Schmidt (eds), *Kreisky, Der Memoiren dritter Teil*, Wien, 2005, p. 325.
3. Cf. Vranitzky, op. cit., pp. 304–6.
4. Vranitzky, ibid., pp. 224–30. Interview with Rudolf Streicher on 22 May 2007.
5. For an extremely critical appraisal, not only from a foreign political point of view, see Trautl Brandstaller, 'Quo vadis SPÖ?' in *Europäische Rundschau*, Wien, 2004/2, pp. 67–79
6. Vranitzky, op. cit., pp. 239–42.
7. Cf. my interview with Rudolf Burger on 14 May 2007; see also 'Abschied von einem Staatsmann' in *Der Falter*, Wien, 26 February 1997.
8. See his brilliant characterization of Haider in 'Romantisches Österreich', *Wespennest*, Wien, December 1999; 'Austromanie oder der antifaschistische Karneval' in *Ptolemäische Vermutungen*, Lüneburg, 2001, pp. 99–123, 239.
9. Anneliese Rohrer, *Charakterfehler*, Wien, 2005, p. 173.
10. See the *Der Westentaschen-Haider* and *Haider, beim Wort genommen* collection of quotations, both Wien, 2000.
11. Hans Pretterebner, *Der Fall Lucona*, Wien, 1987.
12. Rohrer, op. cit, pp. 96–9.
13. Brandstaller, op. cit., p. 78.
14. Rohrer, op. cit, pp. 188–9.

183

17. SCHÜSSEL, RISE AND FALL OF A PLAYER

1. Max Weber, *Politics as a Vocation*.
2. Cf. for my comments the new, revised and enlarged edition of *Auf schwarzen Listen*, 2004.
3. Cf. Nachlese spezial, *Das Magazin des ORF*, March 2000.
4. Wolfgang Böhm, Otmar Lahodynsky, *Der Österreich-Komplex*, Wien, 2001, p. 60.
5. For Burger, ibid., p. 117; for Juncker, Böhm /Lahodynsky, ibid., p. 74.
6. *FAZ*, 7.2.2000, p. 11.
7. Interview on 14.2.2007.
8. Interviews with Wolfgang Schüssel on 23.2., 8.3. and 3.4.2007; see also Gerfried Sperl, *Der Machtwechsel*, Wien, 2000, pp. 20–22. The statements and arguments in the interviews with me were basically repeated at great length in Wolfgang Schüssel's reminiscenes (noted by Alexander Purger) in the book 'Offengelegt' (Salzburg 2009).
9. Cf. Heinz Fischer, *Wende Zeiten*, ibid., pp. 95–104; Sperl, ibid., pp. 57–66; Böhm/Lahodynsky, ibid., pp. 49–65; Peter Pelinka, Wolfgang Schüssel, Wien 2003, pp. 94–101; Hugo Portisch, in *Nachlese*, ibid., p. 41.
10. ORF TV interview with Franz Kreuzer, televised in the autumn of 1982. For an abridged version edited by Franz Kreuzer see *Europäische Rundschau*, Wien, 1983/1.
11. Interview with Rudolf Burger, 14.5.2007. The letter is dated 9.1.2001.
12. Interview with Heinrich Neisser on 5.2.2007.
13. Interview with Jörg Haider on 14.2.2007.
14. Interview with Riess-Passer on 12.4.2007.
15. 25.6.2007.
16. See Matthias Horx, *Glückliches Österreich*, Wien, 2006.
17. See *Profil*, 5.3.2007.
18. G. Sperl, *Die umgefärbte Republik*, Wien, 2003.
19. Quoted in *Die Zeit*, Hamburg, Joachim Riedl, 21.6.2007
20. Stuart E. Eisenstat, *Unvollkommene Gerechtigkeit*, München, 2003 pp. 352–69.
21. See my memoirs for details, *Blacklisted*.

18. BATTLE FOR POWER: THREAT TO STABILITY

1. Beginning with the election in 1990 the voter participation fell from 86% to 78,8% in the year 2008. The proportion of the majority held by the two major parties ÖVP and SPÖ has fallen since 1983 (90,9%) continuously and reached an absolute nadir with 55,3% in 2008 thus losing the two-thirds majority needed for passing constitutional laws.

POLITICAL CHRONOLOGY AUSTRIA 1945-2008[1]

General Elections

Year	ÖVP	SPÖ	FPÖ	GREENS
1945 (165 seats)	85	76		
1949	77	67	16	
1953	74	73	14	
1956	82	74	6	
1959	79	78	8	
1962	81	76	8	
1966	85	74	6	
1970	78	81	6	
1971 (183 seats)	80	93	10	
1975	80	93	10	
1979	77	95	11	
1983	81	90	12	
1986	77	80	18	8
1990	60	80	33	10
1994	52	65	42	13
1995	53	71	40	9
1999	52	65	52	14
2002	79	69	18	17
2006	66	68	21	21
2008	51	57	34	20

[1] Other parties: The Communist Party of Austria (KPÖ) had 3 to 5 seats between 1945 and 1956. The Liberals (Liberales Forum) had 11 seats in 1994 and 10 seats in 1995. The BZÖ (Bündnis Zukunft Österreich), the splinter group founded by Jörg Haider in 2006, had 7 seats in that year and 21 seats in 2008.

Heads of State and Government Since 1945

Federal Presidents

Karl Renner (SPÖ)	December 1945–December 1950
Theodor Körner (SPÖ)	June 1951–January 1957
Adolf Schärf (SPÖ)	May 1957–February 1965
Franz Jonas (SPÖ)	September 1965–April 1974
Rudolf Kirchschläger (non-party)	July 1974–July 1986
Kurt Waldheim (ÖVP)	July 1986–July 1992
Thomas Klestil (ÖVP)	July 1992–July 2004
Heinz Fischer (SPÖ)	July 2004–

Federal Chancellors

Karl Renner (SPÖ)	April 1945–December 1945
Leopold Figl (ÖVP)	December 1945–April 1953
Julius Raab (ÖVP)	April 1953–April 1961
Alfons Gorbach (ÖVP)	April 1961–April 1964
Josef Klaus (ÖVP)	April 1964–April 1970
Bruno Kreisky (SPÖ)	April 1970–May 1983
Fred Sinowatz (SPÖ)	May 1983–June 1986
Franz Vranitzky (SPÖ)	June 1986–January 1997
Viktor Klima (SPÖ)	January 1997–February 2000
Wolfgang Schüssel (ÖVP)	February 2000–January 2007
Alfred Gusenbauer (SPÖ)	January 2007–December 2008
Werner Faymann (SPÖ)	December 2008–

SELECT BIBLIOGRAPHY

Barker, Elisabeth, *Austria, 1918–1972*, London, 1973.

Bischof, Günter, Pelinka, Anton, Karlhofer, Ferdinand, *The Vranitzky Era in Austria.* New Jersey, 1999.

Böhm, Wolfgang/Lahodynsky Otmar, *Der Österreich-Komplex*, Vienna, 2001.

Brook-Shepherd, Gordon, *The Austrians: A Thousand-Year Odyssey*, London, 1997.

Bruckmüller, Ernst, *Nation Österreich*, 2nd enl. edition, Vienna, 1996.

Carr, E. H., *What is history?*, London, 1978.

Eizenstat, Stuart E., contributor Wiesel, Elie, *Imperfect Justice: Looted Assets, Slave Labor and the Unfinished Business of World War II*, USA, 2003.

Fischer, Heinz, *Die Kreisky-Jahre*, Vienna, 1983.

Fischer, Heinz, *Reflextionen*, Vienna, 1998.

Fischer, Heinz, *Überzeugungen*, Vienna, 2006.

Fischer, Heinz, *Wende-Zeiten*, Vienna, 2004.

Hanisch, Erst, *Das Große Tabu* (eds. A. Pelinka /E. Weinzierl), Vienna, 1987.

Hannak, Jacques, *Karl Renner und seine Zeit*, Vienna, 1965.

Horx, Matthias, *Glückliches Österreich*, Vienna, 2006.

Jahanbegloo, Ramin, *Conversations with Isaiah Berlin*, London, 1992.

Jelavich, Barbara, *Modern Austria: Empire and Republic, 1815–1986*, Cambridge, 1987.

Klaus, Josef, *Macht und Ohnmacht in Österreich*, Vienna, 1971.

Kreisky, Bruno, *Der Memoiren dritter Teil* (Eds. O. Rathkolb/J. Kunz/M. Schmidt), Vienna, 2005.

Kreisky, Bruno, *Zwischen den Zeiten*, Vienna, 1986.

Kriechbaumer, Robert, *Die Ära Josef Klaus*, Vol. 2, Vienna, 1999.

Lendvai, Paul, *Blacklisted*, I.B. Tauris, London, 1999.

Lendvai, Paul, *Antisemitism without Jews*, New York, N.Y., 1972.

Leser, Norbert, *Salz der Gesellschaft*, Vienna, 1988.

Liegl, Barbara/Pelinka, Anton, *Chronos und Ödipus. Der Kreisky-Androsch-Konflikt*, Vienna, 2004.

Luza, Radomir, *The Resistence in Austria, 1938–1945*, Minneapolis, 1984.

Palme, Liselotte, *Androsch—Ein Leben zwischen Geld und Macht*, Vienna, 1999.

SELECT BIBLIOGRAPHY

Pelinka, Anton and Plasser, Fritz, *The Austrian party system*, USA, 1989.
Pelinka, Peter, *Wolfgang Schüssel. Eine politische Biographie*, Vienna, 2003.
Petritsch, Wolfgang, *Bruno Kreisky*, Vienna/Zurich/Munich, 2000.
Pisa, Karl, *1945, Geburt der Zukunft*, Vienna, 2005.
Pretterebner, Hans, *Der Fall Lucona*, Vienna, 1987.
Rathkolb, Oliver, *Die paradoxe Republik*, Vienna, 2005.
Rauscher, Hans, *Das Buch Österreich*, Vienna, 2005.
Reimann, Viktor, *Zu groß für Österreich, Seipel und Bauer im Kampf um die Erste Republik*, Vienna, 1968.
Secher, H. Pierre, *Bruno Kreisky, Chancellor of Austria: A Political Biography*, Pittsburgh, 1984.
Seidel, Hans, *Österreichs Wirtschaft und Wirtschaftspolitik nach dem Zweiten Weltkrieg*, Vienna, 2005.
Simmel, Georg, *Soziologie, Collected works*, Vol. 2, 4th ed., Berlin, 1958.
Sperl, Gerfried, *Der Machtwechsel*, Vienna, 2000.
Sperl, Gerfrled, *Die umgefärbte Republik*, Vienna, 2003.
Steiner, Kurt (ed.), *Modern Austria*, California, 1981.
Steininger, Rolf, Bischof, Günter, Gehler, Michael, *Austria in the Twentieth Century*, USA, 2002.
Stiefel, Dieter, *Entnazifizierung in Österreich*, Munich, 1991.
Sully, Melanie, *A Contemporary History of Austria*, London, 1990.
Sully, Melanie, *Continuity and Change in Austrian Socialism*, USA, 1992.
Sweeney, Jim and Weidenholzer, Josef (eds.), *Austria: A Study in Modern Achievement*, Aldershot, 1988.
Szabolcs, Szita, *Verschleppt, verhungert, vernichtet: die Deportation von ungarischen Juden auf das Gebiet des annektierten Österreich 1944–45*, Vienna, 1999.
Thurnher, Armin, *Das Trauma, ein Leben—Österreichische Einzelheiten*, Vienna, 2000.
Tóth, Barbara, *Karl von Schwarzenberg, Die Biografie*, Vienna, 2005.
Trost, Ernst, *Figl von Österreich*, Vienna, 1972.
Vorhofer, Kurt, *Die Ära Kreisky* (eds. W. Gatty/G. Schmid/M. Steiner/D. Wiesinger), Innsbruck/Vienna 1997.
Vranitzky, Franz, *Politische Erinnerungen*, Vienna, 2004.
Weinmann, Beatrice, *A Biography of Josef Klaus, Ein großer Österreicher*, Vienna, 2000.
Wiesenthal, Simon, *Recht, nicht Rache*, Berlin, 1988.
Wirth, Maria, *Das Beispiel der SPÖ in „Der Wille zum aufrechten Gang"* (ed. M. Mesner), Vienna, 2005.
Withalm, Hermann, *Aufzeichnungen [Notes]*, Vienna, 1973.
Wodak, Ruth and Pelinka, Anton, *The Haider Phenomenon in Austria*, USA, 2002.
Zuckmayer, Carl, *Als wär's ein Stück von mir*, Frankfurt am Main, 1966.

INDEX

Adler, Victor: and Trade Union Federation, 41; first leader of Austrian Social Democracy, 41
Advisory Council for Social and Economic Affairs: established (1963), 36
Aiginger, Professor Karl, 49
Alliance for the Future of Austria (BZÖ), 175: founded by Haider, Jörg, 170; electoral victories, 173–4
Avineri, Prof. Shlomo: Director-General of Israeli Foreign Ministry, 135, 154; support for EU sanctions (2000), 154
Androsch, Hannes, 120, 140; and Benya, Anton, 120; and Lacina, 113; and Salcher, Herbert, 113; and Vranitzky, Franz, 113, 137, 142; conflict with Kreisky, Bruno, 40, 95, 109, 113, 115, 121–2; Consultatio, 109, 121; Deputy Chairman of SPÖ, 109; dismissal (1980), 109–10, 113; Finance Minister, 32, 82, 109, 111, 120; Director-General of Creditanstalt bank, 111, 123; trial of, 110–13; Vice-Chancellor, 4, 109, 120
Anschluss, 10, 20; and Bauer, Otto, 12; and Kreisky, Bruno, 25; and Renner, Kurt, 12, 28; and Schuschnigg, Kurt, 10; and SPÖ, 25; resistance to, 13

Arafat, Yassar: and Kreisky, Bruno, 98
Arbeiter-Zeitung, 103
Austria: and USSR, 43, 46; denazification period (1945–47), 19; economic performance, 48–9; First Republic, 11, 24, 48; Jewish population, 12; Provisional Government of, 19; reduced to Ostmark, 13; Second Republic, 3–6, 13, 17, 20–1, 23, 35, 44, 48, 51, 53–4, 59–60, 145, 160, 175; Soviet occupation, 29; State Treaty (1955), 6, 21, 35, 42–4, 46, 50–1, 54, 59, 143
Austria-Hungary; dual monarchy of, 8, 50, 55
Austrian Broadcasting Corporation (ÖRF), 59, 89, 127, 150: and Bacher, Gerd, 74, 89; and ÖVP, 75
Austrian Freedom Party (FPÖ), 162; and Creditanstalt Bankverein, 160; and Habsburg, Otto, 55; and Olah, Franz, 116; and Vranitzky, Franz, 137–8; and Peter, Friedrich, 94; and Wiesenthal, Simon, 96; association with Nazis, 167; coalition with ÖVP, 5, 149–50; electoral defeat, 162, 173; electoral progress, 157, 159; EU opposition toward, 153–6; expels Haider, Jörg, 163, 170; led

INDEX

views on Schüssel, Wolfgang,
170; views on Vranitzky, Franz,
142–3
Busek, Erhard, 141; and CV, 157;
and EU, 152; and Graff, Michael,
131; and Klestil, Thomas, 158;
and KSJ, 70; and Schüssel,
Wolfgang, 39, 157–8; Chairman
of ÖVP, 157–8; Deputy Chancellor, 141; deputy mayor of Vienna,
111; retirement, 164; Secretary
General to Sallinger, Rudolf, 39,
102; Vice-Chancellor, 4, 39, 41,
152, 158
Butler, Rab, 112
Bütler, Hugo: editor in chief of
Neue Zürcher Zeitung, 151

Canada, 3
Cap, Josef: Chief whip of SPÖ, 125,
142
Cartellverband (CV), 87; and
Busek, Erhard, 157; and Federal
Chancellery, 69–70; and Judaism,
69; and Klestil, Thomas, 140;
and KSJ, 70; and ÖVP, 69; and
Withalm, Hermann, 70; persecu-
tion under Nazis, 69
China, 2, 158
Chirac, Jacques: President of
France, 156
Chňoupek, Bohuslav: Czechoslovak
Foreign Minister, 97; former KGB
agent, 97
Christian-Social Party: and Dolfuss,
Engelbert, 9; formation of
Heimwehr (Home Guard), 9;
trade unionists of, 41
Churchill, Winston: Prime Minister
of UK, 23, 157
Clemenceau, Georges: Prime
Minister of France, 8
Clinton, President Bill, 168
Cold War, 29
Communist Party (KPÖ), 10, 13,
26; and Pittermann, Bruno, 64;

and Renner, Karl, 27; and USSR,
36; electoral defeat, 28; hostile
reactions to, 15; trade unionists
of, 41
Concordia Press Club, 34, 63, 92
Corfu: Treaty of, 141
Creditanstalt Bankverein: and FPÖ,
160; and ÖVP, 160; and Schüssel,
Wolfgang, 160; SPÖ dominance
of, 160
Croatia: alliance with Nazi Ger-
many, 18
Czechoslovakia, 28: and USSR, 46;
Warsaw Pact Intervention (1968),
76
Czettel, Hans, 119; Deputy
Governor of Lower Austria, 81;
Nazi Party membership, 119

De Gualle, Charles, 61
Democratic Progressive Party
(DFP), 64
Dichand, Hans: and Kreisky, Bruno,
89; Editor-in-chief of *Neue
Kronen Zeitung*, 89, 128, 172
Dolfuss, Engelbert, 61, 95: and
Christian-Social Party, 9; and
Schuschnigg, Kurt, 10; murder
of, 9

Eastern Bloc, 19, 55, 72
Ebner-Eschenbach, Marie, 76
Eizenstat, Stuart E.: and Schau-
mayer, Maria, 168–9; US Special
representative for Holocaust
Issues, 168
Europe, vii, 19, 28, 31, 34, 38, 44,
46, 48, 50, 72, 75, 79, 81, 87,
135,151; conflict in, 12, 14, 96;
Council of, 72
European Free Trade Association
(EFTA), 43
European Union (EU): and Busek,
Erhard, 152; and Schüssel,
Wolfgang, 158, 160; criticism

191

Judt, Tony: views on EU, 154
Juncker, Jean-Claude: Prime
   Minister of Luxembourg, 152–3

Kaiser, Robert: managing editor of
   Washington Post, 134
Kamitz, Reinhard: and Helmer,
   Oskar, 92; and Klaus, Josef, 58;
   and ÖVP, 92; Finance Minister,
   58, 92; Nazi Party membership,
   92; President of National Bank
   (1960–67), 58; SS, 92
Katholische Studierenden Jugend
   (KSJ): and Busek, Erhard, 70; and
   CV, 70; and Riegler, Josef, 70;
   and Schüssel, Wolfgang, 70
Kausel, Anton, 48–9
Kery, Theodor: Governor of
   Burgenland, 88, 97, 126
Khruschev, Nikita, 52
Kirchschläger, Rudolf: ambassador
   to Prague, 77; and Kreisky,
   Bruno, 88, 120; and Wiesenthal,
   Simon, 96; Federal President, 4,
   77, 88, 96, 120, 122; Foreign
   Minister, 77, 88, 120
Klaus, Josef: and Bacher, Gerd, 74;
   and Belgrade, 72; and Bulgaria,
   72; and Fischer, Heinz, 61–2; and
   Gruber, Karl, 78; and Hungary,
   72; and Kamitz, Reinhard, 58;
   and Neisser, Heinrich, 78; and
   ÖVP, 57, 59, 68–9; and Romania,
   72; and Taus, Josef, 58, 71; and
   Tito, Marshall Josip Broz, 72;
   and Yugoslavia, 72; government
   of, 61, 75, 77–8, 84, 156; Federal
   Chancellor, 44, 60–1, 64, 67, 71,
   79; Finance Minister (1961), 51,
   53, 57, 68; Governor of Salzburg,
   51, 57; loss of daughter, 67–8;
   retires, 78
Klestil, Thomas: and Busek, Erhard,
   158; and CV, 140; and Mock,
   Alois, 141; and ÖVP, 140; and

Schüssel, Wolfgang, 161; and
   Vranitzky, Franz, 140–1; and
   Zilk, Helmut, 141; declining
   reputation of, 161; diplomat to
   USA, 140–1; Federal President,
   70, 77, 135, 140, 149, 155–6,
   158; Secretary-General of Foreign
   Ministry, 141; secretary to
   Chancellor, 76–7
Klima, Victor: Federal Chancellor,
   147, 154; successor to Vranitzky,
   Franz, 147; weakness of power
   base, 154–6
Köning, Cardinal Franz, 4, 133
Koren, Prof. Stephan: and Kreisky,
   Bruno, 88, 121; chief whip of
   ÖVP, 97, 121; Finance Minister,
   75: President of National Bank,
   88, 121
Kosovo: War (1999), 3, 154
Krainer Jnr, Josef: Governor of
   Styria (1948–71), 4, 53
Kreisky, Bruno, 11, 36, 92, 111,
   113, 131, 160; ancestry of, 82;
   and Anschluss, 25; and Arafat,
   Yassar, 98; and Austrian Imperial
   Assembly, 82; and Avnery, Uri,
   98; and Belgrade, 72; and Benya,
   Anton, 40, 81, 122; and Broda,
   Christian, 117, 122; and
   Dichand, Hans, 89; and Federa-
   tion of Foreign Correspondents,
   96; and Firnberg, Hertha, 122;
   and Fischer, Heinz, 94; and
   Gadaffi, Muhammad, 98; and
   Genscher, Hans-Dietrich, 83; and
   Gusenbauer, Alfred, 166; and
   Habsburg, Otto, 55; and
   Hanisch, Ernst, 15; and Israel,
   94, 96, 98; and Jonas, Franz, 62;
   and Kirchschläger, Rudolf, 88,
   120; and Koren, Prof. Stephan,
   88, 121; and Lower Austrian
   Farmers' Federation, 93; and
   Mubarak, Hosni, 98; and Olah,